Helping the Sexual Addict

Patrick Carnes, Ph.D.

Connie and Denis — Best wishes and thanks for your help! Patrick Carnes

CompCare® Publishers
2415 Annapolis Lane
Minneapolis, Minnesota 55441

Published in the United States
by CompCare Publishers

Carnes, Patrick, 1944–
Contrary to love.

Bibliography: p.
1. Psychosexual disorders. 2. Compulsive behavior.
I. Title.
RC556.C368 1989 616.85'83 89-556
ISBN 0-89638-156-0

Cover design by Susan Rinek

Inquiries, orders, and catalog requests should be addressed to:
CompCare Publishers
2415 Annapolis Lane
Minneapolis, Minnesota 55441
Call toll free 800/328-3330
(Minnesota residents 612/559-4800)

5 4 3 2 1
93 92 91 90 89

To Professor Richard Clendennan,
Dean of the Juvenile Officer's Institute,
University of Minnesota

We know better than others the limits of our sexual addiction:
that it is solitary, furtive, and satisfies only itself,
that, contrary to love, it is fleeting,
that it demands hypocrisy,
that it enfeebles strong sexual feeling,
that it is humorless and cruel,
that it destroys good feelings about ourselves,
that it is hollow,
that it distances us from our feelings,
that it works to exclude our family,
that it exploits power over others,
that it causes us to abuse our bodies,
and
that we end up broken and alone.

An Anonymous Addict

Contents

List of Figures

Acknowledgments

There are many people who helped me in the preparation of this book:

David Olson of the Family Social Science Department of the University of Minnesota for his generous support and for the use of his Circumplex Model.

David Walsh, Judy Smith, Patrick Daughrety, Shirley Carlson, and Mary McBride of the Family Renewal Center of Fairview Southdale Hospital for their contributions to the ideas presented in this volume.

Sarah Sandberg, Ty Weslie, Tammy Horstman, and Carol Schneeweiss and the staff of the Sexual Dependency Unit at Golden Valley Health Center for their critique of the manuscript and support while it was written.

Mark Davidson and Dennis McGuire of the University of Minnesota Psychological Foundations Department of Curriculum and Instruction for their help with data analysis.

Ron Smith of Georgia State Prison, Bill Steele of Minnesota State Prison at Oak Park Heights, and the Twin Cities Intergroup for Sexual Addicts Anonymous and group members—both women and men for assistance in gathering data.

Michael Hunter, Warren Schaffer, David Horst, Sherod Miller, and Jim D'Aurora whose professional encouragement and help were invaluable.

The CompCare Publishers staff including Nan Holland and Margaret Henningson-Marsh who have had to go so many extra miles for this project.

Bonnie Hesse, who as a skilled editor and long-time friend supported me through some of the most difficult moments of my writing career.

Professor Richard Clendennan of the Juvenile Officer's Institute of the University of Minnesota to whom this book is dedicated because he has few peers in both scholarship and generosity.

Terri O'Grady, whose involved editing vastly improved the book.

My children—David, Stefanie, Jennifer, and Erin—without whose love and support nothing really makes much sense, including writing books. . . .

Patrick Carnes, Ph.D.
Senior Fellow
Institute for Behavioral Medicine
Golden Valley Health Center
Golden Valley, Minnesota

Foreword

In his groundbreaking book, *Out of the Shadows*, Patrick Carnes confronts the sexual taboo by revealing the pervasiveness and destructive aspects of sexual addiction for individuals, their families, and society. By drawing a clear parallel with other addictive behaviors, he reveals a four-step addiction cycle which intensifies with each repetition: preoccupation, ritualization, compulsive sexual behavior, and despair.

The addictive system is maintained by the belief system and impaired thinking which keep the behavior unmanageable. He describes three levels of addiction and indicates how to assess the sexual, physical, and emotional abuse in one's childhood which make one vulnerable to sexual addiction. Addiction is also maintained by the co-addict who unwittingly supports the addictive behaviors. Carnes clearly demonstrates the significance of the family in the etiology and maintenance of the addiction.

Out of the Shadows not only addressed a taboo topic, but made professionals more aware of the prevalence of the problem. It also tapped into an unmet need of sexual addicts who had been unable to find help for their problem. Like alcoholism a decade ago, sexual addicts are still generally ignored and seen as an untreatable minority in this society.

In *Contrary to Love: Helping the Sexual Addict*, he builds on the theoretical foundation provided in the earlier book. Conceptually, he demonstrates the ecology of all types of addiction and indicates why cooperation from a range of disciplines is needed to effectively treat this problem.

Building on the Circumplex Model which I developed to describe types of family systems, Patrick Carnes creatively bridges family behavior and sexual addiction. He describes how "extreme" types of family systems in the addict's family of origin help create the climate for sexual addiction to develop. In addition, the current families of these addicts also have extreme behaviors which help to maintain this addictive cycle. More specifically, while nearly half (49 percent) of the sexual addicts surveyed grew up in families that were extreme on the Circumplex Model, two-thirds (66 percent) of the current families were extreme. In using the Circumplex Model, Carnes also describes how addicts ineffectively deal with intimacy and dependency issues and how this helps to maintain the addictive process.

Diagnostically, he demonstrates how the Circumplex Model can be used to describe the family of origin and current family system of the addict. Another diagnostic tool he developed was a Sexual Addiction Screening Test that clearly distinguished sexual addicts from those not addicted. The scale also describes the specific sexual behaviors that cluster together at the three levels of addiction.

Treating the sexual addict is a major focus of his book, and he demonstrates the usefulness of the Twelve Step model which has been used so effectively with Alcoholics Anonymous. He describes both the process of first order and second order change that is required for effective treatment.

This book provides a comprehensive systemic framework for understanding and treating a range of addictive sexual behaviors. He describes how the addictive cycle can be applied not only to understanding sexual addiction, but all types of addiction. In addition to bridging the family system theory and addictive processes, he illustrates how families are instrumental in both creating the climate for the addiction to develop, but also for maintaining and reinforcing the addictive process.

This book is well written, involving, and full of rich, insightful anecdotes. It clearly sets the stage for a major revolution in the treatment of sexual addiction. This book is destined to become a classic for expanding our understanding and enhancing our ability to treat the sexual addiction within a family context.

David H. Olson, Ph.D.
Professor, Family Social Science
University of Minnesota
St. Paul, Minnesota

President
National Council on Family Relations
1988-89

1
Sexual Addiction
An Overview

At a southern university medical school, a staff sexologist saw her first clients of the day. Dan and Lauren, in their late thirties, hadn't had sex in three years. During a series of sessions, other issues affecting their lives together had emerged. Lauren's resistance to Dan's sexual approaches had roots deep in addictive and abusive patterns. Sexually abused as a child, she had had several bouts with anorexia over the years. Dan was chemically dependent and had been compulsively having affairs and visiting prostitutes. The therapist diagnosed him as having a sexual addiction. Their case was familiar to her; she often found that sexual addiction co-existed with one partner's inhibited sexual desires, in the midst of a dysfunctional family system that enabled multiple addictions.

When Dan and Lauren were asked to complete a "genogram" of their families, some important background information came to light. Two of Dan's brothers were chemically dependent; one boasted a massive pornography collection. Ironically, Dan's father was a Baptist minister, well known for preaching against pornography and alcohol. Dan's paternal grandfather was a notorious womanizer and alcoholic. To complete the picture, his grandmother had been married four times and at one time was a working prostitute. Lauren's father was an overweight, alcoholic physician who several times had been charged with the sexual abuse of patients. Her uncle had recently joined a Sexual Addicts Anonymous group in a nearby city.

While such revelations made the session painful, the genogram had done what it always does. The clients developed a clearer picture of their family history and of the role addiction played in their lives. They weren't bad people; rather they had an illness that affected the whole family. As the therapist watched the couple walk to their car, she reflected on the fact that knowing each person's dysfunction had not been sufficient to make an accurate diagnosis. The family was the missing link. She wondered how many patients she had treated with futile results before understanding the family connection.

Similar professional soul-searching was going on in a treatment facility for impaired physicians where the director had just secured a bed in the inpatient sexual addiction unit for Phillip, a forty-two-year-old family practice physician. This was the third time he had been admitted for alcohol and drug addiction. In both of the earlier treatments, serious sexual problems had also been identified, including multiple affairs and the sexual abuse of patients. However, the loss of his license and practice was initiated by nurses' charges of sexual harassment, not the abuse of patients.

Phillip's sexual indiscretions had previously been seen as an extension of out-of-control alcohol and drug use. But in the most recent round of sexual escapades, he wasn't drinking. In fact, the sexual acting out seemed to flourish with sobriety.

It was only when the authorities intervened that Phillip started to use drugs again. Realizing this, the director and staff finally concluded that Phillip wouldn't be able to remain alcohol and drug free until his sexual addiction was dealt with. In fact, the director told the admitting physician that he was convinced that sexual addiction was really Phillip's primary illness. Chemicals gave Phillip a way to kill the pain resulting from his compulsive sexual behavior. As he walked down the hall to talk to Phillip's family, the director wondered how many others he and his staff had missed.

A university sociologist sat in his office late at night, fatigued and outraged. He had been writing all day on the concept of sexual addiction and the damage it could do in a society already inundated with misinformation about sexuality. Essentially he saw the concept of sexual addiction as part of a moral crusade, representative of the current fundamentalist religions influencing the nation. By calling sexual addiction an illness, so-called experts were pathologizing moral notions without any basis in scientific fact, extending the American tradition of social control of people's sexual behavior.

Only recently a colleague had told him about a tormented client who thought he was a sex addict because he masturbated twice a week. The sociologist mentally constructed scenarios in which people could be damaged by the concept of sex addiction. Worse, there were self-help groups now based on the model of Alcoholics Anonymous groups in which there was no facilitator trained in sexual science. He sighed as he thought of all those misguided people.

In a midwestern city, Alex prepared dinner for his two small children, ages four and seven. A victim of AIDS, Alex's body was being destroyed by the advanced stages of cancer. His arms had accumulated so much fluid that such simple tasks as cooking and setting the table were excruciating. He struggled to do his best, since his wife, Kim, also diagnosed with AIDS, was in the hospital with pneumocystis pneumonia. He felt terrible remorse about transmitting the virus to her. Between his anguish and his physical disability, he moved as if he were in slow motion.

Alex and Kim faced up to the realities bravely without trying to analyze or blame. There wasn't time for anything else. The hardest decision was to select guardians for their children. Alex watched as they played on the living room floor, oblivious to the changes about to occur in their lives. His eyes filled with tears as he thought about the pain his sexual addiction was causing. Alex had been in treatment for chemical dependency at one time. What if one of the therapists had identified his sexual addiction? Could he have been saved from contracting AIDS?

Yet he was grateful for many things, especially the support of his Twelve Step sexual addiction group and his physician. He believed they were the primary reasons he still had the will to live when all the others in his diagnosis group were now dead.

His wife's commitment to maintaining their relationship in the face of the harsh reality of their illness deepened his gratitude. But he often wondered how different their lives might have been if he had sought help for his sexual addiction before it was too late.

Sexual Addiction as an Illness

Sexual addiction is an illness with many masks. Like other addictions such as alcoholism, a confusing array of problems serves to obscure our understanding. One such source of confusion is the extremely wide variety of behavior patterns that are included under the label of this addiction. Yet, sex addiction is clearly an illness with a definite set of symptoms and it is treatable. Further, research in sexual addiction is transforming our knowledge of addiction in general and expanding our awareness of human sexuality as well. But the concept that someone can be addicted to sex generates controversy, because it raises problematical issues and confronts both professional and popular prejudices. Amid media controversy and academic debate, we must not lose sight of the seriousness of sexual addiction.

In *Out of the Shadows: Understanding Sexual Addiction,* I provided an operational definition of sexual addiction as a "pathological relationship" with a mood-altering experience.[1] The notion of sexual addiction is sometimes confused with the positive, pleasurable, and intense sexuality enjoyed by a "normal" population. It is also sometimes confused with simply enjoying frequent sex—what's "frequent" to some is the norm for others. Also, many people experience what they would term sexual excess. But they learn to moderate their behavior. They are able to stop and say no. Sex addicts have lost control over their ability to say no; they have lost control over their ability to choose. Their sexual behavior is part of a cycle of thinking, feeling, and acting which they cannot control.

Contrary to enjoying sex as a self-affirming source of physical pleasure, the sex addict has learned to rely on sex for comfort from pain, nurturing, or relief from stress, etc., the way an alcoholic relies on alcohol, or a drug addict on drugs.

Contrary to love, the obsessional illness transforms sex into the primary relationship or need, for which all else may be sacrificed, including family, friends, values, health, safety, and work. As life unravels, the sex addict despairs, helplessly trapped in cycles of degradation, shame, and danger.

No one personality profile can describe a sex addict, although a number of common characteristics can be identified. The sex addict may do one, more than one, or all of the following:

—exhibit a constellation of preferred sexual behaviors, arranged in a definite ritualized order, which are acted out in an obsessional scenario

—experience periods of escalation, de-escalation, and acuity

—continue to act out despite serious consequences, including health risks, severe financial losses, injury, loss of family, and even death

—have delusional thought patterns, including rationalization, minimization, projection, reality distortion, and memory loss

—make futile repeated efforts to control the behavior even to the point of extreme hardship or self-mutilation

—experience little pleasure, often feeling despair even in the midst of sex

—spend most of the time in a state of obsession which subordinates life decisions, feelings, and self-awareness until reality comes crashing in

—feel shame and depression so severe that suicidal tendencies are one of the most common concurrent mental health issues

—experience withdrawal symptoms that parallel the depressive states of withdrawing cocaine addicts

—behave in a severely abusive and exploitive way, often violating his or her own values and common sense

—live a secret life surrounded by a web of lies and dishonesty which add to the accumulated shame

—go to extreme efforts to maintain appearances, including high achievements and excessive religiosity

—allow family relationships and friendships to become secondary in importance to obsessional and delusional patterns that are pathological and self-destructive

—incur significant economic costs due to lost productivity, increased health care costs, and financial losses associated with maintaining the addiction

In addition, a number of common preconditions have been identified which contribute to an individual's vulnerability to sex addiction. These risk factors include:

—a high probability of having been sexually abused as a child, although the addict may not recognize the abuse or see its connection to current behavior

—a high probability of having been raised in a dysfunctional family in which self-esteem has been damaged, resulting in severe problems with intimacy (how to be close) and dependency (whom to trust)

—a history of emotional and physical abuse, intensifying a sense of unworthiness and fear of abandonment

—sex addiction or other types of addiction among parents, siblings, and other family members

—an extremely high probability of other addictions and compulsions, including chemical dependency, eating disorders, compulsive gambling, and compulsive spending

Our knowledge of the addiction, as outlined above, has emerged out of two major growth areas of research in behavioral medicine. First, in the field of addictionology it is now understood that the dynamics common to alcohol or drug addiction can extend to other obsessive behaviors, including eating disorders, compulsive gambling, sex addiction, and others. Compulsive, addictive behavior patterns often co-exist in the same person or in the same family. In fact, the second major growth area, the expansion of our knowledge in family therapy, has supplied the essential perspective of how the shame-based family system supports compulsive behavior, whether it be out-of-control addictions such as alcoholism or extremely controlling obsessions such as anorexia. To treat an individual's addiction without assessing the web of obsession and shame in the family leaves the family system intact to perpetuate more shame and obsession.

Guided by current developments in addictionology and family therapy, professionals now view sex addiction from a clearer perspective. Still, our understanding has been obscured by our reluctance to face sexual issues both professionally and personally. The addiction has been further masked by the secrecy and shame that characterize the illness.

Within the field, progress has been made since *Out of the Shadows* was published. Inpatient as well as outpatient services have been established throughout the country. Twelve Step support groups with names like Sexaholics Anonymous, Sex Addicts Anonymous, Sex and Love Addicts Anonymous, and Sexual Compulsives Anonymous can be found in most major cities in the country. Academicians and clinicians now share research and explore issues at an annual conference. Despite the progress, sex addiction is a relatively new area with much that is unknown and much that is confusing.

Figure 1-1 suggests an image to clarify the issue. Professionals have come to understand all of human sexual behavior as falling along a normal distribution curve. As I noted above, the range of people's sexual experience and behavior is quite varied. Besides the diversity in type of sexual experiences, the frequency and intensity of sex behavior varies: some people choose to have more sex and it enhances their lives; some choose to have less sex and still are content. Two subgroups exist at the extremes of this spectrum, however. On one hand some people have a great deal of difficulty choosing to be sexual. They find it difficult to participate in sex, and when it is not an organic problem, it is one of attitude and belief. For example, of the millions of men who suffer with impotence, a great many struggle with psychological issues, including the fear of being sexual. A great deal of progress has been made in these areas of sexual dysfunction.

At the other extreme are people who have lost the ability to control their sexual behavior. They have, in effect, become powerless over their choice. Sex becomes an addiction which governs their lives, often dictating behavior, partners, and situations they do not want, i.e., would not otherwise be involved in.

Both subgroups at the ends of the behavior spectrum experience life consequences and share in desperation and

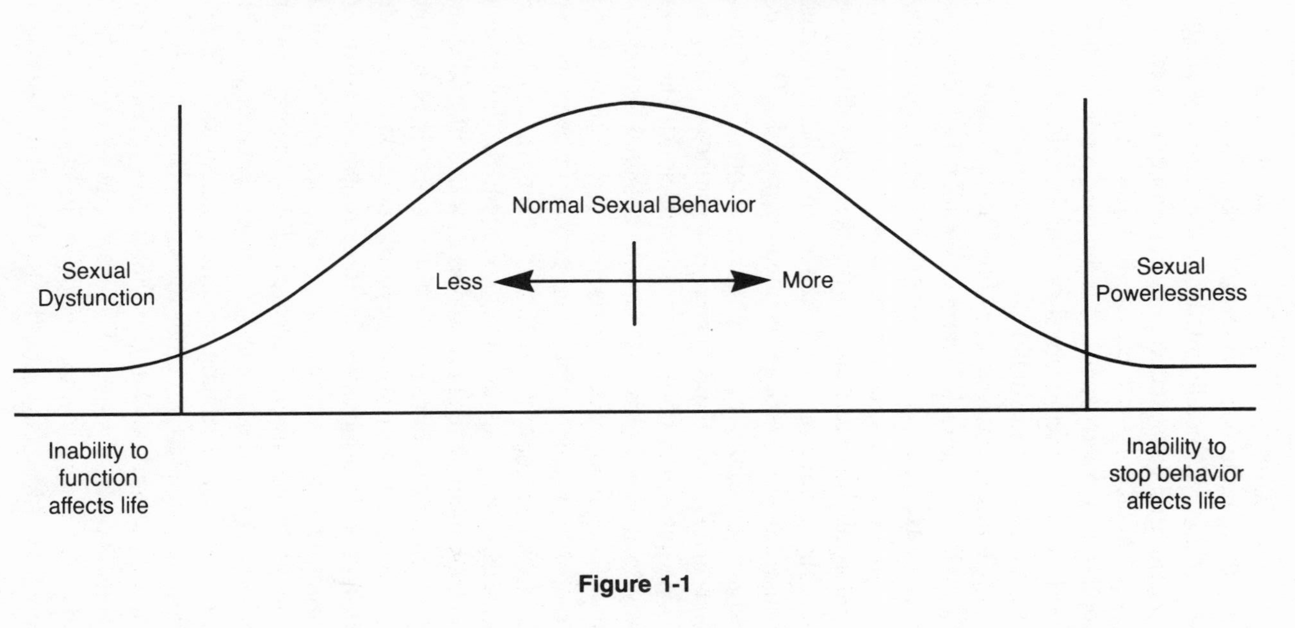
Distribution Curve of Sexual Behavior
Sexual Dysfunction
Normal Sexual Behavior
Less
More
Sexual Powerlessness
Inability to function affects life
Inability to stop behavior affects life

Figure 1-1

obsession. They may even have similar family dynamics, but they differ radically in behavior.

While significant differences exist in physiology, development, and consequences, significant parallels exist between sexual addiction and eating disorders. The most obvious common characteristic is our human capacity to take the most natural, essential, and pleasurable life processes to the extreme of compulsive illness.

Even more suggestive is how the two disorders co-exist. Consider the couple, each of whom has one or more addictions. Here is one scenario: He is both chemically dependent and sexually addicted and she tries desperately to control his behavior, even to the point of hiding his alcohol and throwing away his pornography. She is compulsively nonsexual and weighs two hundred pounds. He constantly berates her about her weight. He deeply resents her sexual unavailability and this serves as a rationale for his sexual acting out and alcohol abuse. Subconsciously, her weight is a way to distance herself from any potential sexual advances and a statement of her anger and hurt. The further out of control he becomes, the more sexually closed she becomes, as if balancing some equation in their relationship. Eating, sex, and chemicals are used to numb the unbearable pain both of them suffer in a complex mosaic of addictive cycles that neither one can seem to stop, separately or together.

Such addictive mosaics force addiction professionals to expand their perspective for those situations when multiple obsessions exist within the individual and/or within the family. What are the theoretical implications of the co-existence of compulsive excesses in human needs, whether the excess is *over*consuming or *under*consuming? What sort of treatment is effective, given the intensely personal nature of the excess and also the obviously essential and powerful family forces at work? These are crucial questions for all addictions. And so the struggle to understand sexual addiction has added significantly to the understanding of the addictive process in general and, in fact, toward a total redefinition of addictive illness as a whole.

Problems for Professionals Who Want to Help

In John Cheever's challenging short novel, *Oh What a Paradise It Seems*, the central theme is organized around the main character Lemuel Sears' efforts to save the town's pond from pollution and destruction. In counterpoint to this theme, Sears and other, minor characters play out scenes that raise questions about what is "pure" and constructive versus "polluted" and destructive in the complex context of human nature, including sex behavior. Sears develops a relationship with a woman. She regularly attends meetings which at first make no sense to him:

> Sears heard the group recite something in unison. He guessed from the eagerness and clarity in their voices that it could not be an occult mantra. It was difficult to imagine what it could be . . . . Then the doors opened and they came out—not like a crowd discharged at the end of an entertainment or a lecture but gradually, like the crowd at the close of a social gathering, and he had, after all, seen them blow the candles out on a cake.[2]

Eventually, Sears learns from a janitor that "these gatherings aimed at abstinence in sex, food, alcohol, and tobacco." Unmistakably, these are characteristics of a meeting based on the Twelve Steps to Alcoholics Anonymous. Sears struggles to find a common denominator among those who attend these meetings. He never succeeds—and never quite understands his new friends:

> He was at once struck by his incompetence at judging the gathering. Not even in times of war with which he was familiar, not even in the evacuation of burning cities had he seen so mixed a gathering. It was a group, he thought,

> in which there was nowhere the forces of selection. Since the faces—young, old, haggard and serene—conveyed nothing to him, he looked at their clothing and found even fewer bearings. They wore the clothes of the poor and a few cheap imitations of the rich.

In many ways, the problem of Lemuel Sears parallels the experience of professional helpers. Sexually compulsive people challenge, and often compound, professional understanding because of their incredible diversity. Wealth, poverty, cross dressing, bestiality, incest, affairs, various sexual preferences—man, woman, hispanic, black, white, young, old, legal, and illegal. How to make sense out of it?

Like Lemuel Sears, we observe people leaving self-help meetings with names such as Sexual Abuse Anonymous, Sexaholics Anonymous, or Sexual Addicts Anonymous, vaguely distrusting what we are not familiar with. We wonder what the common bond is, and whether they really help each other. Further, how do we—the pastor, lawyer, physician, mental health professional, and concerned other—help?

We live in a complex world. New knowledge emerges rapidly, and those of us who are professional helpers must struggle to integrate it into existing disciplines, or create entirely new disciplines. In the midst of this kind of juggling, along comes the phenomenon of sexual addiction, which does not fit neatly with existing professional "territories." Using Italian psychiatrist Palazzoli's term, we need to become a "transdisciplinary" team, using a common systemic approach. Through a common effort, we can bring new perspective to the problem of Lemuel Sears and produce a broadened vision of the life patterns common to those who suffer as sexual addicts.

Creating a common perspective out of different disciplines will generate significant questions, and the sex addiction concept has already generated a number of scholarly controversies, including:

—Sex addiction does not account for the wide variation of sex practices in different cultures. An illness model must transcend cultural differences.

—Sex addiction is a misnomer. It is really love addiction—or a mixture of both.

—Sex addiction is not really an "addiction" but rather a problem of compulsivity. The term addiction is too heavy a label and compulsivity is more accurate a term.

—Sex addiction is a concept that could be used to oppress minorities such as homosexuals or those with sex practices that do not conform to conventional moral codes. Creating unnecessary pathology normalcy could lead to repression of sexual expression.

—Sex addiction can be misused by those who have negative sex biases. It is a dangerous concept in the hands of those with conservative political and religious views.

—The concepts of sex addiction are based on an alcoholism model, and being applied by people with no training in sexuality and no experience dealing with different cultural influences or appropriate treatment strategies.

—Sex addiction is being dealt with by people who have no knowledge of addiction including intervention, diagnosis, treatment, or relapse prevention.[3]

Along with these controversies come the related mental health questions. How does sex addiction differ from psychopathy? How to differentiate it from the borderline personality? What is the relationship between the addiction and the depression that commonly accompanies it? When is someone abusing his or her sexuality as a situational stress reaction and when is someone an addict? When there are other addictions present, what do you treat first?

Extraordinary parallels exist between the history of alcoholism and our somewhat limited experience with sexual addiction. Controversies that began in the pioneering years, such as those about the etiology of alcoholism, still exist. Others have been put to rest.

In an effort to be open to accepting the existence of sex addiction, it is helpful to remember that in the early years, reputable scholars stated that there was no such illness as alcoholism. If such an illness did exist, the numbers were very small and had little significant impact since these people harmed only themselves. Besides, it was thought there was no effective way of treating these people since they were considered basically incorrigible. Alcoholism was also seen as a male problem since it was (and still is) much less visible in women.

Scholars have made identical statements about sex addiction. What helps enormously is that the pioneers in treating alcoholism paved the way for comprehension of an illness in which an individual is "out of control." Those whose early work specialized in understanding eating disorders opened the door for accepting the fact that addiction can exist that focuses on a natural physiological function. Our professional goal, in treating sexual addiction and resolving its controversies, is to build on the foundation that has already been laid in addiction and mental health research. And, as a matter of fact, in many ways serious research in such a sensitive and volatile area would not have been possible without the work of our predecessors.

One major goal of this book is to create an expanded description of the world of the sexual addict. While writing this book over the past six years, I have attended to the controversies, which have served over time to focus and clarify my descriptive efforts. As with alcoholism, the debate will continue. But hopefully, with greater clarity.

Since the publication of *Out of the Shadows*, several shortcomings of the book have emerged despite its growing, general acceptance. For one, female addicts have pointed to the relatively few samples portrayed in the book of women caught in the addictive system. An effort has been made in this book to recognize the impact of the illness on women. Another valid question has arisen about identifying addicts whose lives are not so unmanageable as some of those described in the earlier book, but who clearly have a sexual addiction problem. Diagnostic and assessment criteria are provided to account for and assess the less clear-cut cases.

Previously, I developed a concept of three levels of addictive behaviors to provide a framework for the addict to identify the scope and particular patterns of his or her addictive sexual behavior. The question has since emerged as to whether the three levels of addiction are progressive, meaning that a person's addictive behavior might begin with the more acceptable forms of sexual compulsivity such as masturbation or prostitution (Level One behaviors) and leading necessarily to sex crimes such as rape or incest (Level Three behaviors). The answer is no, not necessarily. However, someone who says "I'm only a Level One addict" denies the seriousness of the problem and distorts what the levels are about. An addict may, for example, start out as an exhibitionist (Level Two), but then engage in Level One behaviors to the point of personal destruction. This book will clarify the role of the three levels as functional categories that contribute to identifying and understanding addictive patterns.

Beyond responding to questions about the addictive dynamics, the second goal in writing the book is to provide a working map for professionals in many disciplines. The map is intended to serve as a guide, assisting the professional to access the world of the sex addict. Chapter 2 details the conceptual barriers which have prevented us from acknowledging sex as a potential addiction. Chapters 3 and 4 specify how the addictive system develops for sex addicts and how the various phases of the addiction can be distinguished. In chapters 5 and 6, factors are surveyed within the family system that contribute to the addiction as well as sustain it. Chapter 7 explores the healing role the Twelve Steps of Alcoholics Anonymous can play when applied to sexual addiction. The remaining two chapters of the book discuss assessment, intervention, and treatment.

As a guide for the treatment of sex addiction, *Contrary to Love* connects the world of the professional with the world of the Twelve Step self-help groups patterned after Alcoholics Anonymous. Professionals have been accused of distrusting self-help groups because these groups are a potential threat to the role of the professional helper. But reservations among professionals probably have more to do with honest doubts about how a nonprofessional group can deal effectively with serious—even life-threatening—problems.

The issue has been accentuated by the Twelve Step communities themselves. First, in preserving their traditions of anonymity and nonaffiliation, these Twelve Step fellowships do not explain much about themselves. Also, some AA members are vaguely suspicious of professionals meddling in what they haven't personally experienced. Some relate stories about professional help that was destructive. Behind the antiprofessional bias may lurk a fear that the help received from their support group will somehow be diminished or degraded by professional scrutiny. I hope that this book provides a means to help the Twelve Step program member and the professional reach out and support one another.

There is much to be discovered and revised. With a steady flow of new contributions to addiction theory, it is naive to think there are final answers about addiction in general—let alone sexual addiction.

What I have written here is a guide to treating sexual addiction. The tasks at hand are practical ones: Who is the addict? and, How can I help? Those who wish to pursue theoretical or research issues will find sources in the chapter notes.

Consider this book an invitation to join Lemuel Sears. His problem was to make sense out of a group whose membership seemed to defy the "forces of selection"—and then to reach out. As professionals, we share the same goal.

2
Sexual Addiction
Obstacles to Understanding

Therapists, like other human beings, are a product of their society. They are . . . members of a guild who are trained by the same method, read the same books, and transmit similar ideas . . . . The idea that the patient contains her own pathology retains its grip on modern therapists who defend their interventions eloquently. In the field of helping people, beliefs speak with a clearer, sharper voice than results.

Salvador Minuchin, Bernise Rosman,
and Lester Baker
Psychosomatic Families

In the convoluted domain of sexual addiction, the power of popular myths, cultural practices, moral precepts, legal consequences, and theoretical orientations combine to distort and disguise the problem. This means that therapists who hope to help sex addicts need to do professional and sometimes personal soul-searching of their own beliefs. In an excellent essay, Howard Liddle suggests that every therapist needs such an ideological checkup in order to make an epistemological declaration:

> The family therapists' epistemological declaration, then, would be our own idiosyncratic statement of what we know and how we know it, what and how we think, and what and how we make the clinical decisions we do.[1]

Pioneers like Jay Haley, Paul Watzlawick, and Milton Erickson insist that what the therapist's clients *believe* to be true may have greater impact than what in fact *is* true. The same can be said of the therapist's belief system. The therapist needs to be open enough to accommodate the client's realities and unrealities.

What obscures the therapist's ability to understand sexual addiction? What are the barriers to be faced in working with sexual addicts?

Three problems are immediately apparent. First, the addict's shame and secrecy limit the therapist's access to information. Second, adequate concepts are lacking to help to understand addicts and their families. Third, professional bias—the therapist's personal belief system—may interfere with a comprehensive picture of the addict and the addictive system.

Secrecy: The Analogy of Gollum's Ring

Late one afternoon in his therapy group, Frank told his fellow addicts and therapists that when he thought about the bad times, he often felt like he was protected by Gollum's ring. He explained that Gollum, the mythical figure in J.R.R. Tolkien's trilogy, *Lord of the Rings,* possessed a ring of power that made its wearer invisible. Only in direct sunlight could the wearer's presence be detected, and then only as a faint, wavering shadow.

This analogy can help us understand the double life of the addict. The addictive system uses secrecy as a shield, and as such it becomes a source of power. The addiction thrives on secrecy because the addict can often avoid public consequences and family confrontations. However, the sense of being alone with the secret increases the addict's despair. The discrepancy between Frank's public persona and the reality of his addictive life created ongoing anxiety which he medicated by intensifying his sexual activities.

Therapists often work with clients a long time without seeing the shadow of addiction. The therapist ends up feeling frustrated about spending so many hours working on the presenting auxiliary problems, marital issues for example, without ever reaching the real source of the turmoil. To the addict's family and close friends, something appears to be wrong—that faint, wavering shadow of the addiction—but often they cannot tell what that something is.

As a sexual addict, Frank told his therapy group that his addictive life was virtually undetectable because, feeling so ashamed, he worked hard to appear normal, pursuing activities in church leadership that made him seem moral and upright. Ironically, he was serving on an antipornography committee the same day he lied to a prostitute about his name and occupation so she wouldn't know who he was.

Denial and delusion are also part of sexual addiction. Although Frank frequently regretted his prostitution contacts, he denied that his affairs were a serious manifestation of his addiction—let alone part of the same problem. Frank had just had lunch with an old lover, claiming they were now just friends, and he believed this facet of his addiction still remained hidden. But the group's reality check reminded him of his history with her—and that he was just kidding himself if he thought this was not a mutually destructive relationship.

In addition to the client's cloak of shame and secrecy, which makes it difficult for the therapist to get information, the treatment of sexual addiction lacks substantive research.

To date, no interviewing method or data-gathering process guarantees candor from people whose sexual compulsivity has become unmanageable. Even if total honesty could be achieved, most addicts have such a high level of denial they could not admit to others what they cannot yet admit to themselves.

In addition to research, a model must be developed that accounts for the patterns of sexual powerlessness and unmanageability that transcend many behavior categories. We have studies of individuals who have enjoyed multiple affairs, exhibitionism, or have been involved in excessive use of pornography or masturbation. But what about exhibitionists, for example, whose affairs and pornography form interlocking behavioral segments of a larger, destructive pattern? To label a set of behaviors too narrowly may mean that the illness is not correctly or adequately diagnosed, and so it may rage on unchecked, unnamed, unperceived.

In recent years sex researchers have done a great service by describing the breadth of human sexual experience and by pinpointing ways to enhance sexual performance. By and large, however, they have not focused on sexual compulsivity. Most of the literature on compulsivity has come from researchers who are connected in some fashion with the criminal justice system, and they never see the many addicts who have not been arrested. Those sexual addicts who have been arrested and/or incarcerated are unlikely to provide much information. In fact, the last person an addict would be honest with is the arresting officer, probation officer, or prison researcher.

The power of Gollum's ring to protect the sexual addict has not kept the problem from surfacing, however, along with a number of explanations for addictive sexual behavior, which brings us to the problem of creating a viable paradigm.

Models That Don't Work

The director of a social work training program calls that part of his curriculum dealing with sexual addiction "The World's Oldest/Newest Perplexity." In many ways, this is a good title. Professionals have long struggled to make sense out of compulsive sexual behavior. There are, however, some general categories, or models, which have been used to solve the perplexity.

Viewing Sexual Addiction as a Failure of Morals

One model sees sexual behavior as a moral choice. Thus, failure of morals or lack of character would underlie sexual excess. This position parallels the early views on alcoholism; twenty years ago it was considered a moral lapse not to be able to turn down a drink. Considering the American Medical Association's official declaration that alcoholism is a disease, it's obvious there has been an enormous change in professional attitudes and also progress in helping alcoholics and their family members.

This comparison is important. The alcoholic believed he was totally responsible for his drinking; society and his family certainly held him accountable. However, the pain caused by repeated failures to control his drinking through will power in effect intensified the problem. Family members operating under the same assumptions would also try to control the alcoholic's drinking, which added destructive energy to the alcoholic's self-defeating cycles.

Alcoholics Anonymous has known for years that the secret to recovery for the alcoholic and the alcoholic's family members is first to admit they are powerless. Acknowledging loss of the power of choice precedes recovery. Looking at the problem of alcoholism as an illness with a definite symptomology has moved the problem from the moral to the medical. Fortunately, most professionals, who work every day with the paradoxical nature of human systems, appreciate the fact that a person regains choice by admitting powerlessness and that values can be reclaimed by moving out of the realm of morality.

Sex addiction also parallels alcoholism in its multigenerational characteristics. An exhibitionist discovers that he has two uncles and three cousins with police records for exhibitionism; a woman traces incest and sexual promiscuity in her family back at least four generations. Matters of individual morality pale in the face of cycles which have generations of power behind them.

Tracing family patterns of sexual addiction can help the client stop making moral self-judgments. In a sample of members of Sexual Addicts Anonymous described later in this book, a high percentage of the respondents reported sexual abuse as children. In no way does this mean that the cause of sexual addiction is sexual abuse as a child, or that a person has to have been abused in order to be an addict. Abuse is simply one indicator that children who were powerless over what was done to them can become powerless over their own behavior in later years.

People generally fear the notion of addiction because they believe the addict will not be held responsible for the consequences of his or her unacceptable or even life-threatening behavior. Again, the parallel with alcoholism helps alleviate these apprehensions. For example, drunk driving is the major cause of deaths from car accidents, yet our knowledge of alcoholism as an illness has not lessened the legal consequences for the alcoholic. If anything, the trend is toward tougher penalties.

So, too, sexual addicts must be accountable for the consequences of their behavior.

The Biological Model

A popular folklore version of this model suggests that when God made some people, there was a mistake and too much sex was put in their genes—they turned out "oversexed." Unfortunately, many addicts see themselves this way. Feeling so unique, they can excuse their behavior to themselves as the result of an irrepressible sex drive, a drive so powerful they feel they must end up sacrificing everything they value.

Thus far, serious efforts to document a consistent relationship between sexual compulsivity and biological factors have failed. Most research has focused on differentiating between sex offenders and normal populations. Studies of temporal lobe lesions or excessive neuronal discharges in subcortical brain areas have been inconclusive. Studies of testosterone and other endocrine secretions have simply underlined the difficulty of isolating and separating physiological variables from the analysis of a complex behavioral problem.

A few recent studies report success in treating both sex offenders and "hypersexual" individuals by using a group of compounds known as antiandrogens. Small studies with tentative conclusions, they raise some interesting questions about treatment but do not establish any causal relationships. As one reviewer, John Bancroft, observes, those "looking for simple biological explanations of human behavior would be advised to search elsewhere."[2]

Researchers have noted one important point that separates sex offenders from other populations and has biological implications: the noticeable presence of alcohol as part of sex crimes. This pattern holds in studies of diverse populations, including incest parents, rapists, and child molesters. For example, George Barnard at the University of Florida College of Medicine and his colleagues have summarized some of the relationships that researchers hypothesize exist between alcohol and rape:

1. The pharmacological effects of alcohol release an individual from the usual constraints, thus permitting rape as one of many possible antisocial acts.
2. The use of alcohol provides a psychological and social context in which the usual restraints on deviance are not considered relevant.
3. Chronic alcoholism produces psychological and social disorganization in the individual which may result in sexual violence.

4. A person with a deviant personality structure may engage in a wide variety of sociopathy including, but not restricted to, disturbed interpersonal relations, sexual violence, and alcohol abuse.[3]

Barnard suggests that all may have truth and, in fact, complement one another.

Another hypothesis holds that some people are naturally addiction-prone to pleasure. This posture assumes that high stimulation or pleasure situations—including drinking, eating, sex, gambling, or even sky diving—can take the form of an addiction. Perhaps one of the most systematic and carefully documented statements was made by Brown University psychologist Richard Solomon. His "opponent process" theory of addiction suggests that psychological and physiological responses of pain and pleasure have a common pattern which in the right sequence can turn anyone into a pleasure "junkie."[4]

An intriguing framework has been developed by Milkman and Sunderwirth in which they divide addictions into three categories: (1) the arousal addictions, including amphetamines, gambling, high risk experiences, and sex; (2) the satiation addictions, including compulsive overeating, depressant drugs, and alcohol; and (3) the fantasy addictions, including psychedelics, marijuana, and mystical and artistic obsessions.[5] They propose a matrix using the three categories and nine hormones which govern the electrochemical interactions of the synapses of the brain, seeking possible psychobiological connections among the various addictions. Such research is promising because it may help further explain how addicts get high without using mind-altering substances.

When these hypotheses are combined with Barnard's about alcoholism and rape, the possibility emerges that another subset of the criminal population exists: those with two primary addictions, sex as well as alcohol.

Before speculating further, however, we need to explore some other explanations for sexual compulsivity beyond biology, including the great debate—personality structure versus learned behavior.

Personality and Behavioral Models

Most available research on sex offenders or "perversions" offers two competing frameworks: the psychodynamic or personality construct view, and the behavioral view. Psychodynamic or personality approaches seek to understand how past experiences form a personality type such as "psychopathic" which could account for sexual acting out. Behavioral approaches focus on the current behavior and the treatment processes necessary to change it.

Both frameworks are far from definitive. Arizona State University psychologists C. David Blair and Richard Lanyon, in a review of the literature on exhibitionism, make some observations which could well be generalized to all literature on the subject. They observe that "despite the abundance of case reports and clinical speculation, remarkably little research exists to substantiate theory, to substantiate treatment, or to link theory to treatment."[6]

When personality researchers give a personality instrument to a group of rapists or exhibitionists, they can conclude on the basis of an average profile that the group "tends" to be introverted, psychopathic, or whatever category fits. At best, such generalizations need to be qualified because the range of scores is usually too varied to be definitive. In some studies no conclusions are warranted. As Smukler and Scheibel write about a group of exhibitionists: "The data does not support any definitive character type or evidence of severe pathology. If specific reference to their symptom of exhibiting is omitted they do not appear to be strikingly abnormal."[7]

Consider the Minnesota Multiphasic Personality Inventory (MMPI). Generally, it has an established record as a reliable clinical instrument. The "4" scale measures psychopathic deviancy based on a number of questions about whether the client has exceeded normal sexual boundaries. The sexually compulsive person who responds honestly will have an elevated 4 scale—which would mean a failure to develop the capacity to live within "conventional" standards of behavior. In reality, this person may have a very strong value system which is being affected by the addiction, in which case the label of psychopathic deviant would not be accurate.

Classification in the disease of alcoholism is also inconclusive. In the latest edition of the *Diagnostic and Statistical Manual of Mental Disorders*—or the DSM III—of the American Psychiatric Association, alcohol and drug abuse are no longer classified as personality disorders. Thus, from a personality perspective, an alcoholic could also be depressed, or psychopathic, or psychotic—or all of the above. Or perhaps have no personality pathology at all.[8]

Although researchers in the personality school of thought have not reached conclusions on the origins and treatment of sexual compulsivity, at least a common ground is forming: most are starting to acknowledge the role of "addiction." Some researchers note a pattern in the literature on excessive or compulsive sexuality which can be described as "addictive." In his review of professional descriptions of loss of control in sexual behavior, Jim Orford comments that many terms for this phenomenon have been used: the Casanova type, compulsive promiscuity, Don Juanism or Don Juanitaism, erotomania, hypereroticism, hyperlibido, hypersexuality, idiopathic sexual precocity, libertinism, the Messalina complex, nymphomania, oversexuality, pansexual promiscuity, pathologic multipartnerism, pathologic promiscuity, satyriasis, and sexual hyperversion.

Orford also points out that most reported cases involve individuals who have pursued many types of behavior including "perverse" and aggressive, but common to all of them is the element of uncontrollable desire:

> Preoccupation with the object of these desires and with the means of consuming or partaking of it is another recurrent theme. The behavior itself is felt inappropriate and in excess of what the individual or other people or both would consider normal. The activity is often engaged in response to the experience of unpleasant affect. Most significantly is described the experience of conflict and the attendant ambivalence and guilt. Attempts at self-control, through a variety of tactics, are usually described as well. These and others are features common to the experience of excessive appetitive behavior whether the object be the consuming of alcoholic drinks, the placing of bets, or heterosexual activity.[9]

Behaviorists, too, have begun to consider addiction as a viable paradigm. William Miller in his book, *The Addictive Behaviors*, writes:

> What do the following have in common: alcoholism, obesity, smoking, drug abuse, and compulsive gambling? Until a few years ago, these were thought of as relatively independent and separate problem areas. Psychologists, psychiatrists, social workers, and other mental health professionals have often specialized in the treatment of one of these behaviors, but few have extended their therapy and research efforts to cover more than one or two of these disorders. In addition, specialists in each of these areas have worked in relative isolation from one another, seldom communicating with each other about treatment and research issues. . . . The past few years, however, have witnessed a remarkable amount of growth and change in professional knowledge within these areas. The emergent concept of "the addictive behaviors" points

to possible commonalities among these seemingly diverse problems.[10]

The establishment of journals like *Addictive Behaviors, The International Journal of the Addictions,* and *The British Journal of Addiction* indicate that professionals from a variety of theoretical camps have begun to use addiction as a working model. In 1983, the American Academy of Addictionology was established with support from the Kroc Foundation to support the development of addictionology as a specialty in behavioral medicine.

Given the amount of literature and clinical experience on sexual compulsivity that we now have, to include sex as one of the more potent addictions would seem a natural progression.

To understand what resistance exists to its inclusion along with the other addictions, we need to appreciate the competing cultural and environmental explanations as well as professional biases.

Cultural and Environmental Explanations

A comparison of cultures reveals a great diversity in what are acceptable sexual practices. Prostitution in Japan has long been viewed as an honorable profession. Legalization of pornography in Sweden and Denmark is considered responsible for the decrease in incidence of child molestation, perversions, and other sex deviations. A California psychologist conducts workshops teaching women how to have successful affairs which are supportive of their marriages.[11] Undoubtedly, culture helps define "normal" sexuality.

But to some, sex is an index to all that is wrong with a culture. Consider the following statement made in 1950 by then assistant attorney general for the State of California, Eugene Williams. It is still worth quoting at length:

> In a world where living has become most complex, where nerves are keyed to a higher pitch; where spiritual values have been entirely forgotten; where religion has been displaced by a pseudo-intellectual and pseudo-scientific conglomeration of half-baked superficialities which individuals are pleased to call their "philosophies of life"; in a world where there are no ethics except that of "not getting caught"; where there is no set principle of right and wrong, where children are brought into the world and educated according to the principle that a child should be permitted to express its own personality without restriction; where discipline and self-restraint and consideration for the rights of others are neglected as old-fashioned and too difficult; in a world where the philosophy that asserts that "I'll try anything once" is considered a satisfactory attitude for the young and inquiring mind; in a world where there is too little religion and too much idle time; there has developed a startling and dangerous increase in sex perversion.[12]

In this view, loose morals cause the collapse of "normal" sexual behavior. Sex remains supercharged in the 1980s for the Moral Majority as a sign of impending disaster. To suggest that sexual compulsivity might be an addictive illness similar to alcoholism engenders deep rooted fears on the part of those who see it as a signal of how far we have fallen.

In one sense, the "decline of civilization" theory helps us find answers. We do live in unsettled times. The threat of nuclear conflict, technological development, and economic dislocation are just part of a list of new or added stresses. These changes correlate highly with anxiety, alcoholism, child abuse, and family violence. Under such conditions, some people will cope with increased pressure by an addictive relationship with sex; that is, sex becomes another means of dealing with stress.

But those who contend that compulsive sexuality signifies cultural decay oversimplify a complex problem. The fear of calling sexual compulsivity an addiction testifies to the enormous significance we attribute to sex in our culture; and our reluctance to name the addiction for what it is reflects our overall discomfort on the subject.

This discomfort has deep roots. Master historian Phillipe Aries makes an intriguing series of observations about death and sex as connected sources of obsession and dread in the rise of modern scientific thought. Aries' book, *The Hour of Our Death,* carefully documents how Western culture shifted from a comfortable, knowledgeable acceptance of death as part of nature to an attitude of fear, ignorance, and denial.

Sex, too, went through a major transition, becoming in Aries' words "as fascinating and obsessive as the other."

Aries points, for example, to the words of eighteenth-century physicians writing about death and about masturbation:

> The doctors lose their composure as they approach the floodgates through which the chaos of nature threatens to invade the rational city of man. In the solitary vice and the "comatose" state, they discover sex and death in unusual and untamed forms, which they denounce with the conviction and authority of guardians of civilization. In both cases one senses in these men of science and enlightenment a rising fear: the fear of sex—and a more basic fear, which is the fear of death. A connection has been made between death and sex: the one has become as fascinating and obsessive as the other. They are the signs of a fundamental anxiety that does not yet have a name.[13]

As humankind in the eighteenth century deified reason, we became more and more uncomfortable with those aspects of life which are clearly beyond reason—sex and death. Our view of death is key to understanding the addiction to sex, and we'll return to it in chapters 7 and 8 as the "dread" that has to be faced in treatment. For now, we need only acknowledge how culturally fundamental is our fear of "uncontrolled" sex.

Besides Aries, many historians have documented shifts in our sexual attitudes in the eighteenth and nineteenth centuries. In a masterpiece of historical detective work, *Education of the Senses,* Peter Gay traces the increasing denial and distance we placed between ourselves and our sexuality in the nineteenth century. He also documents the fact that despite Victorian cultural trends, people were intensely sexual and enjoying it. They simply did not think others did.[14]

Gay's picture of Victorian middle class sexuality parallels our own current attitudes and makes clear that there is another reality to acknowledge that limits the acceptance of a sexual addiction—the reality that modern culture in the mainstream denies the intensity and the psychological importance of the sexual experience. Despite Freud, Kinsey, and Masters and Johnson, many people, including professionals, are surprised at how sexual we humans are, although this is not readily apparent because despite our natural need to express ourselves sexually, we cling to an outward appearance of naivete.

In addition, sexual politics add heated feelings to any discussion of sex and culture. Feminists like Kate Millet *(Sexual Politics)* and Susan Brownmiller *(Against Our Will)* have argued effectively that sexual abuse and exploitation of women is part of a naturally "sexist" social order.[15] One of the most thoughtful statements on this issue is *Psychic War in Men and Women* by Helen Block Lewis. She writes of an exploitive society which injures the sexes differently. Men are made into "expendable warriors" and women are made into "inferior childbearers" who, in Block's view, "alternate paths to madness." She underlines the pathological beliefs about sex—man as the aggressor/performer and woman as the passive object—which perpetuate the tension between men and women. For example, in cultures where sexual initiative is shared equally, exploitation and violence against woman are notably absent.[16]

Separating sexual compulsivity from pathological sexual beliefs and sexual oppression issues is complicated enough, but, in addition, there are those who ask us to look at the environment. A range of environmental factors is used to explain unusual sexual behavior. For instance, there are quite convincing studies which show that incidence of sexual abuse is related to the weather. Also, there is research which shows that sexual assault is related to opportunity, e.g., a bus strike which causes young women to be hitchhiking can account for dramatic increases in the incidence of rape.[17]

Isolating variables in the environment is difficult. To illustrate, take money as a variable. In one case, a very wealthy client had ongoing sexual relationships with over thirty women in cities all over the country, three of whom he supported financially. When asked what would happen if he suddenly no longer had any money, his response was immediate: "I know what I would do, I would become a rapist." Or consider the wealthy attorney whose daughter's report of incest was quickly covered up due to his legal expertise and political connections. How much desperation in how many lives will remain invisible to the researcher simply because of economic resources?

Or, why is it some cities have an extremely high incidence of sexual abuse of children? Is this due to socioeconomic factors or the composition of local ethnic and minority populations? Or is public awareness sufficient to encourage the reporting of abuse? Or is it because police and child protection workers are particularly effective at bringing abuse cases from discovery to prosecution? Any of these separately or in combination could account for comparatively high numbers of incidence.

In general, most people recognize that cultural and environmental factors make for an exceedingly complex set of causes for compulsive and/or criminal sex behavior. For example, when two University of South Dakota researchers, Thomas Jackson and William Ferguson, polled over four hundred students on what they believed caused incest, they found that "individuals consider the roles of offender, victim, society, and situation in their attribution of incest blame."[18]

To give credence to a sexual addiction is difficult at best when sexuality serves as a touchstone for so many other significant issues and when there are so many variables to be understood. Further, we haven't approached yet some of the more controversial issues such as homosexuality or transvestism. But primarily there is our fear. To admit to the possibility of a sexual addiction would force us to acknowledge the level of our fear about sex, collectively and individually. This fear is reflected in the professional biases of some people pledged to help the addict.

The Problem of Professional Bias

The head of a federal regional office responsible for establishing funding priorities for alcohol and drug abuse observes during his talk at a state conference, "We will be able to do serious research once A.A. and Alanon die out."

A well-known therapist gives a workshop session on how redefinition of the client's problem can help. He uses a case example of an exhibitionist whose real problem—according to the therapist—was not his behavior, but that he got caught at it. Therapy involved having the exposer's wife help him find situations to act out where his chances of being reported would be less.

A forty-two-year-old man is admitted to an emergency room for an injury from his large male dog with whom he had been sexual. His parish priest and the hospital chaplain recommend that he be admitted to the hospital's incest program because the man is also sexual with his two daughters—and sometimes involves the dog with them. The consulting psychiatrist refuses to refer the man to the hospital program ostensibly because the program is not run by a physician. The psychiatrist sees the man privately. The daughters report two years later that the abuse continues.

At a national conference, videotapes are being shown of a child molester who is talking of his relief after using the drug Depo-Provera. He describes in an emotionally moving way how the side effects, such as weight gain and increased breast tissue, are a small price to pay for not having to struggle anymore. While he speaks, the therapist presenter showing the videotape, clearly uncomfortable, makes derisive and jarring comments about this client.

A university professor is admitted to a hospital mental health ward for depression brought on by some students who reported seeing him leave a massage parlor. During his three-week stay, the issue of his repetitive use of prostitutes is treated as a peripheral issue. Within four weeks he is using prostitutes again. He feels a total failure and attempts suicide.

An incest father is sent to an alcoholism unit for his drinking problem. By the end of treatment he feels the best he can ever remember feeling. In addition to being chemically free, it is the first time in years he has been at peace sexually as well. However, the counselors do not address the sexual issues, insisting that he has to deal with his real problem: alcoholism. After treatment when he faces his first crisis, he is tempted to act out sexually. Since he feels that would be by far the worst thing he could do, instead, he chooses the next worst—he starts drinking. Later, in recovery, he comments that by comparison, drinking was much easier to stop.

An independent review group, a committee of research experts appointed by a federal agency, meets to examine a series of proposals for funding. One of the best proposals being reviewed includes the Twelve Steps as adapted for incest families. The program would refer to a community-based group that used these steps. One researcher mocks a dramatic reading of the Twelve Steps, ridiculing the use of such a resource. Despite the efforts of experts in attendance who recognize the merit of the proposal, the impact of the ridicule effectively puts the proposal out of the running.

The need to have control over patients, distrust of lay programs such as those based on the Twelve Steps of AA, distrust of other professionals, a lack of understanding, or worse, outright contempt of sexually compulsive clients can all be factors in professional decision-making. Particular damage to clients occurs when therapeutic decisions are made on the basis of faulty cultural beliefs.

Professional Prejudice

The attitudes of professionals today are not without precedent. Consider the words of Peter Steinglass a decade ago discussing therapists' reluctance to treat alcoholics:

> In exhibiting a singular lack of interest for the treatment of alcoholism, family therapists have merely been following the predilections of their colleagues in the mental health professions. Professional stereotypes toward alcoholism and the alcoholic have been well documented. The alcoholic is viewed as a distasteful, self-indulgent, weak individual involved in a pernicious cycle of self-destructive behavior. Motivation for change is thought to be extremely low and therapeutic work therefore felt to be unrewarding. Although originally viewed as scientifically objective, these stereotypes have more recently been characterized as culturally determined, and if applicable at all, applying only to a very small percentage of the alcoholic population. Therefore, in part the family therapist is merely suffering from cultural prejudices.[19]

Substitute "sexual addict" for "alcoholic," and the statement would unfortunately be accurate today, although feelings of disgust or contempt for the sexual addict may be stronger. What kind of woman or man would do such things?

Hard to treat, self-willed, indulgent, contemptible, weak, and incorrigibly self-destructive are descriptors used for sexual addicts. Add words like pervert, animal, sleaze, slime, abuser, or deviant, and whole new levels of meaning are added. Perhaps the worst condemnation would be to put the labels "sex fiend" or "nympho" and "drunk" together.

The therapist's own experience will dramatically affect his or her perspective on the illness. First, is the therapist a man or woman? Gay or straight? A victim of sexual assault or child abuse? Personal factors such as these most likely intensify the therapist's reactions and heighten the probability of fusing cultural prejudice with professional judgment.

Perhaps the greatest personal factor that can influence professional decision-making is the therapist's own addiction. Consider, for example, the psychiatrist who has scandalized a community for years because he is sexual with patients.

Even the consequence of losing his medical license does not stop his behavior. When he sees sexual compulsivity in his clients, he ignores the damage of the illness, just as he does in himself.

In fact, people who are professional helpers—nurses, physicians, ministers, psychologists—are especially prone to the illness, partly because they sometimes chose this life's work of "helping people" out of their own neediness as well as their low self-image. They also experience high-pressure training and demanding professional lives, which are often predeterminants of sexual addiction.

In addition to prejudice stemming from the fusion of personal experience, cultural beliefs, and professional stereotype, there is also the problem of professional "hardening of the categories."

Rigidity of Professional Concepts

Professionals use conceptual frameworks to organize reality and investigate ideas. However, after being used and relied on, these concepts become hard to abandon. When hypothesis-proving becomes rigid, we lose the capacity to be hypothesis-seeking.

Even the transition to a system approach in therapy suffers because of our investment in the old, more familiar categories. Minuchin, Rosman, and Baker write:

> Psychotherapy is now in a period of scientific revolution or paradigm shift. Therapists seem at present to be working with mixed theories. As a result, systems thinkers using old terms to explain new concepts, sometimes arrive only at global formulations. Psychodynamic clinicians, expanding their language to incorporate new meanings, may try to save old paradigms by creating complex elaborations, which serve only to confuse.[20]

Operating from rigid conceptual categories has serious concrete implications. For example, if a professional does not have a conceptual model to make sense out of client sexual behavior, but does recognize depression, he or she will treat what appears to be the problem. An alcoholism counselor who is very familiar with the alcoholic system of defenses quickly recognizes when an alcoholic brings in extraneous issues to avoid the reality of his or her drinking behavior. But, if that patient describes a concurrent sexual addiction of equal or greater power, the therapist may fail to recognize its significance. The professional's knowledge base must include the concept of sexual addiction in order to identify and treat it.

Sometimes inadequate concepts also limit the resources a professional can use. Some professionals criticize groups like Alcoholics Anonymous or Gamblers Anonymous for relying on inadequate resources and insufficient knowledge. The following comment from Claudette Cummings (et al.) illustrates this distrust of Twelve Step programs:

> These organizations foster dependency on the group and God that serves as the "cure" for the disease. This conversion to group support and external control makes therapeutic sense as a means of substituting dependency in place of the addiction. However, little is given to the client about what to do when he or she encounters a

> high-risk situation for relapse. These programs avoid the issue of breakdown of abstinence perhaps because they lack an understanding of the relapse process and the requisite behavioral skills necessary to handle such situations. In place of skills to prevent relapse or moderate the effects of relapse if it occurs, slogans are presented that unfortunately sound more like dogmatic tenets or axioms than like self-instructional or coping statements.[21]

Clearly, some professionals fail to understand the underlying principles and the operation of these groups. Twelve Step groups are very behavior-oriented, using modeling and feedback about past, current, and future behavior. Behavioral rehearsal in a group creates a sense of competence to operate in a nonsupportive world and supports behaviors associated with increased competence. As we shall see in later chapters, contrary to creating dependence, Twelve Step programs foster autonomy. They are, in effect, a systems intervention which operates at many levels and their widespread development and success can be regarded as one of the major intellectual events of this century. To dismiss the power of these groups because the members may lack professional expertise reveals a limited understanding of the psychologically therapeutic dynamics integral to the Twelve Step process.

To compound the problem, rapid and dramatic changes are occurring in the health care industry, creating an atmosphere which is not conducive to the growth of "new" illnesses. Unanswered questions such as, who can treat it and who will pay for it simply serve as catalysts for conflict.

So, finding an adequate model that helps to explain the experience of sexual addicts to professionals is not enough. We, as professionals, need to be open to all the many ways help can be given to our clients, even when the treatment doesn't involve us in a professional capacity. We also need to acknowledge our professional prejudices and the changing character of our professional life.

All professional helpers bring a set of beliefs to the problem of sexual addiction—beliefs forged out of experience, culture, and professional training. Given this, therapists need to be aware that they may have beliefs that limit their understanding and acceptance of sexual addiction.

Therapists need to understand each of the models that currently exist and to acknowledge that no one model, not even their own, is entirely accurate. Any model of sexual addiction is just a working tool which helps us come closer to understanding a particular patient's reality.

But what model or paradigm can help explain so complex a phenomenon as sexual addiction and what can penetrate the power of Gollum's ring? The next chapter describes a systems approach for creating a model of sexual addiction.

3
The Beginning of the Addictive System

. . . whereas in the beginning the difficulty had been to throw off the body of Jekyll, it had of late gradually but decidedly transferred itself to the other side. . . . I was slowly losing hold of my original and better self and becoming slowly incorporated with my second and worse self. . . .

Robert Louis Stevenson
The Strange Case of Dr. Jekyll and Mr. Hyde

Labeled a sex offender at age eighty-one, Ben, a grandfather of six, could not understand what had happened or why. Charged with the sexual abuse of his eleven-year-old granddaughter Joanie, Ben did not deny that they had been sexual, but he maintained, in his quavery, fading voice, that she had initiated their first sexual contact.

Ben had been babysitting Joanie and was taking a nap. She came in from playing and found him sleeping in the nude. Curious about his penis, she touched it, awakening him. He maintained that since she had started it, he should be held less accountable. Each time Ben brought up this argument, the court-appointed psychiatrist John reminded Ben that he had been the adult in the situation. Even if Joanie had initiated sexual contact, Ben, as the adult, should not have taken it further.

John was puzzled. Ben had a childlike quality that was much like a cooperative five-year-old. When asked questions,

Ben answered as honestly as he could, but without volunteering additional information. Despite the seriousness of his situation, he seemed to need nothing from John. Mostly, he retreated into himself and appeared to be in a trance-like state. At times he acted very naively; he did not know, for example, how to take a bus to get to his therapy sessions.

John began to doubt whether he was competent to deal with Ben. His professional career to that point had not prepared him to reach this man. He wondered if Ben was using an elaborate con; if a specialist should be called in to establish that Ben was too senile to treat; if he was overlooking something.

A turning point came one day after an explosive family session, especially dramatic for Ben's son Michael, who was Joanie's stepfather. Arrested twice for exhibitionism, Michael had thought he was the only one in the family with sexual problems, although he knew that alcoholism was a family issue. Michael and his wife Sue had been through treatment and were active in AA. Michael's older brother Benny had a serious drinking problem but refused all offers of help. Michael and Sue even guessed that the death of Michael's mother Emma some years earlier had been caused by her drinking.

Both father and son learned about the sexual secrets of their family in that session. They discovered that Michael's younger brother Loren was also an exhibitionist, that older brother Benny had at one time been charged with rape, but the charge had been dismissed, and that a "nephew," who had been raised in the family supposedly because of the death of the boy's parents, was in fact the son of Michael's elder brother and sister.

After other members of the family and the other therapists involved in the case had left, John and Ben remained to talk over the session. For a long time Ben gazed at the piece of newsprint on the wall on which their family had been diagrammed. The names of family members who were alcoholics or probable alcoholics were circled in red. Members whose sexual compulsivity or behavior had created a problem were circled in blue.

Ben sighed deeply. He began to talk to John while still gazing at the diagram on the wall. He talked of the last four years of his wife's life. Her illness had prevented any sexual contact between them. In the three years since her death he had not been sexual with anyone. In effect he had not been sexual in over seven years. At that time, he had reconciled himself that the sexual part of his life was over.

But this first breakthrough session was a relief to Ben, who, prior to the seven years of celibacy, had struggled secretly with his sexuality—mostly masturbation, prostitution, and incest with his daughter. His conversion to an extremely fundamentalist splinter group of Lutheranism helped, but he acknowledged that his "curse" had only gone underground. In fact, he read St. Paul's letters and often thought that Paul had struggled as he did, a fact he took great comfort in.

Until the incident with his granddaughter, Ben had thought he was free. But now, tears welling in his eyes, he turned to John and whispered, "My God, it never stops!"

John held Ben's frail shoulders as he sobbed. Ben talked about how he had been stunned during the session by the sexual happenings in his family he had not known about. He was sure however, it was God's punishment for his inability to deal with the curse—a curse now extending to his whole family.

Sexual addiction is so strong that it can span a person's entire life and spread through whole generations of a family. It is so virulent it can survive in many environments and even become dormant only to emerge at the least expected time. It is so deceptive that even intimate family members can be in its presence and not know its impact.

The addiction is a pathological system of great strength that envelops individuals and their families as it grows, drawing further strength from its environment. Defining this system and describing its growth are the tasks that will be undertaken in subsequent chapter sections. In many ways, this description will portray the loss of one personality as it is overcome by a second personality—the addictive personality. This almost Jekyll-and-Hyde-like transfer is often talked about by addicts themselves. In intervention and treatment, as we'll see in later chapters, addicts recover their true selves.

To define and describe the addictive system, we first need to establish the essential criteria for a model of the world of the sexual addict.

Guidelines for a Model of Sexual Addiction

Jim Orford did an extensive literature review examining the concept of sexual addiction in a 1978 issue of the *British Journal of Addiction*. While evidence of such an illness spanned centuries of professional and historical literature, he found that the term "sexual addiction" was not used until 1956 when Eisenstein used it to describe hypersexuality in marriage.[1]

Based on his review, Orford concluded that there are two compelling reasons why sexual addiction should be included in the larger domain of addiction theory. First, he suggested we should expect it simply on theoretical grounds. That is, there will always be some people who do behave compulsively:

> Our knowledge of drug taking, gambling, television watching, and consuming behavior in general must lead us to expect that the availability of a reinforcing activity will result in the population distributing themselves along a skewed frequency distribution curve. Whatever the activity, the majority engage in it in moderation or not at all. Fewer and fewer people do more and more of it. Very heavy, frequent, or immoderate indulgence in the activity is abnormal only in the statistical sense, but almost always

> carries greater risk of the incurring of various "costs" (loss of time, loss of money, social rule-breaking, bodily damage, impairment of performance, etc.) . . . it would be most surprising if there were no dissonant or "compulsive" heterosexuals. (Orford, pp. 307-308)

The other compelling reason is that the cases in Orford's study are "remarkably parallel to accounts of the experience of excessive drinkers, drug addicts, and gamblers" (Orford, pp. 307-308).

But Orford points to three inherent problems presented by developing a model for "dependence" on sex: (1) it is difficult to separate normal and abnormal sexual behavior; (2) it is difficult to determine when loss of control occurs; and (3) it is difficult to assess the role of culture in this addiction. By identifying these three problem areas, Orford points the way for us to begin to generate a set of guidelines for the development of a working model of sexual addiction.

Guideline One: A model of sexual addiction must account for the wide range of sexual behavior.

The first frequent criticism of the concept of sexual addiction is that it is difficult to separate normal and abnormal sexual behaviors.

Orford notes: "The distribution of amount of sexual behavior in a population follows a continuous unbroken curve with no evidence of a separate sub-population of people whose behavior is excessive and qualitatively different from that of the others" (Orford, p. 302).

Thus, for example, a homosexual person can be addicted to sex as well as a heterosexual. And a person who has affairs may or may not be addicted; a heterosexual who masturbates may or may not be addicted. To further complicate things, a person's addiction may include behaviors in one or more different categories, such as homosexual, transvestite, and heterosexual behavior. For a model of this addiction to work, it must describe the elements of the addiction that are common to various populations with any number of combinations of behavioral patterns.

Guideline Two: A model of sexual addiction must see "loss of control" on a continuum as opposed to a yes/no dichotomy.

Defining when the addict actually loses control over his or her sexual behavior has been a major issue in sexual addiction as with other addictions. Orford comments that "the field of alcoholism studies has been bedevilled by an all or nothing concept of control and uncontrol in precisely the same way as have discussions of excessive sexuality" (Orford, p. 308). He suggests that by seeing control as a continuum we can avoid some of the greater pitfalls of all or nothing diagnostic criteria for behavioral disorders.

We know that addicts frequently report periods of abstaining from addictive behaviors alternating with periodic bingeing—a situation which defies an arbitrary cutoff point in terms of control. Further, the periods of abstinence can be quite extended. Therefore, to accurately describe the world of the addict, a model of the addiction must accommodate the many fluctuations in sexual activity that exist in the lives of addicts.

Guideline Three: A model of sexual addiction must factor in the role of culture as part of the illness.

Orford further notes that describing compulsive sexual behaviors as pathological is incomplete, and therefore risky, because "it relegates differences in social habits and customs, and reactions to deviance, to a position of relative unimportance" (Orford, p. 304). Understanding culture is critical to understanding the growth of this addiction. At a minimum, cultural perceptions can support addictive behavior. One example in our culture is the movie hero Agent 007, whose sexual conquests are perceived as part of the good life. At the maximum, cultural proscriptions can enhance the excitement of sex behaviors by declaring them forbidden, illicit, or illegal.

Even within a certain culture, subcultural and individual differences exist that have an impact on the development of an addiction to sex. The Catholic female addict from Boston and the Baptist male addict from Atlanta will have great differences in their beliefs regarding religion and gender roles—beliefs that serve as driving forces in their respective addictions. However, in talking with one another they would soon discover that their experience of the addictive process is very similar.

What is considered deviant and what normal should vary within our definition of addiction, and whether or not addiction exists will be determined by other criteria, such as use or motive on the behavior and the consequences of acting out. A good working model will accommodate these differences.

Two observations are necessary. First, all helping professionals struggle with two levels of pathology: the illness of the people who need help and the cultural pathology. When does sexual victimization represent cultural, ideological, and/or sociological problems, and when is it an aspect of one person's addiction? The therapist consistently struggles with what appears to be an invisible line between the two levels—a fact that illustrates the functional relationship between culture and behavior. The problem compounds in that the perspective of the professional person may also be significantly affected by the larger pathology.

In the spirit of honesty and objectivity, we must remember that this book is a product of its culture. While the attempt here is to provide an expanded paradigm, it is still a paradigm that will be transformed and changed as our knowledge base grows.

Guideline Four: A model of addiction must indicate a definition of positive principles of change useful to the

therapist and understandable to the client and concerned family members.

Systems theory has helped therapists make sense out of the fact that it is hard for people to change behavior even though it is self-destructive, degrading, and even dangerous. The French expression, *Plus ca change, plus c'est la meme chose* (the more things change, the more they remain the same) is often used by Paul Watzlawick and his colleagues at the Mental Research Institute in Palo Alto, California, to encapsulate the addictive experience. The woman who marries the same type of abusing, alcoholic man three times makes a certain kind of change. However, the system she lives in remains the same. This example, and many others like it that are observable in lives where addiction exists, points to the principle or logical conclusion that a change in circumstance or situation does not equal a change of focus or direction.

In many families, alcoholism simply repeats its vicious cycle generation after generation. Some children of alcoholics resolve to go to the opposite extreme and become teetotalers. However, with alcohol still a central focus in their lives, the dynamics of control and obsession remain. As parents, they are stunned when their own children develop alcohol and drug dependency problems. Unwittingly, they have perpetuated exactly the nightmare that they wanted to escape.

The same pattern is common in sexual addiction. Addicts who become panicked at the unmanageability of their lives may use monumental self-control to eliminate their sexual misbehavior. Yet they remain just as obsessed about sex in an effort to obliterate the source of their shame and pain. In unrelenting messages to their children about the need for sexual control, they create an aura of excitement and fascination which ignites the addictive system in their own children. Similarly, spouses of addicts who suppress their own sexuality, and constantly search for evidence of sexual misdeeds as a way to control the addict, surpass the addict in terms of obsession with sex. What is worse, they add energy to the addictive system of the addict.

Perhaps most extreme are the cases where an addict launches a moralistic campaign about a sexual issue while his or her own addiction rages unchecked. A working model will accurately describe how to escape the addictive system and prevent the extreme lifestyles which serve only to keep things the same.

Guideline Five: A model of sexual addiction must specify the relationship between the internal system which drives the addict and the exterior interdependent support systems which give the addiction its life and power.

The growing acceptance of systems theory—particularly as a framework for marriage and family issues—stems at least in part from recognition of the superior therapeutic results achieved when the systems model is used compared to traditional intrapsychic efforts. The ill person is seen as an inextricable part of the interaction of a larger system which should be the target of the intervention.[2]

However, professionals using a systems framework have overlooked the internal system of the "identified patient." The critical question remains: What is the internal experience of the addict and how does that interface with family, friends, and culture?

Researchers who write about hypersexuality use terms like "a disorder of the self" to describe how excessive sexuality becomes a way to organize the personality. Many accounts describe the Jekyll-and-Hyde change in which the "real" person disappears and the addict takes over.[3] From a systems point of view, addiction presents an apparent paradox. How can a person as an addict, autonomous, increasingly isolated, and out of touch with reality, have at the same time a central role as the "symptom bearer" or "identified patient" in a larger system of family and friends? In concept, according to systems theory, both can be true. In fact, common sense would lead us, as therapists, to consider carefully both the addict and the system. Focusing on one to the exclusion of the other would necessarily limit our information and perspective. In a significant essay on the development of family therapy, Bradford Keeney observes:

> As many family therapists are aware, individuals are overlooked as separate, autonomous units in favor of seeing them as parts of a family organism or system. . . . Without any regard for autonomy, we are logically led to consider the whole universe as the appropriate unit of treatment. . . . The complete therapist . . . has an enriched vision that enables him to see both autonomy and connection of diverse forms of pattern.[4]

Our task in the remainder of this chapter and the next is to describe the addictive system as the internal experience of the addict. Chapters 4 and 5 will then show the addiction as part of an interactive system deriving sustaining energy from other members of the family system.

The systems model is ideal for describing sexual addiction, particularly its repetitive aspect. Essential to the definition of a system is that it is recursive and interdependent. If it repeats, it is a system. If it exists, it exists in context. The same is true for sexual addiction.

The key question is, how does it start?

The Beginning Stage of Sexual Addiction: The Initiation Phase

In the earliest phase, sexual behavior that is a percursor to addiction is difficult, if not impossible, to distinguish from normal sexual behavior.

Many people have intense sexual experiences as early as their grade-school years. Experimentation and curiosity are a natural part of psychosexual development. Guilt may result, but most people are able to move beyond it. Many addicts, however, report that the impact of these early activities was exceptionally intense. Sex seemed to be more important to them than to their peers. Also, addicts can often recall that self-stimulation was not merely experimentation; it was already a way to anesthetize emotional pain.

In general, much time in adolescent and young adult years is spent coping with emerging sexual desire. Normal development usually involves some trauma, frustration, anxiety, and disappointment. Often young people get involved in situations that have unfortunate consequences. These are used as learning experiences and simply are not done again.

Addicts often perceive their maturing years differently. They see this period as punctuated by a series of events in which their sexual behavior risked serious disapproval. Instead of learning experiences to draw upon for wisdom, they acquired a string of shameful memories that cast doubt on their normalcy. Another aspect of this time in addicts' lives is that sex became a way to get through life's difficulties and pressures.

Many adults continue to experiment by expanding their sexual experiences. In one recent and quite conservative study, 48 percent of men and 43 percent of the women reported having affairs while married.[5] Some people experiment by having a homosexual relationship, trying open marriage, joining a nudist club, or having group sex with other couples. Sometimes couples try to recover some of the intensity in their lovemaking through the use of pornography.

Some even seriously abuse themselves, such as sexually bingeing after a particularly painful divorce. Others, in surviving a difficult or lonely period, may be "temporarily promiscuous" with a number of persons. Whatever the outcome of the experiences, even though some degree of regret may exist, most of these people are able to make sense out of what happened and move on.

An addict, however, does not recover from these experiences but rather forges them into a ritualized pattern for coping with life. Not all addicts report this development history, however. Some addicts report—and all evidence supports their claim—that their growing up was quite normal. No sexual abuse. Relatively normal family lives. No unusual sexual problems. Even very limited sexual experience. But given an extraordinary situation with great stress and intensely pleasurable sexual experiences pursued to excess, they will begin to form a potent pattern of sex as stress relief with lifelong consequences.

Clinicians working with addicts need to search for the catalysts for these patterns. There are two major varieties: catalytic environments and catalytic events.

Catalytic Environments

Catalytic environments are characterized by extremes. For example, situations that combine high performance expectations with a low degree of structure seem to be particularly potent. Addicts who are professionals in various fields report that their addictions started and flourished during their training experiences—medical school, seminary, law school, graduate school. The demands of the curriculum, the competitive pressure to be one of the "survivors," and the high expectations of the family were coupled with lack of structure—a great deal of unscheduled time and only periodic accountability, when tests and papers were due.

The business world may also generate an environment that has high expectations and low structure. For example, a new salesman may be given a year to demonstrate his ability by developing a new territory.

Other examples of extremes include:

—the factory worker who spends a highly structured day doing extremely unskilled routinized labor and who aches for an escape

—the government official who has the extremely high expectations of the elected representative and also the total accountability under the unceasing scrutiny of the media and political opponents

—the professional sports figure who feels the pressure to serve as a "model" American hero and to be at a peak each season with the off-season requiring nothing

—the out-of-work minority individual who has no structure on time and few expectations to do anything about it

Common to all these extreme environments is a progressive self-doubt. Addicts typically say they never had much faith in themselves; even those who once were self-confident agree that at the onset of their addiction they were in an environment where they experienced a serious loss of faith in themselves.

As in many other addictions, procrastination seems to be the nemesis for sexual addicts. Many addicts talk about being unable to meet productivity expectations at work. Sometimes an addict will go into a last-ditch work binge to save the day, will use sexual behavior as a reward, and then will start procrastinating again.

Note that *anxiety* and *control* are common aspects of these experiences. The uncertainty of mastering unknown, uncertain, or extreme environments and inability to ensure acceptable outcomes are cornerstones of all addiction. The addiction supplies a temporary solution by allaying anxiety and giving momentary purpose to the self, but ultimately it compounds life problems. Anxiety and control will be themes throughout this book because of their central role in the addiction and its treatment.

In addition to noting the catalytic environments that are often part of the initiation phase of sex, the helping professional must help a client identify the catalytic events.

Catalytic Events

Catalytic events may be seen as falling into two major categories: abandonment events and sexual events. Usually, abandonment events involve a significant loss or a perceived significant loss.

For example, loss of parents—especially when a child is very young—is often interpreted as abandonment. From a child's point of view, a parent can be physically, emotionally, or even sexually abusive, and the child can still feel a sense of belonging. But if the parent leaves home, there is only one conclusion: the child was not acceptable—not worthy enough to stay for. Divorce, extended separation, and death—all can be perceived as abandonment.

Milton was a classic teenage sexual addict. By the time he was twenty, he had a string of arrests for exhibitionism and had been involved in organizing a teenage prostitution ring. He was also chemically dependent but had received court-mandated treatment for that. He counted his sexual addiction as worse, however. He had started when he was eleven, three weeks after his mother died. Part of therapy for Milton was to reinterpret what his mother's death meant to him. The eleven-year-old Milton had concluded that her death was a statement about him and his unworthiness. With help, the twenty-year-old Milton could grieve his loss and accept the pain he had avoided throughout his adolescent years.

Abandonment comes in many forms. Most of us regard the birth of a child as a welcome addition, but for male addicts who are married fathers, pregnancy and birth may be exasperating experiences in which they can no longer claim the same amount of attention from their spouses. Feeling unnecessary and uninvolved, they attempt to relieve their anger and distress by their excessive sexual behavior.

In another example, Martha started having clandestine affairs when her husband became so involved in work that he had little time for her. While maintaining her extra relationships, she started being sexual with her boss, which was very exciting for her. When he started to "take her for granted," she slept with *his* boss. With both men suspicious of the other, she played them off against each other. She found the power exhilarating, but her "games" left their corporation in a shambles.

In therapy, after the loss of her marriage and job, she began to make sense of her profound disappointment at the turn her marriage had taken. She realized that, in addition to using sex to medicate her loneliness, she had incorporated new, self-damaging beliefs: that she would never rely on just one person for her sexual needs and that she would never be in a sexual relationship she did not control. Changing those beliefs was critical to her recovery.

Identifying abandonment events allows clients to begin to replace faulty beliefs with accurate beliefs—to restructure those false conclusions addicts carry within them causing them to lose faith in themselves.

While abandonment events are unquestionably damaging, equally harmful in terms of igniting addiction are the catalytic events in the other main category—sexual events.

Arthur's life was filled with incidents of sexual unmanageability. Plagued by engaging in sex behaviors such as affairs, prostitution, and live porno shows, his major obsession was picking up transvestites and having sex with them. Sometimes these peak adventures were physically dangerous. Always they were degrading and always Arthur would resolve never to do it again.

When Arthur was young, his father had taken him out one evening and purchased the services of prostitutes for both of them. That was the beginning. Later, Arthur found out his father lived in a crazy, out-of-control world. Ever since that night with the prostitute, Arthur had lived with the distorted belief that as part of life's inevitabilities he was doomed to live a life like his father's.

Sandy was proud of the fact that she had had sexual relations with every man in her family by the time she was sixteen, including her father, three brothers, an uncle, and two cousins. This was a foreshadowing of sixteen more years of prostitution, sexual acting out, and the demise of two marriages. At age thirty-two, when confronted by a physician who told her that her fallopian tubes were too scarred by venereal disease to have children, she sought help. In treatment, she identified the first time she had sex with her father at age eleven, two months after her mother died, as the critical event that started her addiction.

Retrospectively, addicts can usually identify the initiation phase of their addiction. Sometimes aspects of the addictive system are present for many years before becoming the ritualized pattern of addiction seen in the subsequent establishment phase. Sometimes it is only a matter of months.

Clinicians may have the experience of working with someone whose behavior may be in the initiation phase, exhibiting all the potential of fully establishing an addiction. However, this behavior also may be just experimental. Therapy focusing on the restoration of faith in oneself and responsibility for self may be all that is required. Just as it's important to diagnose addiction, it's also necessary to remember that not every individual who has acted out sexually is on a doomed track to the addiction—although some people have a history with inevitability written throughout.

What are the signs of an addict in the making? The following aspects are common:

—coping with stress by using sex to relieve tension

—determination to find ways to maximize sexual behavior opportunities

—episodic periods of excessive acting out, or abusive sexual behavior

—concerns, disappointment, or guilt about sexual behavior

—loss of faith in oneself, feelings of unworthiness and distrust, while living in an extreme environment

—incongruency between feelings of exhilaration and degradation

—catalytic events which correspond with first episode of sexual excess

—perception of behavior as experimental, occasional, or short-lived, when in reality, it is regular, periodic, or increasing in frequency or intensity

—feeling exhilarated while sexually acting out when there is real danger from the act itself or from the possibility of detection

Once a pattern of behavior is developed, the addict enters the establishment phase of the sexual addiction. Once this stage is reached, the addiction casts a perpetual shadow on the addicts' lives and the lives of those who care about them.

Sexual Addiction's Second Stage: The Establishment Phase

Understanding sexual addiction has the effect of putting on a new set of lenses. New patterns emerge where none had been discernible before. The risk, of course, is that we will overinterpret and start to see addiction everywhere. Certainly, this risk should not be ignored. However, I believe we do not yet appreciate how widespread and entrenched in our culture sexual addiction is.

Our media—TV, magazines, radio, news, movies, and popular literature—all reflect a cultural preoccupation with sex and, in fact, indicate the prevalence of sex addiction. But it is not until a bizarre story breaks that we are willing to acknowledge that clearly something is wrong. And then we are so horrified at the extremity of the sexual crime that we see the event as unique, one of nature's monstrous and unexplainable absurdities, as opposed to the extreme end of a continuum of very common self-destructive patterns.

National headlines track the story of staff members of a preschool who face charges of having abused children over an appalling number of years. A story out of Colorado describes a series of highly ritualized homosexual murders. A report in the *Journal of the American Medical Association* receives much press because it documents over forty AIDS victims who had sex with the same man. As long as we dismiss these as random aberrations rather than an extension of a progressive pattern of addictive behavior, we will not be able to detect the majority of addicts whose illness is masked by secrecy and denial.

As professionals, we can learn to discern sex addiction if we develop an eye to detect its shadow. Once this eye-opening occurs, it is painfully easy to draw parallels between the cases seen in the therapist's office and the seemingly isolated notorious events in the media. Consider the following excerpt from "Valentina," an intriguing science fiction story in an issue of *Analog*. The story features Paul, an attorney whose sexual encounters, especially with underage women, served to complicate his life with deceit and intrigue. Worth quoting at length, the story truly captures the progression from the initiation to the establishment phase:

> Fridays were good for daydreaming. . . . Friday was followed by Saturday . . . and the best part of Saturday was Saturday night, when his wife Eva made her weekly trek to Houston to visit with her parents in the nursing home. She rarely ever called home and had never yet cut a Houston visit short. She always relied on Paul's assurance that the kids were all right on those occasions when she did call to check.

> His entry into the world of adultery had been both accidental and fortuitous. He knew better, of course. He knew that what he was doing was both socially unacceptable and criminal, but he counted on being able to cover his tracks well enough not to get caught.
>
> It had begun with Lila . . . who first crossed his path in life when she came to sit with his children, (and) had been the first, perhaps the most interesting, and certainly the most dangerous. Others followed, and it became a weekly ritual, planned carefully, executed with precision grown out of practice, until it became a polished routine.[6]

The Addictive Cycle

The first clue for the clinician that an addiction is established is regularity. In the story above, if Paul's experience were examined as a case history, it would be noted that his sexual life became predictable as opposed to spontaneous, and that the organizing principle of his life was the Saturday night trysts.

As an integral part of established, addictive behavior, a cycle emerges with four distinct and sequential components: preoccupation; ritualization; sexual compulsivity; and shame and despair.

Preoccupation

The addictive cycle begins at the point where the addict's thoughts become focused on the behavior. In the story above, Paul's Fridays were filled with hours of obsession in which he anticipated the events of the weekend to come and euphorically recalled the weekend before. His mental state was a kaleidoscope of feelings, fantasies, memories, hopes, and expectations. Paul provides a good example of the way that all addicts can mobilize from their own psychic resources a mood-altering "high" without actually being sexual. Just thinking about sex can initiate a trance-like state of arousal that can blot out the current demands of real life.

Using obsession as a coping mechanism leads to low productivity and procrastination. This kind of preoccupation is time-consuming. In fact, most of the sex addict's time spent in the addictive cycle is spent in preoccupation. The office, the shopping mall, the bus on the way home—all the everyday situations are transformed with sexualized energy. Work, responsibilities, and deadlines fade by comparison. In Paul's situation, Friday was the day of the weekly staff meeting of the firm's partners—from Paul's point of view, a great day to tune out.

The exciting sexual feelings will be intensified when the addict seeks stimulation for his or her obsession. Addicts refer to the search for stimulation as "cruising," which means deliberately seeking an object or environment that is provocative or opportune. Driving around to look at women, sitting as one of the few women in a singles bar, or even going to a health club can have the quality of "teasing oneself."

With this obsessive preoccupation, the addict has already lost control. Once a certain level of preoccupation is reached, rarely is there turning back. For example, addicts who use their cars for cruising often make statements like "Once I started thinking, it was as if the car had a mind of its own."

For recovery, it is critical to identify the cues—time of day, place, situation, or other—which trigger the onset of the preoccupation stage.

Ritualization

Addicts enhance their mental preoccupation with rituals, regularly followed methods of preparing for sexual activity to take place. Anyone who has worked with hypnosis, meditation yoga, or even competitive sports knows the use of ritual to induce trance, alter mental states, and enhance sensory experience. Anything can become a ritual for the addict. Again in the story of Paul, one ritual was arranging for the telephone company to forward home calls to the office where he had his Saturday night flings, in case his wife called. Other examples are:

—the exhibitionist driving regular "routes" or settings

—the incest parent making elaborate preparations to be alone with the child

—the professional speaker scanning the audience for potential partners

—the prostitute patron frequenting the noontime topless show

—the female addict showing up at the local hotel's cocktail hour

—the compulsive masturbator browsing in adult bookstores

—the fetishist or cross dresser shopping for clothes at a rummage sale

Rituals involve context. Certain places, especially cruising areas, focus the ritualization and trigger sexual obsession: bars, singles spots, city parks, lakes, beaches, campuses, public restrooms, stairways in buildings, elevators, shopping malls, parking lots, and porno shops. Sometimes rituals include movies, pornography, drugs, alcohol, and even articles of clothing.

Rituals that are deliberately negative in nature also exist. For example, an addict may routinely pick a fight with his or her spouse and then sexually binge in self-righteous anger. Or the addict may make inopportune or inappropriate sexual advances to the spouse, anticipating rejection, and then proceed to act out again, feeling fully justified.

Work behavior too can become part of negative ritualization. This may mean routine overextension to the point of exhaustion, when addicts become so depleted that (a) they can no longer make decisions for themselves, (b) they are desperately needy for nurturing at any price, and (c) they can use their vulnerability to manipulate others into taking care of them sexually.

Regular self-defeating behavior—living from disaster to disaster—is a consistent underpinning of addictive behavior. The sense of crisis adds energy to the rituals: "I need it to survive," or "I deserve it." With the addition of this kind of faulty logic, the addiction gains momentum and power.

The ritual seems magically to bring order out of chaos. Think of it as a dance—certain steps, certain sounds, ceremony, rhythm, special artifacts—which can be very elaborate but have only one purpose: to put addicts into another world so they can escape the conditions of real life over which they feel they have no control. Fantasy is compounded by delusion at this point, for the mood-altered state is a "world" in which the addicts no longer *care* about control in the same way. Sexual obsession is pursued to its peak regardless of risk, harm, or other consequences. There is only one kind of control that matters now—control of source of sexual pleasure. Once they start dancing, they rarely, if ever, can stop on their own.

It is absolutely essential that therapists and recovering addicts recognize the powerful role of rituals in addiction. In "reckless abandon" the next stage of addiction is entered: the sexual acting out.

Sexual Compulsivity

As this book goes to press, a considerable debate exists over the use of the word *compulsivity* versus the word *addiction*. Primarily, the question has been raised by professionals who see the word *compulsive* as a more accurate alternative to the word *addicted*. Others see the two words as interchangeable—and, in fact, a dictionary reading defines both with the words surrender and irresistible.[7] Rather than contribute to confusion or create an arbitrary definition, let me simply say that the way compulsivity is used in this book builds on a tradition in the chemical dependency field. Compulsive drinking was and is considered one of the signs of the illness, the addiction, of alcoholism. Compulsivity, essentially, is out-of-control behavior.

Sexual compulsivity, then, is the inability to control one's sexual behavior, and the behavior is the cornerstone of the addiction. To be preoccupied and to ritualize are precursors to this stage, but without the acting out the addiction is not established, because the behavior is still under control. However, determining loss of control with sex addiction is difficult because of the wide variety of behaviors possible. Nor is frequency a valid criterion. For example, there is no fixed number of times a day a person masturbates or has affairs, etc., which can be used as a cutoff point.

To start with, many times helping professionals are stunned at the large numbers of people who are involved sexually with the addict. To be sexual with thirty to forty people in a year or to maintain five to ten active sexual relationships simultaneously may seem overwhelming. In a decade's time this could mean sex with three to four hundred people who become a blur of faces and bodies. Actually, as we shall see, people in the acute phases of the addiction report contacts with literally thousands of people.

The number of contacts will mean different things to different addicts:

—number of anonymous sexual contacts

—number of prostitutes

—number of people exposed to

—number of relationships

—number of homosexual contacts

—number of child sex contacts

—number of sex acts seen

—number of nude people seen

—any combination or variation of the above plus many others

The number is important but not the critical factor in determining whether the addiction has reached the establishment phase. These combine to form a baseline of behavior which may not, in fact, involve any other people. For example, addicts who masturbate up to five times every day have a regular or recursive pattern. If they do this behavior even though they recognize that it conflicts with fundamental values held, then the behavior has taken the highest priority.

When the sexual behavior becomes the most important aspect of the addict's life, the addict now has a pathological relationship with a mood-altering behavior. People, job, family, values, the elements that give meaning to our lives, become secondary. The primary relationship, i.e., of primary importance, is with the behavior.[8]

Sometimes perceiving a regular pattern eludes professionals because the addiction may take the form of binge cycles. However, binge cycles also have a pattern. A binge may be a five- to ten-day spree followed by several weeks or even months of controlled behavior. In the establishment phase, these binges cease to be irregular periods of acting out and become predictable. When difficult to assess, if the client does a careful charting of the binges on a calendar, regularity of sexual acting out will emerge.

A helpful clue for the professional who suspects sexual addiction is to consider the client's despair, which is the last stage and the connecting link of the addictive cycle.

Shame and Despair

Pleasure and pain seem to be concomitant feelings in human existence. The addict's intense emotional pain is transformed into pleasure during the preoccupation and ritualization stages, becoming euphoria during the fleeting moments of sexual release. However, following the climax experience, the addict plummets into shame and despair more deeply with each repetition of the cycle. Isolation also increases.

Despair becomes the connecting link in all addictive cycles, creating the need to begin the cycle again. Whether the focus is food, drugs, alcohol, gambling, or sex, the addict relieves the low or "withdrawal" by getting high again. That is, to take away the pain of despair, he or she reenters the obsessive preoccupation, thus completing the cycle (fig. 3-1). Once complete, the cycle becomes self-perpetuating and autonomous. The purpose of the cycle in the addict's life is to keep pain at bay.[9]

Often, addicts in the despair stage of the cycle appear to be depressed. At this point they may make efforts to curb or stop the sexual behavior. These efforts may account for the times of abstinence of the periodic binger. The despair often has to do with shame at the loss of control.

There are two kinds of mistakes clinicians often make about the addict's despair. The first is to diagnose the depression as simply depression and not tie it directly to the addiction. For example, one common error is to view the sexual behavior as symptomatic of the depression. Another error of this kind would be to assess the despair as excessive guilt, masking a depressed state. Such clinical misjudgments are easy to make during the establishment phase of the addiction, in contrast to the obvious extremes reached in the contigency or acute phases to be described later. To help the sex addict, the therapists must carefully assess whether the despair is that which is an integral element of the addictive cycle, or whether clinical depression is present as well.

The Addiction Cycle

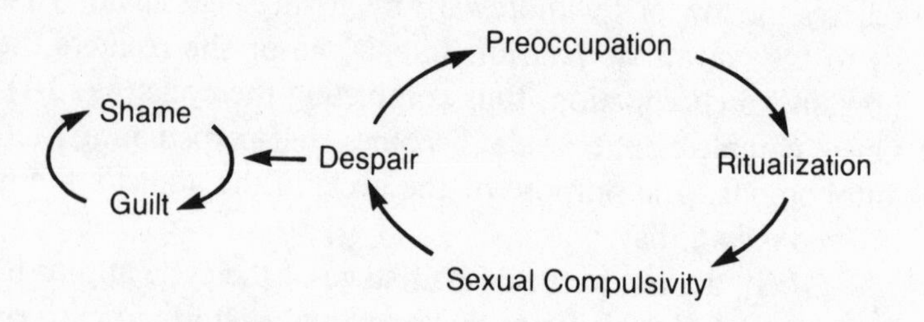

Figure 3-1

The other mistake is to dismiss the possibility of an addictive cycle if there is no despair. No efforts to control or stop the behavior or no emotional letdown after sexual acting out may simply mean that the addict is not connecting feelings with behavior. Sometimes when little unmanageability and few consequences are experienced during the establishment phase of the addiction, the addict may mostly be aware of the exhilaration. These feelings of excitement obscure not only the moments of despair, but also feed the addict's denial.

When the mood swings are less discernible, professional helpers can look beyond the addictive cycle itself. This cycle rests in a larger addictive system that has three other elements supporting the cycle's recursive patterns: the addict's belief system, impaired thinking, and unmanageability (fig. 3-2).

The Larger Addictive System: The Framework for the Addictive Cycle

Just as the addictive cycle is self-perpetuating, the larger addictive system, of which the cycle is a subsystem, also reinforces itself. The four component subsystems are the belief system, impaired thinking, unmanageability, and, as noted, the addictive cycle.

The driving force of the addictive system is the belief system, the addict's filtering lens through which he or she views the world. This includes all the messages, conclusions about self, family rules, myths, meanings, information, "self-evident truths," prejudices, and guesses regarded as fact gathered from life experience and combined to form an interlocking mosaic of beliefs. Through this belief system all decisions are filtered.

The addict possesses faulty beliefs which give the addiction its momentum. Some are cultural beliefs, like the one that says a "good" woman is in charge of her sexuality and is also responsible for male behavior. This belief might be

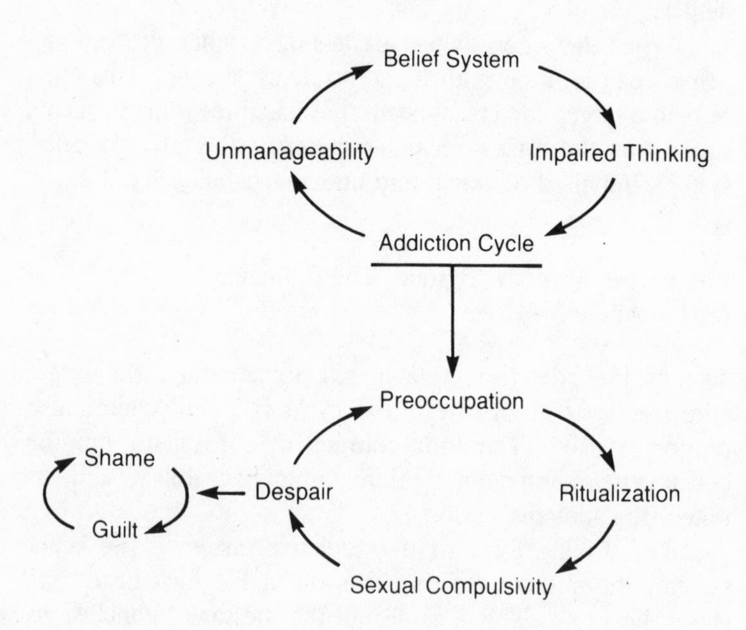
The Addictive System
Belief System
Impaired Thinking
Addiction Cycle
Unmanageability
Preoccupation
Ritualization
Sexual Compulsivity
Despair
Shame
Guilt

Figure 3-2

confirmed by family messages not to enjoy oneself sexually. For a woman to be out of control sexually while holding such a belief would support other fundamental attitudes she held about her own unworthiness. These core beliefs are critical to understanding the addiction and its treatment. Their etiology will be the focus of chapter 4.

During the establishment phase of the addiction, the most important indication of faulty beliefs is when the addiction increases the addict's negative feelings about him- or herself. Being out of control comes to mean, "I am a bad, unworthy person." Flowing out of the faulty belief system is impaired thinking. A female addict may rationalize her multiple affairs with the reasoning that they are all with married men and, as such were not harmful and may enhance her own marriage. Focusing on the rationalization, she ignores the addictive pattern of her behavior, the negative consequences, and growing unmanageability.

Impaired thinking usually involves a distortion of reality. The same woman may see these affairs as significant love relationships with almost "cosmic" implications, ignoring the reality that these sexual encounters are fleeting, degrading, and exploitive.

Other types of impaired thinking include denial, rationalization, self-delusion, self-righteousness, or blame of others.

But the addict's problem is that despite all the denial and distortion, reality does creep in. No amount of self-justification can account for all the complications in the addict's life. Anxiety and alienation occur in the family. Relationships are neglected. The addict violates personal values such as honesty or fidelity. Procrastination and low productivity at work may compound the difficulties. The addict's life becomes unmanageable.

Going back to the short story of "Valentina," Paul was very confident that he would be able to cover up his Saturday night adventures. But all cover-ups require deceit. In Paul's case, when a security computer revealed a record of his activities, he had to tell further lies to cover up his cover-ups. Like most addicts, Paul started to participate in a double life—one public and respectable and the other intensely secret and shameful. In instances like this and in the case of all sex addicts, fear of discovery is a constant companion.

Reality, i.e., the consequences which the addict cannot rationalize completely away, keeps the addict's life unmanageable. The split between delusion and reality eats away at the addict's sense of self. This loss of faith in oneself, originally precipitated by the catalytic factors in the addict's life, deepens with the regular repetition of the addictive cycle. An eroding self-concept adds to the addict's pain and contributes negative emotional energy to core beliefs about his or her unworthiness.

When the addictive cycle has become fully established, the addictive system becomes an autonomous, closed system, feeding upon itself, maintaining regularity and priority.

Signs that an addictive system has formed and that the addict is in the establishment phase are:

—Preoccupation becomes a routine way to avoid problems.

—Rituals emerge which usually precede sexual behavior.

—A baseline of regular behavior can be established.

—Behavior becomes a priority over other meaningful aspects of life.

—Periods of depression are sometimes followed by efforts to curb or stop behavior.

—Behavior and unmanageability confirm destructive core beliefs about self.

—Thought processes distort reality, creating unrealistic confidence and negating potential problems.

—Reversal of life priorities causes complications in family, work, relationships, and values, and the addict starts to live a double life.

When the addiction moves beyond the establishment phase, greater degrees of intensity are experienced, as well as greater suffering. The next chapter focuses on the further phases of growth of the addictive system.

4
Growth of the Addictive System

Don Juan is a character of endless fascination. His story has mythic proportions, resonating with powerful emotions, unconscious needs, and identifications that are fundamental to the nature of man. Poets and playwrights have created many versions of this legendary libertine in their efforts to confront the essence of his character. In literature, Don Juan may take the form of a lovable rake or a dissolute villain. He variously evokes admiration, pity, envy, and condemnation. In Mozart's mythopoetic masterpiece, Don Giovanni becomes the archetype of ruthless hedonism, unrepentant even as he is dragged into hell. Evil and retribution are the central forces of this great work. Don Juan, in his various guises, grips the human imagination because he personifies feelings and impulses which—to a degree—are universally shared. . . . While Don Juan as a patient is a frustrating problem, as legend he is a continuing source of inspiration to the creative artist.

Milton Eber
Bulletin of the Meninger Clinic
July 1981

The Question of Inevitable Progression

The classic model of alcoholism has traditionally defined the illness as progressive, meaning that it inevitably gets worse.

While this may be true for the greatest number of cases, other patterns of alcoholic drinking have been observed by professionals, leading researchers to challenge the notion of "inevitable progression," and to expand the definition of alcoholism to include a wider variety of alcoholic drinking patterns. This discussion of the process of defining alcoholism provides a springboard for advancing our attempt to define sex addiction.

Human behavior in all its complexity defies absolute categories; people don't *always* do anything. This fact combined with the fact that the study of sexual addiction is really in its infancy reminds us that a rigid and categorical definition is not realistic. So, it is with an attitude of openness and a pioneering spirit that we continue to describe and define the terms of sex addiction, arguably the most complex, embedded, and difficult to understand of all addictions.

Given available empirical data, it can be said with considerable certainty that sex addiction is not inevitably progressive. Some addictive patterns are, some are not. Some sex addicts' behavior remains *relatively* constant for their lifetimes. Others quickly escalate their addictive behaviors within a month of establishing a base line. Some escalate to such a degree that the illness becomes acute, governing every facet of their daily lives. Others de-escalate their behavior, controlling it for years. In most cases, these people are still addicts, in a stage comparable to what alcoholics call "white-knuckle" sobriety, since fear and obsession continue to govern their lives. Another much smaller group of addicts escalate to chronic illness.

A model that insists addiction is *always* progressive is a linear model. Sex addiction, because of the complexity and number of variables, is more accurately described by a systems model which is multidimensional and interactional. This model allows us to see order in what had seemed chaos. For example, we can observe that compulsive behaviors appear and disappear, only to reappear in another form. An exhibitionist's fear of arrest may drive him to massage parlors. A person who engaged in compulsive affairs may stop that pattern, but the addiction may then re-emerge as excessive use of pornography and masturbation.

Another aspect of addiction that defies a linear model is that the energy from one addiction can flow into another. The energy from de-escalating sex addiction can be transformed into compulsive working. Or the escalation of sexual compulsivity can be matched simultaneously by increases in compulsive eating or drinking.

The individual's internal addictive system comprised of faulty beliefs, impaired thinking, and the addictive cycle, is autonomous, but it is also interdependent, i.e., affected by the larger external systems, such as family and culture, that support the addiction in varying degrees and in various ways. The term *contingent* is used here to describe this conditional or dynamic effect. So, given certain events and environments, the effect may be that the addiction is in an escalation mode or a de-escalation mode.

The Phases of Sex Addiction: A Brief Summary

In chapter 3, the first two developmental phases of sex addiction, initiation and establishment, were discussed in detail. In this chapter we'll discuss the remaining four. The discussion has been divided in this way because the first two phases describe the beginnings of addiction; the others describe growth. However, before continuing, here is a list and a brief summary statement of each phase so the parts can be seen in relation to the whole. The phases of sex addiction are as follows:

1. *Initiation Phase.* Catalytic events and/or catalytic environments combine with individual tendencies to precipitate addiction. In contrast to healthy, life-enhancing sexual activity, sex now becomes the "drug of choice," used to escape or cope.

2. *Establishment Phase.* Behavior patterns are established. The addictive cycle forms and is repeated: trance-like preoccupation intensified by rituals leads to compulsive sex behavior, which is followed by shame and despair. For descriptive purposes, addicts whose behavior stays more or less consistently at the base line of established addiction are said to remain in the establishment phase.

3. *Contingent Phase: Escalation Mode.* The individual's addictive system is now fully established and given certain events and environments, begins to escalate—more intensity, more frequency, more risk, more unmanageability, etc. Behavior may escalate at a varying rate, or it may de-escalate.

4. *Contingent Phase: De-escalation Mode.* In this mode, the addiction is still fully established, but for various reasons, addictive behaviors are less frequent, less risky; in general, there is less unmanageability. Behavior may de-escalate for the remainder of the addict's life without the addict dismantling the internal addictive system and really recovering. Or behavior may escalate and the addiction may progress to the acute phase.

5. *Acute Phase.* The individual breaks with reality, abandoning his or her value system, becoming alienated from significant others and isolated within him- or herself. Typically, addiction plateaus at a high level of activity; behavior patterns become rigid. The addiction cycle is played out despite obvious risks; preoccupation is almost constant while shame and despair are seldom, if ever, felt. The addiction may continue to an end stage, stopped only by physical or social consequences such as death or confinement. Or addiction may de-escalate.

6. *Chronic Phase.* The addiction is irreversible and, as such, no longer responsive to any treatment. Most chronic phase addicts are institutionalized. Behavior is limited only by opportunity.

The Three Levels of Behavior

The general developmental phases of sex addiction, including their visibility, duration, and effect on both the addict's internal system and external support systems, are dependent on many variables. Among the most significant of these is the actual sex behavior involved. Consequently, we need a framework for describing the range and level of behaviors. As shown in figure 4-1 we use three levels to indicate different ranges of behavior.[1]

Level One includes behavior that is perceived in our culture as acceptable. These behaviors include masturbation, heterosexual relationships, homosexual relationships, pornography, and prostitution. While some of these activities bring disapproval and may be illegal, their widespread practice indicates general public acceptance. In the case of heterosexual relationships, even some hero images exist, such as the playboy who is seen as living the good life or the adventuresome life.

Level Two specifies sexual behavior that is generally regarded as nuisance behavior. These behaviors include exhibitionism, voyeurism, transvestism, bestiality, indecent phone calls, and indecent liberties. Public reaction usually judges these behaviors as sick or pathetic or obnoxious. Often they are dismissed as innocuous, not serious, and usually not dangerous. When prosecuted, however, they may involve stiff legal penalties. The risk of arrest does add excitement for the addict who finds that the exhilaration of the illicit in Level One behavior is not enough.

Level Three includes sexual behavior that is dangerous, abusive, or life threatening. These behaviors include incest,

Levels of Addiction

LEVEL OF ADDICTION	BEHAVIOR	CULTURAL STANDARDS
Level One	Masturbation, heterosexual and homosexual relationships, pornography, and prostitution.	Depending on behavior, activities are seen as acceptable or tolerable. Some specific behaviors such as prostitution and pornography are sources of controversy.
Level Two	Exhibitionism, voyeurism, indecent phone calls, and indecent liberties.	None of these behaviors is acceptable.
Level Three	Child molestation, incest, and rape.	Each behavior represents a profound violation of cultural boundaries.

Figure 4-1

Levels of Addiction (cont.)

LEGAL CONSEQUENCES/ RISKS	VICTIM	PUBLIC OPINION OF ADDICTION
Sanctions against those behaviors, when illegal, are ineffectively and randomly enforced. Low priority for enforcement officials generates minimal risk for addict.	These behaviors are perceived as victimless crimes. However, victimization and exploitation are often components.	Public attitudes are characterized by ambivalence or dislike. For some behaviors such as womanizing there is a competing negative hero image of glamorous decadence.
Behaviors are regarded as nuisance offenses. Risk is involved since offenders, when observed, are actively prosecuted.	There is always a victim.	Addict is perceived as pathetic and sick but harmless. Often these behaviors are the objects of jokes which dismiss the pain of the addict.
Extreme legal consequences create high-risk situations for the addict.	There is always a victim.	Public becomes outraged. Perpetrators are seen by many as subhuman and beyond help.

Figure 4-1 (cont.)

child molestation, sexual abuse of vulnerable adults, and rape. To these acts, the public almost universally reacts with rage and the desire for revenge. The acts are seen as profound violations of cultural boundaries demanding severe consequences. While the risk generates excitement, the act may create profound self-hate if the perpetrators use the same social standards that others use to judge themselves.

It is important to point out that the three levels do not indicate progressive stages of addiction, but rather serve as descriptive categories of behavior whose only progression characteristics are risk—and hence excitement—as well as harm to others. Also, we should note that the concept of levels gives us a way to discuss the behaviors *per se,* while the concept of escalation allows us to examine the progressive severity of the addictive system itself.

Addicts who operate at each level experience shame. However, prevalent public attitudes result in mixed messages about addictive sexual behavior. Being sexual with a large number of people is seen as a success story (although this attitude is rapidly changing in light of the AIDS threat). But neither admiring nor enraged reactions toward people who are sexually compulsive acknowledge the suffering involved. The part that we as outsiders miss, because of our cultural blinders, is that all addicts experience pain. When sex addicts get together and talk about their histories, they find that no matter how their addiction manifested itself, their internal experiences were similar. Husband seducer, masturbator, exposer, child molester, pornography connoisseur, and rapist—all are caught in an excruciating cycle.

A number of caveats are in order. First, to have raped or committed incest or exposed oneself or had an affair does not mean addiction is present. Rapists, for example, often have varied criminal records, having perhaps sold drugs, committed burglary or murder. But a subset of rapists are sex addicts, who may or may not have integrated value systems.

Second, to return to the dynamics of the system for a moment, seldom does an addict focus on one behavior. The exhibitionist voyeur who frequents strip shows and massage parlors and has numerous affairs may also be a rapist. It is futile to use traditional clinical categories and typologies of behavior such as "deviancy" or "perversion," because some sex addicts may pursue one behavior, change to another, only to add a third. The levels of behavior are useful only in helping to chart the pattern of a particular addict, not in classifying addicts into subgroups. By the very nature of their illness, they elude such categorization.

Third, the three levels of behavior are themselves simply another paradigm that reflects our cultural assumptions. Obviously, attitudes toward masturbation, rape, incest, pornography, prostitution, and affairs will change from culture to culture. Thus, the risk/excitement factor will vary. This book, however, attempts to describe a pathological system that transcends cultural bias as much as possible. Although the process described here relies partly on cultural content (principally the culture of the United States), it also relies on the universality of human sexual experience. This sexual experience—in whatever form—can be pursued as a source of nurturing, acceptance, and escape, ultimately becoming the primary relationship, in the life of any man or woman in any part of the world.

With these caveats and the three levels in mind, we are now ready to return to an in-depth discussion of the developmental phases of addiction; we can now explore how the addiction can escalate through increased intensity, extended range, and/or added levels of behavior.

The Contingent Phase: Escalation Mode

Increased Intensity

Increased intensity means that addicts pursue their established patterns of behavior with more energy, greater frequency, and greater investment of time. Indications of increased intensity might include:

—starting to seek out situations with multiple partners

—picking up someone not once but two to three times a week

—finding serial affairs insufficient and starting multiple relationships

—going from nighttime exposing to daytime exposing

—going from cruising two to three hours twice a week to three to five hours each day

Added Levels of Behavior

One of the surest indicators of escalation is crossing into new, more clearly risky or dangerous sexual behavior than had been practiced before. Going from Level One to Level Two, or from Level Two to Level Three suggests at the least that the addict is seeking the greater excitement that increased risk brings. Changing levels may also indicate a degree of desperation. Fred's case is a good example.

In the early stages of his addiction, Fred peeped into windows of apartment complexes and nearby university housing, gradually progressing to masturbating as he watched. Soon he was also exposing himself outside the windows. The peak experience he sought was for a nude young woman to find herself watching him as he masturbated to orgasm. When this goal clearly became part of his fantasy life, he increased the frequency of his activity dramatically to five nights a week. In fact, he often used Friday and Saturday nights, and had to drop much of his social life. Fred was in his late twenties, single, with an excellent job in high-tech engineering. With few financial obligations, he had managed to accumulate an expensive car, furniture, and stereo component system—all the accepted elements of the "good life."

He especially valued having money in the bank and a good credit rating. It was a part of having an orderly life, he said.

Fred came from an incest family. His mother had been sexual with him, including intercourse in his midteens. His distrust of people, especially women, was deep.

Fred's pattern was disrupted one night when he was chased by a group of angry neighbors who had been waiting for him at one of his regular haunts. Although he was not caught, the incident scared him. Recognizing the need to curtail his activities, he searched desperately for a different outlet. As an experiment, he went to a massage parlor, hoping he could expose himself there. This experience was far beyond his naive expectations. Not only could he be nude, but a willing "masseuse" would take off her clothes and help him achieve orgasm. Thus, the scenario he desired the most and which had precipitated the escalation of the exhibitionism was achieved in the new setting. The only differences were that he had to pay, it was somewhat less exciting, and it was safer.

However, prostitution was not enough. Fred still needed to expose himself. This Level Two behavior was the one he could not stop or alter much. For a while he varied his routes but not his pattern. Then he started to run out of money, and his exhibitionism became more frequent. Eventually he reached a point when his credit was no good and he was broke. His job was in jeopardy because of his unexplained absences and his low productivity and fatigue. Fred's exhibitionism literally took over his life. He abandoned all caution. Finally he was arrested by university police outside a sorority house. He had not slept for three days and had not shown up at work that week.

It is important to note that Fred did not start at Level One and progress to Level Two. Rather he started at Level Two and escalated by using Level One behavior. The behavior patterns of the sex addict can weave back and forth across the levels as conditions warrant. When addicts say, "I'm only a Level One,'' they are trying to minimize the power of the addiction. Addicts who stay in Level One behavior are just as addicted as Level Two or Level Three addicts. Level One addicts can just as easily destroy their lives. What makes Level One behavior more insidious is that it is less likely to get the attention of professionals who can give these people the help they need.

The development of Fred's addiction also illustrates the role of fantasy and preoccupation. Fred's favorite scenario gave propelling force to the escalation. During the escalation of addiction, fantasy life not only expands, but develops a problem-solving or creative quality. The addict's preoccupation focuses on new ways to accommodate the increase of sexual energy or to achieve the latest fantasy, while minimizing risk.

The paradoxical part of such preoccupation is that addicts become victims of their own frequent lapses of reality. In attempting to fulfill fantasies or objectives that have become more and more consuming, they abandon logic and caution and ignore values that once were important to them. They attempt sexual behavior at great risk and cost. Their defense mechanisms of projection, blame, and denial increase along with this escalating behavior. Dramatic unmanageability results. Severe family strain as well as work and financial problems appear. Legal complications and even physical symptoms, such as insomnia or hypertension, may indicate escalating addiction.

For many addicts, escalation causes further unmanageability through substantial changes in other addictions (e.g., alcoholism or overeating) or compulsive behaviors (e.g., shoplifting and working). Changes in these concurrent addictions may mean an increase or a decrease in the addictive behavior. For example, drinking may decrease because the sex addiction absorbs all the addict's energy, or drinking may increase as a way for the addict to anesthetize pain caused by the sexual behavior. Increased drinking and the consequent greater feelings of loss of control may serve as a catalyst for escalating the sexual behavior, resulting in the addict's further loss of control.

The addict's despair adds to the complications caused by unmanageability. Addicts use the expression "it hurts so good" to convey the ongoing desperation in this phase. It's impossible for the addict to sustain excitement and pleasure indefinitely; the unmanageability of his or her life confronts him or her, probably daily. Moods shift from peaks of elation to valleys of depression and suicidal thoughts. They may have their first significant bouts with depression and suicidal thoughts during this time of escalation. Unmanageability heightens as the addicts become personally more ineffective.

The shame and despair that come from the powerlessness and unmanageability help crystallize the core beliefs about personal unworthiness that were part of the addict's initial addictive system:

1. I am basically a bad, unworthy person.
2. No one would love me as I am.
3. My needs are never going to be met if I have to depend on others.
4. Sex is my most important need.

These beliefs negate whatever positive beliefs addicts have about themselves. As the addiction escalates, Mr. Hyde starts to overtake Dr. Jekyll. The surest sign that the addiction has escalated to a point of dominance is when the addict dispenses with secrecy. When attempts to deal with the world on the world's own terms are totally abandoned, the acute phase of the addiction is reached.

To summarize, primary indicators of the contingent escalation phases are:

—Fantasy life expands, including new or different behaviors and a problem-solving quality.

—Rituals become entrenched and integral precedents to sex acts.

—Rapid escalation of addictive behavior may include changes of intensity, range, or levels of behavior.

—Excitement is balanced by on ongoing desperation, with peaks of depression and even suicidal feelings.

—Negative core beliefs become more dominant.

—Reality lapses are frequent as logic and caution are abandoned and defense mechanisms increase.

—Severe strain on family, work, and finances compounds with legal consequences, physical symptoms, and shifts in concurrent addictions.

Part of the addiction's strength lies in its flexibility. For as rapidly as it can escalate, it has the power to go underground, lie dormant, and re-emerge at its former strength. We call this the de-escalation mode of the contingent phase.

The Contingent Phase: De-escalation Mode

Susan Griffin's book, *Pornography and Silence: Culture's Revenge Against Nature,* powerfully underlines the dualistic struggle between good and evil that many addicts, indeed many people, use to understand their sexuality. Nowhere in the addict's world is this dualism more explicit than in the de-escalation mode of the contingent phase. Griffin's comments are particularly appropriate:

> In his history of the creation of *Playboy* magazine, Gay Talese tells us that in the earlier years of its existence in

> Chicago, the *Playboy* office lay in the shadow of a great church, Holy Name Cathedral. Writing ironically of this juxtaposition, he tells us: "great cathedrals cannot be . . . maintained without sufficient numbers of sinners to justify them." But when we look at the history of pornography, and the pornographer's obsession with transgressing the morality of the church, we begin to understand that pornography, and the pornographic idea of sin, could not exist without the great cathedrals.
>
> We begin to see pornography more as it were a modern building, built on the site of the old cathedrals, sharing the same foundation. And if one were to dig beneath this foundation, we imagine, one might see how much the old structure and the new resemble one another. . . . And what is called a transgression against the church fathers is finally loyalty.[2]

The moralistic church, in its battle to control the lust-driven sinner, shares a common element with the addict: obsession. The battlefield becomes a narrow continuum in which the only options are to be good or to be bad, to be saved or to be damned. Excluded are spirituality, responsibility, and the joy of sexual expression.

Some addicts, shocked at their own behavior and its consequences, make a radical shift in an effort to control their addiction. The shock may have come from finally coming face to face with the unmanageability of their lives. They may have been arrested or have had a near miss. Their behavior almost became public, or did. Someone in their family found out. They have run out of money. Or they have lost a job. Sometimes they are simply overwhelmed by despair. Whatever the reason, they make a dramatic effort to change their lives. Those addicts who subscribe to the narrow model of good versus evil—essentially a model built on shame and control—may return to the church. They may become not only pillars of the church community but avenging angels out to destroy all lust. But as we know, their crusades mean that they have only switched sides in the battle—not the foundations of their beliefs.

For other addicts whose religious experiences have at best been peripheral, it may be a time for conversion experiences. Their conversion significantly occurs immediately after a major unmanageability event such as an arrest. Unfortunately, they may adopt wholesale the belief system of their new community in place of a thoughtful, long-term spiritual pilgrimage that integrates a new understanding with integrity. This phenomenon is so common that mental health workers who serve populations of sex offenders call it the "jail cell conversion": in jail, the offender will have a conversion experience; when released he will re-offend; upon arrest he will have another conversion experience. Caught in this cycle, he will successfully resist any rehabilitation efforts aimed at making his recovery the fundamental issue. Instead of looking for peace and forgiveness, the crusader and the instant convert find a place to hide. When pastoral counselors become aware of this ploy, they can guide the addict toward a program of true recovery.

Identifying de-escalation is difficult since it may look like recovery. The addict makes every effort to make life manageable and to live an honorable life. If the addict does not get involved in the church, there is usually some special effort to become part of a respectable group. There may be a surge of responsible behavior at work. Other addictions are reduced or brought under control. There is even a honeymoon period with family members, as the addict attempts to make up for the way he or she has complicated their lives.

Most important, there is a rapid de-escalation to safe or acceptable sexual behavior. Addicts may go to extremes and try to obliterate all sexual feelings. Some keep a low level of behavior going, e.g., masturbation to softcore magazines instead of hardcore porn, or keeping just one "meaningful relationship." Others return to activities typical of their establishment or initiation phases.

Some will control their behavior, while their fantasy lives remain intense. Others go for appreciable periods with no fantasies at all. Obsession with guilt and shame over sexual behavior may replace addictive preoccupation at times. But when despair and obsession combine, the core beliefs about unworthiness and sexual needs do not weaken. Addicts in the de-escalation mode often are still isolated. They still feel precariously close to sexually compulsive behavior, because reducing the addictive behavior did not reduce their alienation. They continue to guard their secret world, either to hide their obsession (which convinces them that they are not curable) or to keep intact the web of lies they wove during the time they were acting out. Thus, de-escalation is not recovery. Honesty with oneself and others, self-acceptance that includes one's illness, and support for change by people who know the addiction's power to delude are prime determinants for recovery.

Addicts in the de-escalation mode have, due to some catastrophe brought on by a totally unmanageable life, been stunned into deciding that they must quit. Believing their only options are to be "good" or to be "evil," instead of well versus sick, they feel caught at every turn: they want to be good but cannot stop thinking about being evil. Their impaired thinking tells them that their only alternative to the continuing catastrophe of addiction is a grim determination and a life without happiness of sex. Hopelessness is added to despair.

However, because such a life looks untenable, addicts may continue to "play" with the addiction during the de-escalation phase. They test themselves by going through the ritual to the point of acting out, but then stopping:

—going to a bar, but then leaving

—flirting with someone, but stopping before anything can happen

—seeing old sex partners, just "as friends"

—driving the old routes and perhaps even masturbating, but not letting anyone see

—going into the massage parlor, asking prices, and then leaving

—buying a pornographic item, and then throwing it away

Such toying with rituals reinforces the addicts' beliefs that they can control it, that they are in charge of their behavior. They are in fact getting high while minimizing risk. Sooner or later, in all probability, they will have a slip that may reactivate the addictive cycle. In fact, in the de-escalation mode, the cycle is simply suspended. Its basic elements and its supporting system are intact, active, and ready to be fully engaged.

To summarize, indications that the addictive system is in its de-escalation mode include:

—Fantasy life can remain intense but may diminish entirely for periods of time.

—Rituals may be restricted to "playing" with the addiction by tempting oneself.

—There is rapid de-escalation to safe, marginal, or acceptable sexual behavior.

—Obsession with guilt and shame over behavior may replace or co-exist with addictive preoccupation.

—Core beliefs do not abate, keeping the addict isolated and acting "as if."

—The reality of near catastrophes breaks through delusion, leaving the addicts stunned and even hopeless.

—Efforts to make life manageable and to live respectably may result in excessive religiosity, shifts in concurrent addictions, responsible behavior at work, and honeymoon periods at home.

Remember that seldom, if ever, is there a phase that is clearly or purely one or another. The escalation and de-escalation modes of the contingency phase are primarily transitional. Elements of establishment can occur in the initiation phase. In the contingent phase, aspects of escalation and de-escalation can even occur simultaneously. Or addicts can remain in the de-escalation phase indefinitely with only an occasional slip to remind them of their vulnerability. However, when addiction escalates to the acute phase, everything changes.

The Acute Phase

An internationally known economist and a full professor at a university graduate school, Rich had fully established himself in his career. His teaching load was light and his major projects were characterized by brief, furious periods of work followed by long periods of low demand. He was seldom asked what he was doing by the dean and never by his peers. He was free to enjoy his primary passion, the pursuit of women. In effect, that was all he really did, which was what had created the crisis that brought him to therapy: an affirmative action grievance alleging sexual harassment of students, and almost unbelievably, a concurrent paternity suit. With his wife leaving him and his career in jeopardy, Rich went into therapy.

He did not want to be in therapy. He was angry. He felt caught. He rationalized his behavior, blamed others, tried to justify his mistakes in judgment—all of which Jim, his therapist, listened to patiently. When Jim explained the concept of sex addiction, Rich exploded and called it the craziest fabrication by psychologists he had ever heard. Only the reality of his wife's refusal to talk with him until he got help and the need to put on a good show for the university review panel kept him talking.

Jim proposed that Rich do an honest history of his sexual activities, and that they could decide together if addiction was present. He further pointed out that Rich couldn't lose. If he were addicted and had an illness, he would certainly want to know. If he were not, then he could prove to all those pointing the finger at him that he did not have a problem.

So Rich agreed. He tackled the problem with almost scholarly zeal. He started with what he considered his first "date" in second grade. In his next session, he had just finished talking about high school when Jim asked a sobering question: did Rich have any men friends? No was the obvious answer, which led Jim and Rich into a long discussion about how Rich felt he couldn't trust anyone, male or female; how the pursuit of sex and academic excellence were the only two things he could count on in life; and how his family were never really admitted into his world.

From that moment on, realization followed realization:

—He was the victim of child abuse. He had always thought he was the initiator of some of his early sexual experiences. Jim helped him to see how he had been used by adults.

—He could no longer blame his marriage for his sexual behavior. His affairs really preceded his marriage. In fact, one of his lovers helped to pick out his wedding ring.

—His whole career was organized around his sexuality. Jim pointed out that he slept with his students; that he routinely developed sexual relationships from various speaking engagements; that his consultation contracts with companies were invariably based on a sexual relationship; and that many of his writings were co-authored with women he slept with.

—He had developed an elaborate set of rituals for swinging as his behavior became more and more frequent. After establishing a relationship with someone, it was Rich's pattern to either involve other people or encourage the woman to have other relationships and report about them to him. In fact, it was his increasing rigidity about this that frightened and angered the women who took legal action.

—Sex was no longer casual relationships, but a daily hunt. Rich was averaging five to eight sexual partners per week and up to one hundred per year. He was no longer being discreet. Part of the energy behind the legal action was the growing concern on campus that something needed to be done, but nobody knew quite what.

Jim asked Rich what he would do if he could not have sex. The panic Rich felt at the prospect intuitively helped him appreciate the depth of his problem.

Like all acute phase addicts, Rich suffered from a total sexualization of thought patterns. His fantasy life took on a desperation that never let up. The addictive system became his life, and everything else simply supported it. There was no more starting and stopping, downtime, or de-escalation. Rich's addiction was fully in charge.

In the acute phase, rituals become quite rigid despite obvious danger, risk, or cost. The exposer ceases to vary his routes; the voyeur refuses to modify his cruising even though he's in physical danger.

Behavior is repeated constantly in the acute phase. Usually it is daily, but may involve, for example, forty-eight- or seventy-two-hour cycles. Typically, the addict is involved with large numbers of people; some are sexual with thousands—willing and unwilling. The multiple-affairs addict whose pattern involves eight to ten partners a week, even without counting repeats, can add up to three hundred or more people per year. An exhibitionist who exposes himself to sixty or seventy people in a week may encounter over three thousand people per year.

The accumulation of this kind of data is vital to treatment of the addiction. Prognosis is good if an addict, having looked honestly at the pattern of his behavior, can have sincere remorse at the reality of it. This includes regret about how he has diminished himself and sorrow for what has happened to others. In Rich's case, Jim's efforts to break through the addictive denial brought home significant realizations which, in turn, prepared the way for Rich to acknowledge the depth of his suffering.

Breaking through addictive denial is not easy at this stage, because usually in the acute phase the addict's awareness of repercussions is diminished. In addition to being out of touch with him- or herself, the addict's sense of impact on others has become limited. The pain doesn't disappear; it just becomes so commonplace that the addict literally gets used to it. Despair permeates every facet of the addict's life. Impaired thinking and repetitive behavior cause severe breaks with reality. Delusional thought processes emerge as values are abandoned. This level of desperation can easily be mistaken as psychopathy—and, in fact, they share some traits in common.

All acute phase addicts lead incredibly complicated lives. Other addictions may stabilize or flourish; family and jobs may be lost; physical complications may include insomnia, hypertension, venereal disease, pregnancy, physical abuse, and malnutrition; legal complications abound. These life issues overwhelm the addict, thus sustaining the addict as he or she turns to sex for comfort and escape, obscuring the despair, and further distorting reality. Above all, the situation confirms the faulty inner logic of the addict's core beliefs about being unworthy and unlovable, about having no one to meet his or her needs, especially the primary need for sex. In the acute phase, this inner logic governs every day of the addict's life.

Key indicators of the acute phase, then, are:

—Sexualization of thought patterns takes on desperate quality.

—Rituals become rigid despite obvious danger, risk, or cost.

—Compulsive sexual behavior occurs in constant twenty-four- to seventy-two-hour cycles.

—Awareness of personal pain as well as impact on others diminishes.

—Massive acceptance of the addictive belief system governs daily behavior.

—Breaks with reality generate predatory thought processes and signal abandonment of value system.

—Significant losses occur, including job, family, and finances, as well as legal, physical, and other addictive complications.

Most acute phase addicts are able to recover, depending on other mental health and addiction issues. Some addicts, however, at the most extreme end of the behavior spectrum, can no longer de-escalate, nor are they good candidates for treatment. We simply do not have a technology to reach them. This is called the chronic phase of the addiction.

The Chronic Phase

Classically, the use of the word *chronic* in connection with illness means that the condition resists treatment. Because of severely damaged lives, some addicts are unreachable. Events in early childhood, for example, may have been so destructive that the resulting character disorder is not easily treated. Or severe psychoses exist that prevent contact with reality. Such mental health situations compound the self-destructive elements of the addictive system.

The most severe chronic phase sex addicts end up in our prisons. But most sex offenses are extensions of antisocial behavior and cultural pathology, not addiction. Patterned sex offenders with an addiction problem usually suffer from severe mental problems at the same time. Treatment program directors for sex offenders may have to wrestle with the decision to deny treatment because (1) the cost would be too great, and with limited funds the money would be better spent on people whose rehabilitation is more promising; (2) they do not have an adequate environment and the right resources for the problems presented; or (3) no known modality would work. Another group of chronic phase addicts are institutionalized in mental health facilities. For this population there are severe mental health disorders concomitant with the sex addiction.

A number of clinical criteria can serve to evaluate the chronic phase of the addiction. For one, the addict may have a long history of going to treatment centers and rehabilitation programs, with no progress toward recovery. For another, the addict who totally denies the behavior, even over an extended period of time, when the evidence is absolutely conclusive, may be completely out of touch with reality. An example of this case would be the patient in a psychiatric facility who masturbates continually but does not acknowledge that he does.

For chronic addicts, the damage to the sense of self—the loss of faith in self and others—may be beyond repair. This damage betrays itself in impaired thinking: the addict sees him- or herself as a victim, blames everyone else for all his or her troubles, and admits no personal responsibility. While many addicts start therapy thinking that way, sooner or later their denial gives way to the overwhelming evidence of their powerlessness and the unmanageability of their lives. However, in a chronic case, the addict seems incapable of admitting denial, or even acknowledging the addictive sex acts.

There is no relief for obsession in such cases. For chronic phase addicts, there is no life outside the obsession, and when the obsession combines with psychoses, the challenges for the therapist are legion. The addict's rituals are extremely predictable and rigid, the behavior limited only by opportunity. The addict appears to be totally removed from any personal pain, although there may be occasional grief. In addition, the addict usually has nothing left to hold on to or work for. With so little to lose, plus a good deal of anger, the addict may be prone to violence. The therapist has little leverage unless the addict can become part of some therapeutic community such as an in-treatment chemical dependency program.

Among sex offenders, such as rapists, the number of actual addicts will be few. Most sex offenders are motivated by causes that have little to do with addiction. As Massachusetts psychologists Groth and Cohen, specialists in the diagnosis and treatment of aggressive sex offenders, observe:

> Rape is in fact a sexual deviation in the truest sense of the word: it is sexual behavior in the service of nonsexual needs. Contrary to popular belief forcible rape is not motivated primarily for a need for sexual gratification, and the misconception that it is has led to the curious state of affairs in which the victim is often regarded as more responsible for the crime than the offender, and the existence of emotional problems in the offender that require psychological remedy go unnoticed and neglected.[3]

Addiction may exist, however, in rapists, when in addition to rape, the pattern includes exhibitionism, prostitution, and multiple affairs with their collective unmanageability. Then a different picture emerges.

Symptomology of Phases

PHASE CRITERIA	INITIATION	ESTABLISHMENT	CONTINGENT-ESCALATION
Preoccupation	Sexual obsession helps cope.	Preoccupation becomes routine way to avoid life problems.	Fantasy life expands including new or different behaviors and a problem solving quality.
Ritualization	Determination to find ways to maximize behavior opportunities.	Repetitive patterns emerge which usually precede behavior.	Rituals become variations of a theme.
Behavior	Episodic periods of acting out, abusive behavior.	Regularity and priority of behavior establish a baseline.	Rapid escalation of behavior may include changes of intensity, range, or levels of behavior.
Despair	Concerns, disappointment, or dis-ease about behavior.	Periods of depression sometimes followed by efforts to curb or stop behavior.	Excitement is balanced by an ongoing desperation with peaks of depression and even suicidal feelings.
Belief System	Loss of faith in oneself, feelings of unworthiness and distrust in an extreme environment.	Behavior and unmanageability begin to confirm destructive core beliefs about self.	Dramatic surge of behavior shifts core beliefs into dominance.
Impaired Thinking	Incongruency between feelings of exhilaration and reality of danger or degradation, between perception of behavior as experimental or short lived and reality of regularity or potential of continuing pattern.	Thought processes start to distort reality, creating unrealistic confidence and negating potential problems.	Reality lapses are frequent as logic and caution are abandoned and defense mechanisms increase.
Unmanageability	Catalytic events correspond with first complications of behavioral excess.	Reversal of life priorities causes complications in family, work, relationships, and values and addict starts to live double life.	Severe strain on family, work, and finances compounds with legal consequences, physical symptoms, and shifts in concurrent addictions.

Figure 4-2

of Addictive System

CONTINGENT-DE-ESCALATION	ACUTE	CHRONIC	PHASE CRITERIA
Fantasy life can remain intense but may diminish entirely for periods of time.	Sexualization of thought patterns take on a desperate quality.	No life occurs beyond the obsession.	**Preoccupation**
Rituals may be restricted except to "play" with addiction by tempting self.	Rituals become rigid despite even obvious danger, risk, or cost.	Rigid rituals extremely predictable.	**Ritualization**
Rapid de-escalation of behavior to safe, marginal, or acceptable behavior.	Constant 24 hour to 72 hour behavior cycles.	Behavior limited only by opportunity.	**Behavior**
Obsession with guilt and shame over behavior may replace or co-exist with addictive preoccupation.	Awareness of personal pain as well as impact on others diminishes.	No apparent awareness of personal pain.	**Despair**
Core beliefs do not abate, keeping addict isolated and acting "as if".	Massive acceptance of addictive belief system governs daily behavior.	Damage to sense of self may be beyond repair.	**Belief System**
Reality of near catastrophes breaks through delusion, leaving addict stunned and even hopeless.	Breaks with reality generate predatory thought processes and signal abandonment of value system.	Personal responsibility never acknowledged.	**Impaired Thinking**
Efforts to make life manageable and to live honorable life may result in excessive religiosity, shifts in concurrent addictions, responsibility at work, and "honeymoon" periods at home.	Significant life losses occur including job, family, and finances as well as legal, physical, and other addictive complications.	Nothing to hold on to or to work for.	**Unmanageability**

Figure 4-2 (cont.)

To summarize the indications of the chronic phase:

—No life occurs beyond the obsession.

—Rigid rules are extremely predictable.

—Behavior is limited only by opportunity.

—There is no apparent awareness of personal pain.

—Damage to sense of self may be beyond repair.

—Personal responsibility is never acknowledged.

—Addicts feel complete hopelessness and despair, with nothing to hold on to or to work for.

Much work remains to be done in researching the dynamics of sex addiction, especially the chronic stage. A major contribution would be the development of screening mechanisms for such cases. That may be difficult, however, given the unpopularity of such research, given that the affected population is primarily in penal or mental health institutions, and given the small number of cases involved. Like all other phases of the addiction, however, the chronic phase illustrates the strength of the addictive system.

The next two chapters explore the role of the family system in the development of sex addiction. With that task finished, we will have completed our model of addiction, and we will turn to the process of recovery.

The chart on the previous two pages summarizes the phases of the growth of the addictive system.

5

The Addict's Family and Beliefs

There was the sweet-sad, all encompassing feeling he had for the whole world, all mankind, and in a heightened sense for some individuals. But he never could get sex and love absolutely straightened out. Oh, I can sort it out intellectually, he thought. But in the doing of either or both, I get pretty mixed up. Maybe I do rather love everyone I fuck . . . .

Earl Thompson
The Devil to Pay

An old Zen parable describes two monks traveling together. When they come to a river, a young woman approaches and asks for assistance in crossing. The older monk carries her on his back across the river. She thanks him and goes on her way. For the next two days, the younger monk thinks about the obvious temptation his older colleague risked in carrying the woman. Unable to contain himself any longer, he finally confronts the older monk: "Do you think it wise to have carried a young, attractive woman on your back?" The older monk responds, "I carried her across the river. You have carried her ever since."

In sexual addiction terms, the difference between this story and the typical scenario of the sex addict's family is that the family members—or co-addicts—as well as the sex addict, would be obsessed about carrying the woman across the river. Family members typically spend much time and energy obsessing about the sex addict's behavior.

To understand how an individual comes to carry the obsessional burden of sexual addiction, it is necessary to examine the family system which may have helped create that obsession. Obsession becomes one of several bonds that tie members of the family system to the addictive system of the addict. Meanwhile, the addictive system forges chains that anchor it in the family system. As we shall see in this chapter and in the next chapter (on co-addiction in the addict's current family), both the family and the addict find stability in the addictive system, even when the family is desperately trying to eliminate the behavior. It becomes an organizing principle in their lives as well. Like other addictions and mental illness, the homeostatic bond preserves and protects the behavior.[1] The pathology is rooted in the interaction of two different systems: the family system and the individual's addictive system.

But to discuss the dynamics of the addict's family of origin and current family, the helping professionals need a cognitive map to guide them through what otherwise would seem a labyrinth of paradoxes and incongruities. The map selected here is called the circumplex model of family behavior.

The Circumplex Model

In the mid-1970s, David Olson and his colleagues Douglas Sprenkle and Candyce Russell noted that a number of family professionals were using different words to describe the same phenomenon. Researchers used terms like power, control, dominance, and interdependence to describe family structural responses to change and stress. They also used terms like affiliation, closeness, affection, and expressiveness to reflect a family's capacity to relate to each other. Olson, Sprenkle, and Russell saw the need for a model that reflected the basic realities recognized by various researchers, and that used a common framework and a common language.

They called this theoretical construct the circumplex model because its approach is curvilinear. In other words, unlike most linear approaches, which range from good to bad, this model reflected the reality that there are a number of possible extremes a family can reach. In addition, a family does not move in a line but around a combination of behaviors, which more accurately reflects what many family therapists and researchers observe clinically.[2] The circumplex model provides a means and a vocabulary to examine two essential factors in family dynamics: adaptability and cohesion.

Adaptability

A healthy family has the capacity to organize and reorganize itself as the family grows and changes. The circumplex model recognizes four general levels of adaptability within families. Each of the four levels represents a range of behavior options.

—*Rigid.* Rigid families use extremely autocratic decision-making styles in which there is limited negotiation and strictly defined roles and rules.

—*Structured.* Structured families mix authoritarian with some equalitarian leadership, resulting in very stable roles and rules.

—*Flexible.* Flexible families use equalitarian leadership seeking negotiated agreements, making for easily changed rules and roles.

—*Chaotic.* Chaotic families have erratic and ineffective leadership which results in impulsive decisions, inconsistent rules, and role reversals.

Figure 5-1 provides an overview of various categories of adaptability. Note that the middle range is the optimum for family growth. For example, a family with three children under the age of five would thrive in a structured format given the need for consistency and direction of small children. When the children are between the ages of fifteen and twenty the same family will shift to a more flexible mode.

Every family has its chaotic and rigid moments. Families that remain in the extremes, however, damage their members. For example, children who live in rigid families end up with lifelong struggles around rules and authority—whether it is in excessive rebelliousness or excessive passivity—because of the unreachable expectations of their parents. Chaotic families produce children who have difficulty incorporating a consistent set of standards into their own consciences because no one ever demanded it of them. An intriguing aspect of systems is that opposite extremes have similar consequences. Both rigidity and chaos affect conscience formation.

For the focus of this book, a family's inability to adapt to children's needs becomes extremely important because of the close connection between a child's need to depend on others and addiction. To illustrate, in rigid families a child who asks for help may receive assistance but with a heavy price in the form of lectures, high expectations, and moralizing about failure. Under those conditions, a child learns quickly to not ask. In a chaotic family, when a child asks for help, the assistance is incomplete, inconsistent, or doesn't come at all. Rather than embarrass the parents again and subject her- or himself to further confusion and disappointment, the child simply doesn't ask.

Children need to be able to count on—depend upon—their families for survival, nurturing, love, and approval. If the family doesn't provide it, they will look for what they *can* depend upon, and they find it. Drugs, alcohol, food, and sex always produce a predictable high. If a child develops a reliance on these external sources, pleasurable experiences become the primary relationship upon which he or she relies.

Family Adaptability

	RIGID (Very Low Adaptability)	STRUCTURED (Low to Moderate)	FLEXIBLE (Moderate to High)	CHAOTIC (Very High)
LEADERSHIP (Control)	Authoritarian leadership. Parent(s) highly controlling.	Primarily authoritarian but some equalitarian leadership.	Equalitarian leadership with fluid changes.	Limited and/or erratic leadership. Parental control unsuccessful, rebuffed.
DISCIPLINE	Autocratic, "law & order." Strict, rigid consequences. Not lenient.	Somewhat democratic. Predictable consequences. Seldom lenient.	Usually democratic. Negotiated consequences. Somewhat lenient.	Laissez-faire and ineffective. Inconsistent consequences. Very lenient.
NEGOTIATION	Limited negotiations. Decisions imposed by parents.	Structured negotiations. Decisions mainly made by parents.	Flexible negotiations. Agreed upon decisions.	Endless negotiations. Impulsive decisions.
ROLES	Limited repertoire; strictly defined roles.	Roles stable, but may be shared.	Role sharing and making. Fluid changes of roles.	Lack of role clarity, role shifts and role reversals.
RULES	Unchanging rules. Rules strictly enforced.	Few rule changes. Rules firmly enforced.	Some rule changes. Rules flexibly enforced.	Frequent rule changes. Rules inconsistently enforced.

Figure 5-1

Cohesion

Besides dependency on external sources for pleasure and nurture, the other crucial variables in addiction are self-esteem and the capacity to have intimacy with others. These variables bring us to the other major family dimension in the circumplex model, cohesion. Simply defined, cohesion is how closely a family sticks together. The degree of emotional support available in a family is vital to the development of self-concept. Reciprocally, a person's self-image determines the ability to have relationships.

Cohesion has four levels. Each offers a combination of options in terms of the degree of closeness the family environment will support:

—*Disengaged.* Disengaged family members distance themselves from one another, maintaining extreme separateness and little family loyalty.

—*Separated.* Separated families mix emotional independence with some involvement and joint effort and occasional family loyalty.

—*Connected.* Connected families emphasize emotional closeness, family loyalty, and joint efforts while allowing for some individuality.

—*Enmeshed.* Enmeshed families demand extreme family closeness and family loyalty and allow for little individuality.

Figure 5-2 illustrates these levels of family cohesion. To return to our earlier example of a family with three children under the age of five, the family would optimally be a connected family because of the high support needs of small children. When those children become teenagers with their own peer support groups, the family would shift to a more separated mode. During times of transition, there may be problems with members feeling too close or too far from one another. Everyone experiences moments of being too close or too far from their family. Change, though painful, is usually healthy. Families who remain locked into a specific extreme mode, however, characteristically develop unstable relationships and members with low self-esteem. In disengaged families, for example, children learn that parental love and support is conditional. If children do something wrong, their parents' warmth and approval is (or feels) withdrawn. This pulling away is a potent weapon for parents to use because of the dependent children's fear of abandonment. And as we have learned, abandonment is a critical part of the formation of the addictive system. In healthy families, a child's behavior may be criticized without risking a rift in the relationship. The child is encouraged to learn through trial and error. Children in disengaged families learn only that they have to be perfect in order to be accepted. Since this isn't possible, and they do not want to be rejected, they simply avoid being close.

In enmeshed families, children have little opportunity to develop personally because of the relationship demands of the family. Enmeshed parents, for example, view children's misbehavior as a direct reflection on them. They then shame the children for what they have done to the family. Sometimes they will cover up for a child in order to protect the family name. The children don't learn to accept responsibility for their own behavior, as later on, if this is the course the child takes, the sexual addict can't acknowledge his or her acting out. The child from an emotionally enmeshed family has no sense of boundaries and as a result, little sense of self. He doesn't know where he leaves off and other people begin.

Adults who were raised in an enmeshed family environment struggle with intimacy issues. If they do not want to replicate what their parents did, they might go to the opposite extreme, rejecting closeness out of the fear of being swallowed up again. Intimacy will remain elusive. Like the adaptability dimension, the extremes of cohesion have similar results: low self-worth and low trust of others.

Family Cohesion

	DISENGAGED (Very Low)	SEPARATED (Low to Moderate)
EMOTIONAL BONDING	Extreme emotional separateness. Lack of family loyalty. Infrequent affective responsiveness between members.	Emotional separateness. Occasional family loyalty. Some affective responsiveness is demonstrated.
PARENT-CHILD COALITIONS	Lack of parent-child coalition.	Clear sub-system boundaries.
MARITAL RELATIONSHIP	Extreme emotional separateness.	Emotional separateness.
FAMILY INVOLVEMENT	Very low involvement or interaction between members. Individual definitions of reality are predominant.	Involvement is acceptable but personal distance is preferred.
INTERNAL BOUNDARIES	Personal separateness predominant.	Some personal separateness encouraged.
Personal Boundaries	Rigid personal boundaries.	Clear personal boundaries.
Time (physical & emotional)	Time apart from family maximized. Rarely time together.	Time alone important. Some time together.
Space (physical & emotional)	Separate space needed and preferred.	Separate space preferred; Sharing of family space.
Decision Making	Independent decision making.	Individual decision making preferred but joint decisions possible.
EXTERNAL BOUNDARIES	Open to influences from outside the family.	Somewhat open to outside influences.
Friends	Individual friends seen alone.	Individual friendships preferred and seldom shared with family.
Interests	Disparate interests.	Seldom shared with family.
Recreation	Separate recreation.	Separate interests and recreation but joint participation allowed.

Figure 5-2

Family Cohesion (cont.)

CONNECTED (Moderate to High)	ENMESHED (Very High)	
Emotional closeness. Loyalty to family is expected. Affective interactions encouraged and preferred.	Extreme emotional closeness. Loyalty to family is demanded. Affective dependency is demonstrated.	**EMOTIONAL BONDING**
Some sub-system boundaries with possible generational intrusion.	Parent-child coalition. Lack of clear generational boundaries.	**PARENT-CHILD COALITIONS**
Emotional closeness.	Extreme emotional reactivity.	**MARITAL RELATIONSHIP**
Involvement is emphasized but personal distance is allowed.	Very high, symbiotic involvement, members very dependent on each other. Shared or imposed definition of reality.	**FAMILY INVOLVEMENT**
Need for separateness is respected but somewhat discouraged. Personal boundaries at times unclear. Time together important and scheduled. Time alone permitted. Sharing family space preferred. Private space respected. Joint decisions preferred but not necessary.	Lack of personal separateness. Diffuse and weak personal boundaries. Time together maximized. Little time alone permitted. Little or no private space permitted. Decisions subject to wishes of entire group.	**INTERNAL BOUNDARIES** **Personal Boundaries** **Time** (physical & emotional) **Space** (physical & emotional) **Decision Making**
Somewhat closed to outside influences. Individual friendships allowed and shared with family. Joint interest preferred. Joint recreation preferred.	Closed to outside influences. Family friends preferred with limited individuals friends. Joint interests mandated. Joint recreation mandated.	**EXTERNAL BOUNDARIES** **Friends** **Interests** **Recreation**

Figure 5-2 (cont.)

Combining Adaptability and Cohesion

When the dimensions of adaptability and cohesion are combined, a map of possible family behaviors emerges. Figure 5-3 displays the parameters of the circumplex model. Note that sixteen possible combinations of adaptability and cohesion exist. Graphically they are divided into three ranges: balanced, mid-range, and extreme.

To understand this graph it is helpful to picture a geographical relief map, where elevation is highest at the center. However, in this case, it is the clustering of numbers of families in the center, not height. Most families are in the center, i.e., flexibly separated, flexibly connected, structurally separated, and structurally connected. Fewer and fewer families are in the extremes, rigidly disengaged or chaotically enmeshed, for example.

Being in the center allows families more options. For instance, the family with three children under the age of five could start being structured and connected. But as the children mature and develop support networks of their own as well as greater independence, the family would move into flexibly connected or flexibly separated modes. David Olson has recently documented these movements families make. His study of one thousand healthy families traces the growth of families and couples from newlyweds to retirees.[3]

Not all families move easily between modes. Given the two dimensions, structured versus chaotic and rigid versus flexible, families in the mid-range tend to maintain one extreme level on one dimension. Thus, a family might be both connected and rigid. Some very wounded families reach an extreme on both dimensions. To be rigid in two dimensions, e.g., to be both rigid and enmeshed, places a family in the "extreme" range of the circumplex. Olson and his colleagues suggest that "to deal with situational stress and developmental changes across the family life cycle, balanced families will change their cohesion and adaptability, whereas

Circumplex Model: Sixteen Types of Marital and Family Systems

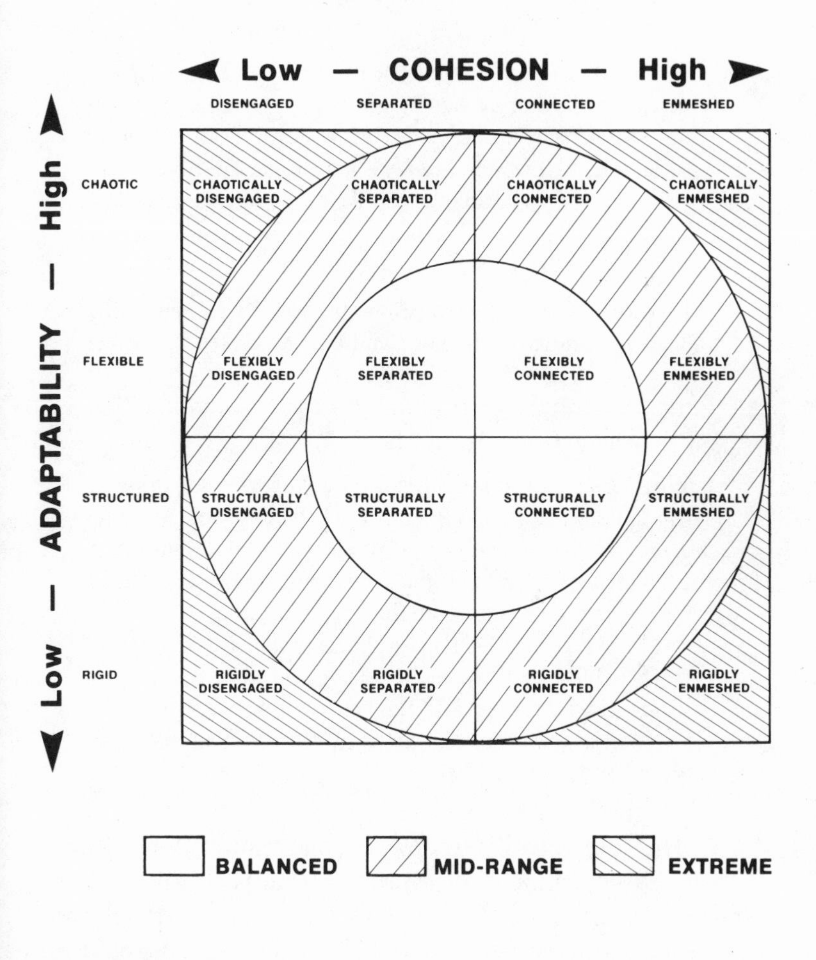

Figure 5-3

extreme families will resist change over time."[4]

The following excerpts from the autobiographical writings of a client named Fred illustrate the impact of the extreme family behaviors. Fred describes his tumultuous childhood, mostly spent trying to escape his father:

> I remember one time when Dad came home intoxicated, he threw the family out of the house. On that occasion my mother carried me in her arms in the dead of winter to a hotel. However, after we arrived at the hotel there were no rooms available so the other kids and myself spent the night with Mother in a restroom, with Mother sitting on the toilet seat and cradling me in her arms. . . .
>
> I remember as if it were yesterday, how I watched, as he beat my mother to the floor and how he kicked her in the face and stomach with his boots as she lay helpless on the floor. My brothers and sisters tried to stop him, but they couldn't. . . .
>
> When I saw my father, I started crying and coughing at the same time. I will remember till the day I die, how he came over to me and said, "You little bastard, shut up or I'll kill you." He then got a butcher knife and grabbed me by the hair and said that he was going to cut my throat. My other brother grabbed a skillet and hit him from behind and when Dad let go of me, one of my sisters picked me up and ran out the door with me. We left Dad in the room and all of us ran down an alley and hid behind some trash. . . .

This excerpt shows how a child can end up feeling extremely vulnerable and helpless in what is clearly a chaotic family. In an effort to escape his father, Fred's family was constantly moving. He writes, "Every time that I would get settled in a new school, I'd have to start in another one." Under the circumstances, it was hard to know what to count on. While families can be chaotic in many different ways, alcohol and physical abuse are especially damaging.

Fred's family went to extremes in terms of cohesion as well. He wrote about his brothers:

> They would come home and fight each other with knives or beer bottles. I watched as they cut each other, then one of them would have to go to the hospital to get stitched up. What I never understood is the fact they were always saying that we were family and it was all right to fight amongst ourselves but if anyone outside of the family gave us any trouble then they had the whole family to fight. . . .
>
> There were times when they came home that Mother was gone to work and they would grab me and try to force me to drink alcohol, and when I refused, they would slap me around and tell me I was Mother's little boy and that I was acting like a baby, I was a Smith [not real name] and I should act like a man. Sometimes they would take turns holding me by the arms while the other hit me in the stomach and they would keep saying that it would make a man out of me. I was also told that a Smith is not afraid of anything or anyone. Since one of my brothers was real good with knives and ice picks, I would be placed against the door and he would throw ice picks at me and stick them in the door around my body. If I moved, it meant a good beating because that showed that I was afraid and, like I said, Smiths were not supposed to be afraid of anything or anyone.

A family united against the world yet fighting among themselves demonstrates the classic features of enmeshment. The Smiths were an extremely chaotic, enmeshed family in which the lack of any structure and the forced family cohesion supported violence and alcoholism. For purposes of comparison, let's look at an example of the opposite extremes of a rigid disengaged family. The following excerpt comes from Sam who describes his life growing up with his sexually addicted and alcoholic father and his co-addictive mother:

> It seemed like our parents were always gone. And when they were around they were either fighting and snapping at us or uncomfortably silent. My parents always had a lot of problems which I never understood then and didn't much care. The main problem it seemed was how much my father was gone and how much he drank. They were always talking about divorce and asking us to decide between them. What really hurt was that neither one of them wanted custody. We made up our minds not to go with either of them. I felt really unloved and neglected. . . .
>
> I really liked it when they were gone, too. I could do anything I wanted and the relief from tension was welcome. The feeling when they were around was like there was a live bomb and any wrong movement, word, or gesture could set it off.

In the rigid, disengaged family, the attitude "every person for himself" becomes a way of life. Although Sam's family and Fred's family were quite different, it is easy to see how a child would feel threatened and develop low self-worth in either one.

Note that both families struggled with alcoholism. Traditional alcoholism theory suggests that different types of families may end up in the same out-of-control situation with the same illness, but how they got there in terms of family dynamics can be radically different. The importance of "differential diagnosis" of families in the field of chemical dependency has been established. The same needs to be done in the field of sexual addiction. Clients need to understand the differing family dynamics that sustain their commonly shared behavior. Toward that end, the circumplex model serves as a helpful diagnostic, clinical, and teaching tool.

Still, despite its major contribution, the circumplex has limits, especially in the area of measurement. Families are very complex to measure. For example, family member perceptions vary. An adolescent might rate his family as rigid, whereas his parents might see the family as structured or even flexible. And there is the problem of coalitions. A mom and son whose incestuous relationship is clearly enmeshed might be considerably disengaged from Dad, making it hard to correctly assess the entire system.

Remember also that families are dynamic and respond situationally. For example, one woman describes her family, using their house as a metaphor. While growing up in her home, no room in the house had a door except the bathroom. That, she says, is what her family life was like: no internal boundaries, no privacy, and no personal space. The one exception to the enmeshment was sex, a totally taboo subject. In this one area, the family was extremely disengaged.

Figure 5-4 presents a graphic representation which approximates how a family might differ according to issue. It is like an EKG in that the family has regular patterns—or rhythms—which can be identified. In fact, from a systemic point of view, that is just what an effective therapist does—identify patterns. Notice in figure 5-4 that a family may have mid-range readings under most circumstances, but with sexual issues, family behavior becomes rigid and enmeshed. Overlooking the fluctuations would mean overlooking the source of the family's discomfort.

Using the circumplex model we can better understand the family of the sexual addict. Our next step is to use this paradigm to describe the family of origin of the addict.

The Family of Origin

In order to understand sexual addiction we need to connect the extremes of the addict's family of origin with the addict's core beliefs, these core beliefs being the foundation of the addictive system. They account for the shame and guilt experienced by the addict, especially sexual shame and guilt.

The importance of shame has long been recognized by clinicians. Shame is qualitatively different than guilt. An

Family "EKG's"

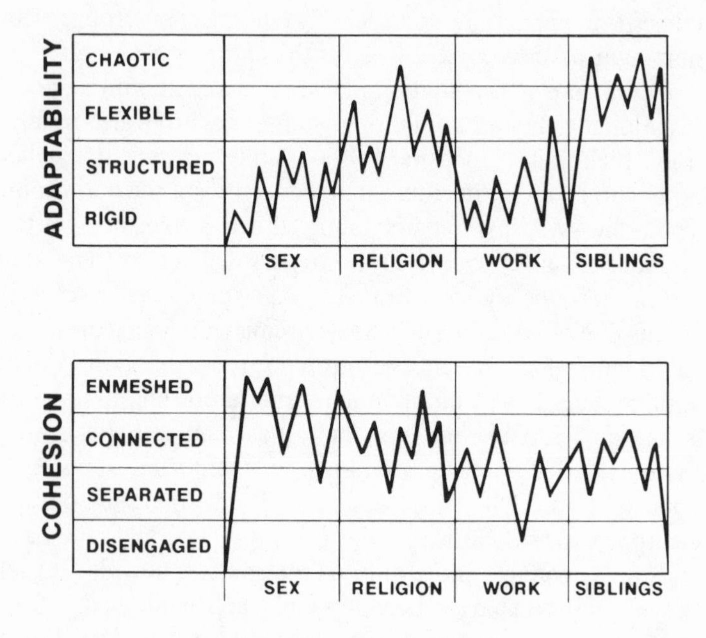

These are examples of family interaction. Rarely is a family simply, for example, "rigidly disengaged" or "chaotically enmeshed" on all matters. Most families tend to wander on the circumplex chart, rules and behavior differing between sexual matters, how siblings are treated relative to one another, and other issues.

Figure 5-4

individual may feel guilty about committing a specific act that he or she knows is wrong. In contrast, shame comes from experiencing oneself or one's behavior as unacceptable. Gershen Kaufman in a widely praised essay describes the shame experience:

> Shame is the experience of being fundamentally bad as a person. Nothing you have done is wrong and nothing you can do will make up for it. It is a total experience that forbids communication with words. . . .[5]

Judging oneself as shameful builds an impenetrable wall keeping others out. The logic is simple: "If I cannot accept myself, I am confident others will do the same." A person who is experiencing shame discounts the efforts of others to reach out, saying, "Either they want something from me, do not see me as I am, or feel sorry for me." When a problem occurs, shame-based people immediately assume that it is their fault—an extension of their own inherent badness. The primitive conclusions of shame prohibit approaching problems as simply issues to be resolved. People who feel shame are quick to defend themselves and are ready to fight even when there's nothing to fight about. A shameful person wants to look good at any price, including dishonesty and self-deception. Kaufman describes why:

> Another dimension of shame is an intense fear of exposure, of having one's badness seen by others. Such exposure of self is intolerable because of the underlying sense of being irreparably and unspeakably defective which somehow separates one from the loneliness of the shame experience, because one cannot express the inner pain and need. (Kaufman, p. 159)

We have described two central features of shame as "core" beliefs: "I am a bad, unworthy person" and "No one would love me as I am." These essentially originate from too little or too much family support and involvement, and, as a result, conclusions about self or family members are diminished. Many people feel shameful, however, but are not seriously addicted. The crucial question is, what turns the failure of family intimacy into addiction?

The critical variable is how the family handles dependency issues. Children depend upon the family structure to get their needs met. When consistent failure to meet these needs occurs, either because of parental inflexibility (rigidity) or inability to follow through (chaos), a child concludes that to survive one can only count on oneself. Other human beings are unreliable. This "survivor" mentality begins to form the third core belief: "My needs are never going to be met if I have to depend on others."

This third core belief extends the logic of the first two: "Since you will never love me anyway because of my innate badness, there's no reason to think you would want to do anything for me. I can't count on you to help, assist, support, or take care of me." This logic obliterates trust and leaves only one option: to survive means to be in control. An equation is established: more distrust equals more controlling behavior. Once established, the distrust/control equation sets the fundamental parameters of addiction. All that is left is to find a source of nurturing over which the addict believes he or she has control—sex. The irony is that when that connection is made—discovering the "high" of exhibitionism, excessive masturbation, or promiscuity—the addict, in effect, becomes powerless.

A further irony is that conscience is now harnessed to the addictive system. In healthy families, children learn standards for appropriate conduct and setting limits. If they transgress those rules and expectations they have internalized, they know they are redeemable. They trust people will not leave them because they have been valued and affirmed enough to be able to value and affirm themselves from within. They can make amends or restitution in some form and be forgiven. The addicts' shame makes a servant of their guilt.

The reasoning goes: "Nobody will ever forgive me, so no effort to reconcile will succeed."

And since being out of control is perceived as the ultimate defect, addicts will experience a series of alternating cycles of shame and guilt which leave them hopeless. Remorse for what they have done confirms their innate badness, which in turn paralyzes their capacity to relieve their guilt. This despair reaches its highest degree of intensity immediately after the addict has been out of control. Within the addictive system of the sexual addict, this moment occurs in the addiction cycle after the sexually compulsive behavior (see fig. 5-3).

We have established that the addictive system is a shame-based system. The addict's shame is made explicit in the internal logic of the addict's first three core beliefs. Addicts make these primitive conclusions while still in their family of origin. Or if the core beliefs are not firmly established, there is sufficient self-doubt from having grown up in their family of origin that damaging life experiences as an adult can confirm the core beliefs. These beliefs about self, relationships, and dependency are shared by all addicts—whatever the form of addiction or dependency. All of which helps explain how a person could be addicted to more than one compulsive behavior. An alcoholic who is also a sex addict or a compulsive gambler has as the common denominator the interior logic of the first three core beliefs.

The remaining question is, how does one become a sex addict? The key variable is the fourth core belief of the addict, "Sex is my most important need." In essence, the addict concludes that since no one can be counted on, sex becomes the one "dependable" source of nurturing that will always be readily available. If the first three core beliefs form the common denominator between all addictions, then the factor that separates the sex addiction from other forms of addiction is the addict's unshakable belief in sex as essential to well-being. Sex is seen as more critical to emotional survival than family, friends, work, and values.

How does sex become so important? Again the family of origin plays a key role, especially in how it teaches sexual shame.

Sexual Shame

Imagine a six-year-old child on a playground. Lonely and having a hard time connecting with other children, he decides to shimmy up one of the support poles of a large swing set. As he reaches the top, he makes an amazing discovery—he experiences an intense pleasure in his groin area. Once the pleasure peaks, he finds himself dazed, disoriented, and even more distant than he had been from his schoolmates. He wants to ask someone, but he has mastered his family's lesson about not asking for help. So he keeps his secret to himself. And wonders whether he is strange. But that doesn't stop him.

Once the discovery is made, the boy often climbs poles. His mother's clothes-line poles are ideal because he can hang on the cross bars for long periods of time, especially when he is lonely. No one else seems to be like him. He watches other kids to see if they climb poles the way he does, but finds no peers. This discovery fits his notion of sex in general: he has an intense interest whereas none of his friends seem to care beyond occasional show-and-tell games. Other kids always lose interest before he does. In his family, although sex isn't talked about, the boy detects an attitude of disapproval about the whole matter. To have it forbidden somehow makes it even more attractive. All he knows for sure is that he feels bad about something he did, which feels both frightening and good.

The fusion of feeling both good and bad become more explicit when the child becomes an adolescent. By this time, he is using other ways to masturbate, including the closet door in his room. His father, aware of his son's behavior, gives him a lecture in which he indicates that to masturbate is a serious character flaw. His father equates manhood with resisting the urge to masturbate, suggesting that "a true man has control of his impulses." That is how the boy learns the word for what he has been doing regularly for six years. Interestingly, from that point on, he actually ejaculates when he stimulates himself.

One incident particularly highlights the fusion of good and bad feelings. This boy had been abused sexually by a number of primary adults in his life by the time he was seventeen. The most striking incident occurs when he seeks counseling for his masturbation "problem." He talks to his English teacher at his high school. As the teacher listens, he places his hand on the young man's penis and gently stimulates it. As the penis gets hard, the teacher tells the boy that he "shouldn't do this alone." The boy leaves filled with shame and confusion about how good it felt. This type of incident crystallizes the shame of the addict who wants something even when it is exploitive and degrading. In the addict's mind, abuse and punishment are deserved.

Once he reaches adolescence, the young man dates a lot. In fact, so much that he develops a reputation as a womanizer. Most of his fantasies, however, are about a young woman in his neighborhood. She is flirtatious with him, and he finds her very attractive. One night he awakes and is very aroused. Earlier he had been thinking about this woman's house which had a porch surrounded by trees. He wondered if he could climb a tree and peer into her bedroom. He gets up, dresses, and goes out to see if in fact this is possible. Perched on a tree branch, he has a clear view of the bedroom. Much to his surprise she walks into the bedroom and undresses. It is the first time he has seen an adult woman nude. Never before has he experienced such excitement. He goes home, straight to bed, and masturbates virtually nonstop until dawn—the first of many such nights.

This young man's story is like those of many other recovering people who report intense sexual experiences in a family environment where sexuality is considered bad. Adult addicts speculate that sexual addiction is so strong because in many cases it starts so early, because sexual satisfaction is easily accessible, and it can be kept secret.

Every addict agrees that the negative family messages had a profound impact. Negative family messages about sex take many forms. Some are very indirect such as:

—heavily loaded value labels like "good girl" and "bad boy"

—"no-talk" rules about sexual issues

—evasive responses to questions about sex

—inaccurate information given purposely

—descriptions which do not match reality and are therefore confusing, such as "curse," "family way," or "birds and bees"

—lack of physical or sexual affirmation

—lack of others who "get into trouble"

—destructive sexual patterns in marriage like "Dad pushes; Mom gives in"

More direct forms include extensive moralizing about sex as inherently bad, evil, or sinful; threats about sexual behavior ("If you ever . . ."); and descriptions of sex as an awful or degrading experience. By far the most damaging forms are physical or verbal abuse when a child is discovered being sexual.

Some families will carry sexual shame from one generation to the next. For example, in one family, generations of unplanned pregnancies perpetuated the belief that "having to get married" was unforgivable in God's eyes. So each new generation would start as "second class" because of their sexual shame.

Some addicts, however, grew up in families where their parents were out of control sexually. For example, parents who are sexually inappropriate in front of their children while intoxicated create confusion. These become "shaming" events in which children conclude there is something wrong with them and their family. Some parents suffer from addiction. One sex addict talks about his alcoholic mother who had over twenty men live in their home while he was growing up. One of his most vivid memories was of a swinging party organized by his mother. There was little chance that he could grow up feeling good about himself or his sexuality.

By far the most damaging way that parents lose control is in sexual abuse of their children. In the research conducted for this book, male and female addicts were asked if they had been abused as children. A comparison group of nonaddicted men and women were asked the same question. Thirty-nine percent of the 160 addicted men and 63 percent of 24 addicted women reported being abused. In the comparison group only 8 percent of the 78 nonaddicted men and 20 percent of the 98 nonaddicted women reported abuse. Of the men who committed incest as part of their addiction, 55 percent were childhood victims of incest.

We believe that these results represent underreporting, that is, a greater percent of the addicts were sexually abused as children. The addicts involved in this study were a mixture of people newly in recovery as well as those who had been in recovery for some time. Persons who are new to recovery will not have as clear a picture of their abuse experience as people with a longer time in recovery. Preliminary results from a new study currently under way would appear to validate that assumption.

Sexual abuse generates shame in several ways:

—Children end up not trusting adults.

—Children are blamed for the abuse, wrongly believing it is their fault that the sexual behavior occurred.

—Children are required to keep the sexual behavior secret, which adds to the feelings of shame.

—Children are harmed physically so that they equate pain with sex.

—Children are invaded, creating feelings of powerlessness.

—Children associate sex with being degraded and losing self-respect.

—Children feel they are not in control of their own bodies.

—Children confuse sex with intimacy and love.

Children can also become eroticized by incest, sometimes at a very young age. Psychiatrist Alayne Yates reviewed cases of very young incest victims about which she concluded:

> These children had several features which seem to me characteristic of eroticized preschool children. Such children are easily aroused by a variety of circumstances and most often cannot discriminate erotic from nonerotic relationships. They are readily orgasmic and also can maintain a high level of arousal without orgasm. . . . In fact, erotic expression may be so gratifying that it is difficult to find comparable rewards to reinforce socially acceptable behavior.[6]

And so the cycle continues. Family researchers Michael Martin and James Walters studied 489 cases of child abuse and neglect. They found a clear relationship between the sexual abuse of children and fathers who were sexually promiscuous and alcoholic.[7] Given the sample in the study, there is a high probability many of those fathers were also childhood victims of sexual abuse.[8]

Nor is the damage limited to direct sexual contact between parents and children. There is also "covert" incest which is devastating because of its subtlety. A parent who is flirtatious, suggestive, or sexually titillating with a child is incestuous even though no physical touch has occurred. A mother who seductively compliments her son on the size of his penis, or a father who repeatedly makes explicit comments about the shape of his daughter's breasts—these parents aren't affirming their children's sexuality—they're being sexual with their children. But since they have done nothing overtly other than talk, their children are left feeling uncomfortable and shameful, not to mention feeling crazy.[9]

Whether the family has a high degree of tension around sexual matters or is out of control, children end up feeling shameful about their sexuality. And when the family is preoccupied with sex, the logic of the core beliefs becomes circular. The belief that "sex is my most important need," combined with the fusion of feeling both good and bad, leads to the corollary: "I am bad or flawed because sex is my most important priority." Addicts then have confirmation of their own innate badness, which is where they started out in the first place:

1. I am basically a bad, unworthy person.
2. No one would love me as I am.
3. My needs are never going to be met if I have to depend on others.
4. Sex is my most important need.
5. I am bad because sex is my most important need.

Figure 5-5 summarizes typical extreme behaviors to be found in the sexual addict's family of origin using the circumplex model. Note the important interaction of intimacy and dependency issues critical to the formation of the core beliefs and intense sexual shame. This interaction gives addicts a firm foundation for their addiction.

A note should be added here: not all sex addicts come from families of origin as described here. Empirical data suggest that most do; however, there are those addicts whose catalytic events occur entirely outside the blood family, such as being raised in a boarding school. Also, some addicts have normal childhoods, but are participants in an affected or catalytic environment later in life. This group is typified by the salesman or graduate student under high pressure to perform in an unstructured environment.

Contrasts in Families

To demonstrate the utility of a model like the circumplex in treatment, thirty-five sex offenders who were in rehabilitation programs in state correctional facilities in Georgia and Minnesota were asked to assess their families of origin. Each inmate was asked to complete FACES II, a family assessment profile based on the circumplex model.[10] First, they were asked to rate their family life when they were adolescents. Given that the results are retrospective and represent only one family member's perception, few conclusions can be made. Interesting contrasts occur, however, when the offenders' memories are compared with a normal sample of 416 adolescents (fig.5-6). Divided into balanced, mid-range, and extreme, the comparisons are as follows:

	Normal	Sex Offenders
Balanced	47%	11%
Mid-range	34%	40%
Extreme	19%	49%

Sex offenders remembered their families as being more extreme than most adolescents did. In fact, 77 percent of the

Typical Extreme Sexual Behaviors and Attitudes in Addict's Family of Origin

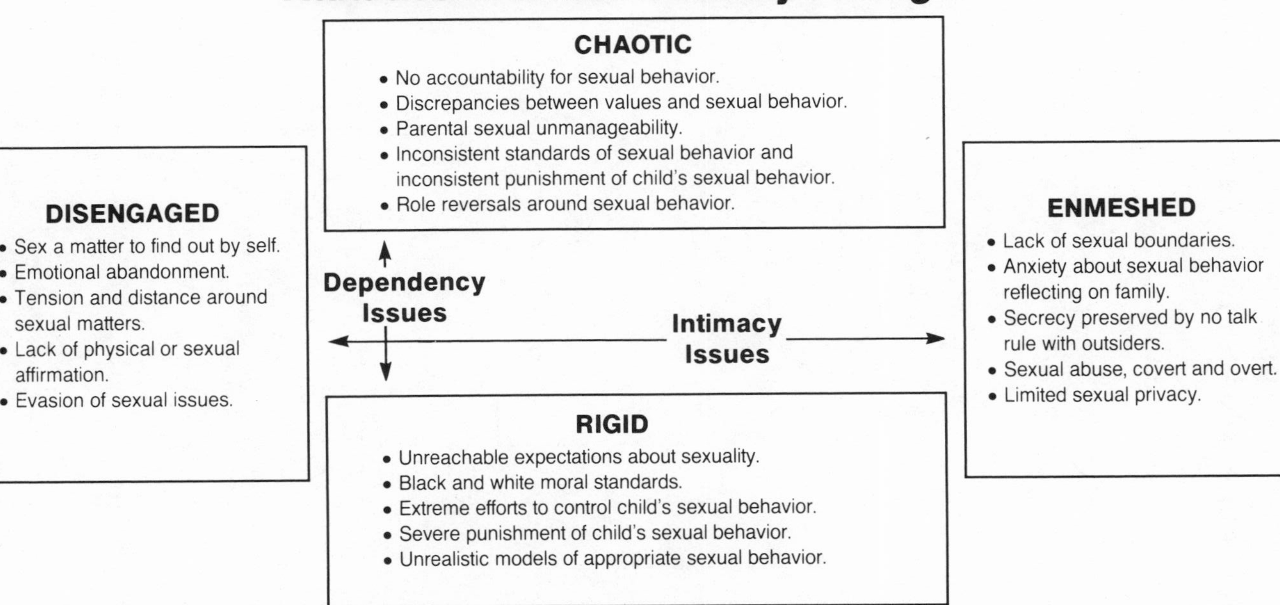

Figure 5-5

Perception of System in Family of Origin
Normal Adolescents vs. Sex Offenders

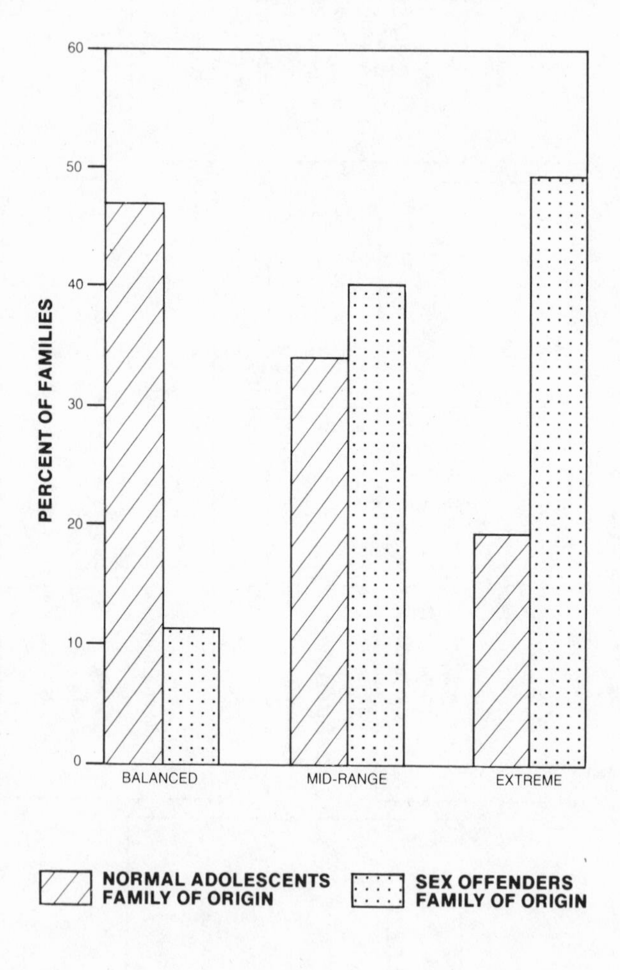

Figure 5-6

offenders saw their families as rigid and 57 percent perceived their families as disengaged. So much commonality in a specific clinical population points to certain critical factors for treatment programs in specific institutions and probably corrections in general. Individual treatment plans need to take these data into account. Further research needs to be done in this area for all levels of addiction. The social policy implications alone are of grave significance.

Some research has been done on the current families of sex offenders. Usually, these efforts represent very small sample sizes ranging from three to thirty offenders. Almost always psychometric tests, as opposed to family assessment procedures, are used when anything beyond case histories are investigated.[11] Again for purposes of illustration, we asked thirty-two of the offenders who were married to complete FACES II, an assessment tool on their current families. Comparing their current families with retrospective assessments of their adolescent family life produced the following contrasts:

	Adolescent	Current
Balanced	11%	19%
Mid-range	40%	15%
Extreme	49%	66%

While a few current were seen as families more balanced, many more were seen as extreme. The largest increase was in cohesion, with 72 percent of the families being disengaged, which might reflect the inmates current prison status. The point remains that these preliminary data support the clinical observation that unhealthy family systems are perpetuated in the current families of these offenders, as perceived by the addicts.

But how does the current family perpetuate the themes of the family of origin? In what ways do the spouse and children participate in the addictive system? To appreciate the roles of the family members, we must explore co-addiction, the illness suffered by those close to and affected by an active sexual addict.

6
Co-addiction in the Family

One of the most difficult aspects of codependency is admitting our powerlessness over the addict. Our continual attempts to affect or control the sex addict render our lives unmanageable.

"Codependents of Sex Addicts: A Program of Recovery,"
Twin Cities COSA, 1983

Herb loved Emily—of that he was sure. But he had never been as jealous of anyone in his whole life. Even after they became engaged, Emily continued to flirt with other men, which really bothered him. When he told her about his feelings, she dismissed them as "male possessiveness," and he always ended up feeling inadequate.

When Herb tried to ignore Emily's behavior, he became angry and sullen, which made him feel even worse about himself. When he demanded that she stop, Emily flirted even more. So he tried to avoid social occasions where there were interesting men. Then Emily accused Herb of being a stick-in-the-mud.

They also fought about Emily's career. She wanted something more challenging, with some travel. But Herb saw this as a way for her to meet more men. Because he believed in women's rights, he agonized over whether he was being sexist. Herb felt the conflict that was going on, but somehow it kept coming back as his problem. Still he checked up on Emily all the time and felt awful doing it.

One day Emily was arrested for shoplifting. After her release, Emily confessed not only to shoplifting frequently but to a whole series of affairs, including one during their engagement. Herb tried to remain supportive, but knowing she had made love with someone else the day before they were married hurt him deeply. Since she was so contrite, he decided to be helpful rather than outraged. He never told her about his feelings. For two months, Herb and Emily entered a "honeymoon" phase which he later remembered as one of the best times in their marriage.

When Emily started graduate school to pursue a new career, Herb became uneasy again. He worried more when she reported that she was taking an art class for fun. His fear became obsessive when he saw nudes in some of her drawings. Emily admitted that she was very attracted to the male model and had, in fact, volunteered to pose nude with him for the class.

Herb decided to go talk with this man, hoping that if the model knew how much pain was involved in this situation, he would abandon a potential relationship with Emily. Herb tracked the man down and talked with him, to no avail. Two nights later, Emily didn't come home. When she finally arrived, she admitted having slept with the model. Herb went on an emotional binge, crying and raging for hours. Emily was contrite. And there followed another honeymoon period.

And so it went for eight years—revelations followed by contrition followed by honeymoon periods. In desperation, Herb finally sought the advice of a former professor who was like a father to him. The professor compared Herb to Charlie Brown in the comic strip "Peanuts." Time after time, Lucy holds a football for Charlie Brown and jerks it out of the way at the last moment. Each time, Charlie says *this* time he is going to kick it out of the park. And each time he falls flat on his back with Lucy's derisive laughter ringing in his ears. The professor suggested that Herb stop playing football. So he left Emily. With a therapist's help, he was able to stop wondering who she was with and worrying about meeting her. The few times he did see her, he desperately wanted to be with her again. As his therapist pointed out, that desire was part of Herb's self-destructiveness, since if he went back to her he would end up feeling a failure again and again.

Herb came to understand his co-addiction to Emily. In therapy he learned that his obsession with Emily's sexual behavior was like his preoccupation with his father's drinking. He had, after all, been trained well. His mother used to send him to the local bar to bring his dad home, for which his dad would always beat him. Yet every time his mom asked, he would go. After each beating he would feel that he had let both of them down. Worrying about whether Dad would drink was a daily concern for Herb.

When he acknowledged his obsession with Emily's behavior, Herb saw how he had denied it before and conveniently overlooked clues pointing to it. For example, his brother reminded him that an anonymous caller had once told Herb, "I've been fucking your wife," and hung up. At the time, Herb wrote off the call as a prank. Now it fit into a larger pattern.

Co-addict Beliefs

Along with obsession and denial, co-addicts like Herb share some of the same core beliefs that addicts do. Both addicts and co-addicts believe that they are basically unworthy persons no one could ever love. Shame and low self-esteem are the common denominators of co-addiction. The woman who marries the same kind of alcoholic three times concludes she can do no better; not only does the situation feel right because it is familiar, but also it is all that she deserves because she is so flawed. Similarly, Herb repeatedly returned to trusting Emily. He pursued the honeymoon periods through incredible pain and frustration.

One woman co-addict wrote about the reasons people hold on to their shame even though it is self-destructive:

> Somehow even in a sick way, shame temporarily relieves the ambiguity, the uncertainty, the lack of control. There is always an answer, "I am a bad person." And for someone like myself who has so very little faith to lean on my higher power, I will easily barter away peace for turmoil—if it means some sort of "reason" or "answer." I just cannot agree or let go of the idea that I am not all powerful, all controlling. . . .
>
> Also, the shame, like styrofoam, has bulk—I can tell that it's in me. Sometimes when I let go of the bulky shame, I feel empty—nothing to fill in the space. I don't see very often that the styrofoam shame keeps me from taking in real nourishment, i.e., food of spirit, feelings, other's love and care.

The analogy is an apt one for co-addictive relationships. They feel like relationships and have form, but they are empty. Despite the honeymoon periods, the true addict is seldom totally present and involved.

Co-addicts also face dependency issues. Along with the addict they believe they cannot depend on others to meet their needs, they go to great lengths to try to guarantee the relationship. Co-addicts, for example, will become super-responsible and reliable to make sure they are indispensible. They may take over more and more household chores as the addict becomes increasingly irresponsible; in Herb's case, he financially supported Emily and did much of the work to keep the house organized. When she still acted out despite all he had done, he could feel self-righteous.

Co-addicts create dependency without realizing it. The woman who says "Having him around is like having another child" probably finds it easier to be close to someone who depends on her than to be intimate with an equal. And concentrating on the addict allows the co-addict to ignore his or her own problems. Thus, intimacy and dependency issues combine to keep the co-addict focused on the addict.

Dealing with the sexual addict becomes the principal life task of the co-addict. The problem takes center stage.

Because sexuality is so personal and so vital to relationships, co-addicts can be seriously damaged. Just as an alcoholic's spouse feels blamed for the alcoholism, co-addicts feel that having a spouse who is sexually out of control is a statement about themselves. Co-addicts doubt their attractiveness, their sexuality, their masculinity or their femininity. They develop performance anxiety because they believe there must be something sexually wrong with them. Herb, for example, went on jogging and swimming binges to get his body in better shape, believing that if he were more attractive, he could influence Emily's behavior.

Thus, addicts and co-addicts share three core beliefs: (1) I am basically a bad, unworthy person, (2) no one would love me as I am, and (3) my needs are never going to be met if I have to depend on other people. But the co-addict develops a different fourth core belief: sex is the most important sign of love. Children who are incest victims are taught that acting sexy or being flirtatious or being sexual are ways that adults provide attention and love. In our culture, women as sex objects are rewarded with male attention, protection, and money. In recovery, the co-addict often recognizes that confusing love with sex was part of the relationship with the addict from the beginning. When the addict who believes that "sex is my most important need" meets the co-addict who believes that "sex is the most important sign of love," a powerfully destructive situation is in the making.

The co-addict attaches great significance to sexual encounters with the addict. For that brief time the co-addict can be sure of the addict's commitment, loyalty, and love, feeling chosen and secure because the addict isn't with someone else. Literally obsessed with how the addict makes sexual choices, the co-addict demands the addict's full attention. If the addict even looks at someone else the co-addict sees the relationship threatened. The spouse of an alcoholic may be able to detach when the partner chooses a bottle over the relationship, but that task is exponentially more difficult when the choice is another sexual partner.

The logic of the co-addictive belief system is particularly deadly: "Since I am unworthy and no one would care for me, my needs will not be met by others unless I do something to control it. In order to preserve this relationship which is perhaps my best or last chance, sex is my one guarantee or my one source of power to make sure that I am loved. If I fail, it is the final proof of my unworthiness as a person." Like the addict's, the co-addict's beliefs are self-reinforcing. Based on the circular logic, the co-addict will go to any extreme to preserve the relationship.

Co-addict Extremes and the Circumplex Model

The circumplex can serve as a guide to the extreme behavior in the addict's current family. Figure 6-1 categorizes typical (but by no means all) co-addictive behaviors into dependency and intimacy issues. Co-addicts who look at this chart often remark, "I've done all of those." While that can be very true, usually there is a pattern or collection of behaviors which favor one set of extremes. Taken together, this behavioral constellation works only to support and to intensify the addictive system, rather than limit or de-intensify it.

One way that co-addicts cope is to remove themselves in some way from the addictive relationship, remaining emotionally unavailable—and safe—to punish the addicts. Along with the detachment goes a self-righteous disdain that pressures the addicts to change. Given what sex signifies to the co-addict, withholding sex is one of the most important messages co-addicts try to send addicts about the depth of their pain.

Unfortunately, addicts totally miss the message of the co-addict's pain. They feel the co-addict is punishing and

Typical Co-Addict Behavior Extremes

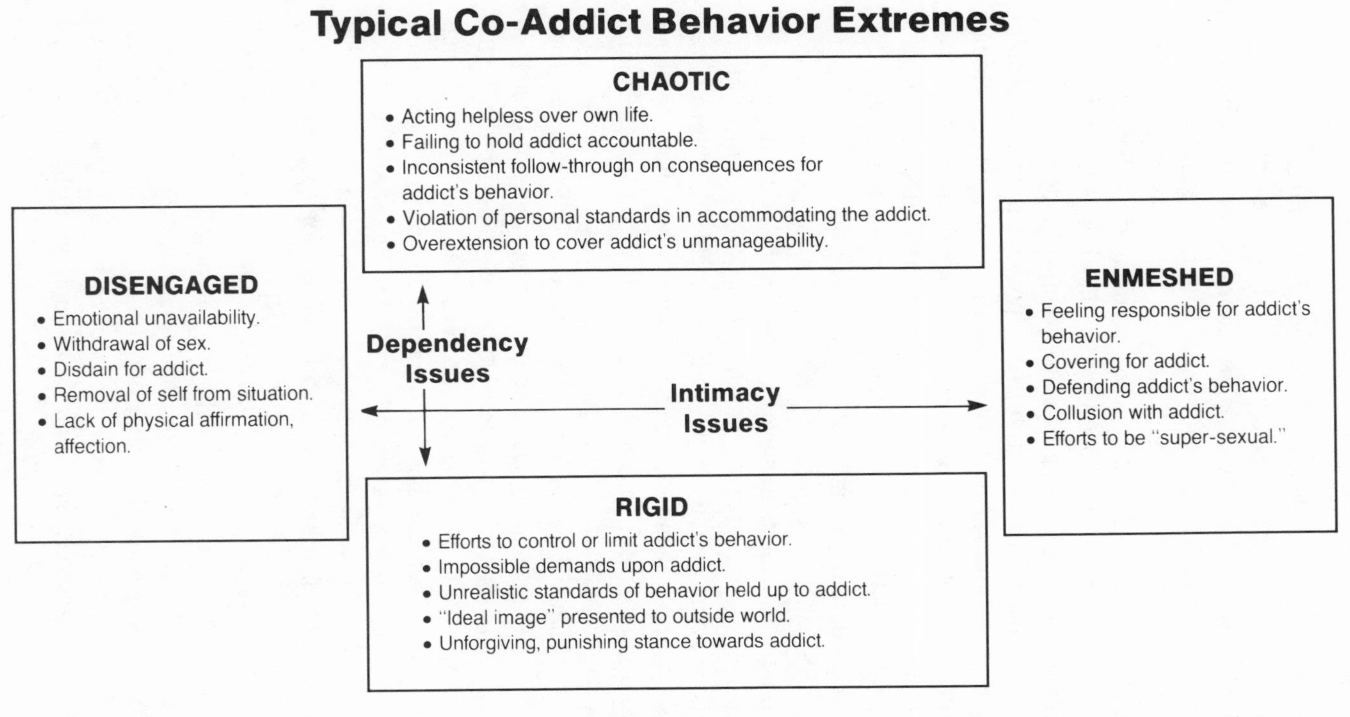

Figure 6-1

unresponsive; all their beliefs about unworthiness, unlovability, and the undependability of others are validated. The withdrawal of sex when it is the addict's most important need creates panic. The addict's impaired thinking blames the co-addict for the behavior: "I need to do this because she (he) will not meet my needs." The "disengaged" behavior of the co-addict, intended to act as self-protection, works instead to increase the addict's despair and compulsive behavior.

Other co-addicts go to the opposite extreme, participating in the compulsive sexual behavior of the addict. Rather than fighting they try to join. For some, involving themselves in their partner's behavior continues the pattern of enmeshment learned in their own family of origin. For others, it is simply a matter of not wanting to be left out.

Sarah's husband convinced her to be part of a threesome. He said a ménage à trois would add zest to their marriage. And since the first threesome would involve another man, Sarah would be the one to benefit. So she said yes. Soon her husband George was regularly recruiting someone to join them. While that person had intercourse with Sarah, George would watch and masturbate.

From the beginning of their marriage, Sarah had tried to be "super-sexual" because of George's intense interest in sex. Although she felt terrible about some of the sexual events George orchestrated, she never told him. She did what he wanted because she felt she had to in order to keep him. Once he had her pose nude with her legs spread and then submitted the photograph to a porno magazine's special section about reader's girlfriends. She couldn't sleep worrying that people she knew would see the picture.

Many co-addicts cover for the addict or even defend the addict's behavior because they feel responsible. Some blame themselves for their own inadequate sexual performance. Sarah felt personally responsible because of her own participation. At one point, George became sexually involved with a neighborhood teenage girl. Although Sarah knew, she felt she couldn't complain because of having been involved in the threesomes. When the girl's angry parents confronted her, Sarah found herself not only lying, but attacking them for allowing their daughter to dress and act in a seductive manner. Then she felt ashamed for defending George's behavior.

Through their enmeshment, some co-addicts become sexual addicts as well. Female addicts report that they started out in a co-addictive posture, seeking love and nurturing, but eventually changed their primary obsession to sex. Their core belief that sex is the most significant sign of love changed to the belief that sex is the end goal.

Sarah's life with George became progressively more chaotic. The threesome scenarios became so violent that Sarah was physically harmed and had to fabricate elaborate stories to explain her injuries. She had frequent vaginal infections and contracted gonorrhea. When George started videotaping the sessions, Sarah felt she had reached her limit. She told him she would never do another threesome. Still, George talked her into it again and again.

By this time, George had become involved with a number of other women he also talked into having threesomes. When Sarah objected, George pointed to the many times she had sex while he watched; after all, he reasoned, how could she object if he had sex with someone else when she didn't even have to watch? Because of his involvements, George spent less time at his work, earned less, but spent more. Sarah had to borrow money to keep the household going; every time she considered moving out she was held back by finances. Her life felt increasingly out of control. The man she had married had been replaced by an awful stranger.

Not all co-addicts respond in the same helpless fashion as Sarah. Some declare war against the addict, the addiction, and in fact anything sexual. These co-addicts will go to any lengths to control or limit their partner's behavior. In the case of Herb earlier in the chapter, when he went to talk to his wife's lover, as opposed to dealing with his wife directly, he did it out of his need to control. Since he couldn't change his wife, he tried changing other people. This co-addictive controlling response is parallel to other co-addicts who try to curb the addiction by avoiding social engagements or refusing to leave town because, left alone, the addict might do something.

The addict's demands come up against the co-addict's unrealistic standards. The co-addict starts with the assumption the addict is not going to meet the standards, in effect setting into motion the self-fulfilling prophecy that the addict will fail. Convinced of the righteousness of his or her own position, the co-addict maintains a punishing, unforgiving stance. It is a siege mentality which dares the addict to step out of line. Threats are immediately carried out, with one exception—the co-addict rarely leaves the relationship. More than anything, the co-addict tries to maintain appearances that everything is under control, that the family is a "Better Homes and Gardens" family. To leave would break the image and acknowledge to the world the weakness of the relationship. In a rigid family, failure equals not trying hard enough, which is part of why Herb kept trying to "kick the football."

The unyielding pressure of the rigid system unwittingly adds great power to the addictive system. The control demeans the addict and invites defiance of a spouse who in effect is acting like a parent. Going back to the story of Herb and Emily, one of Herb's problems was that by controlling the money and social access he made acting out seem more attractive for Emily. All Herb's attempts to control served as justification in Emily's impaired thinking. Herb's reasoning also had become impaired—that is, not based on reality—because he believed against all evidence that his efforts were justified and would succeed. The rigid system—like the chaotic, enmeshed, and disengaged systems—only perpetuates the addictive system.

The phases of growth of the addictive system, introduced in chapters 2 and 3, can also be used to describe shifts in the co-addict's behavior. The following behaviors might typify co-addict extremes at various phases:

—*Initiation:* participation in the process such as in "swapping" or "swinging" (enmeshed)

—*Establishment:* denial of addictive patterns and incorporation of irregularities into life (chaotic)

—*Contingent Escalation:* extreme efforts to control out of fear of collapse of family (rigid)

—*Contingent De-escalation:* joining the addict in presenting a united front to the world (rigid)

—*Acute:* reorganization of the family without the addict, either through intense denial or separation and divorce (disengaged)

—*Chronic:* leaving the relationship (disengaged)

Not all co-addicts experience these phases. Some will start with one set of extreme behaviors and simply intensify them as the addiction grows. Recovery for all co-addicts requires reflection on the changes in intensity or direction of their extreme behavior, and the recognition that these efforts were useless to prevent the sexually compulsive behavior.

Common Errors in Co-addicts' Thinking

Although extremes differ, co-addicts are prone to make three mistakes. *First, they mistake intensity for intimacy.* Life in the addict's family is seldom boring. Crisis, unmanageability, struggle, and pain become a steady emotional diet. Ironically, the disengaged are often the most intense, for it takes a great deal of energy to maintain the obsession from a distance. Because the emotions are so immediate, intensity feels like intimacy—but there is no closeness. Co-addiction fills up a person's life, but leaves needs unmet.

Angry tirades get the adrenaline running and in the short term feel good. At least something is happening. But co-addicts invariably are out of touch with their own feelings. They don't share their own sadness, fear of failure, pain, and loneliness. To share personal feelings would be an invitation to intimacy, too great a risk for the co-addict. So the siege continues. Ironically, the addicts never hear the one message that might help break through the denial about the impact of the addiction: that they are loved.

As time goes on, the co-addict vacillates being understanding one moment, enraged the next. Both these responses fail, which leads the co-addict to believe that he or she hasn't pushed hard enough. So, the co-addict stays in a vicious cycle of rage, understanding, sexual intimacy with the addict, and rage again.

Second, co-addicts mistake obsession for love or care. Like care, obsession focuses on another person, but makes that person into an object. Obsession stems from the terror of being left alone, while care trusts in another person's ongoing availability. Obsession fosters manipulation, whereas care creates respect for self and others. Obsession with another person obliterates self-awareness, while care assumes that fidelity to anyone else begins with faithfulness to oneself.

At its worst, obsession takes over the life of the co-addict. Like the addict, co-addicts lose a sense of their own lives. Pain, boredom, and lack of direction disappear as obsession gives new meaning and even excitement to life. Many co-addicts talk of how they've changed; they don't like the person they've become. Frequently, phrases like "losing myself" are used by co-addicts to describe a personality shift that almost parallels the Jekyll-Hyde experience of the addict. But obsession does have payoffs. One payoff is that obsession guarantees a connection with the addict—even when the addict isn't there. Obsession helps prevent feelings of abandonment. For example, Herb's obsession with Emily for years after he had left her was a way to keep her present in his life. His preoccupation helped stave off the grief of losing her to the addiction.

Another payoff of obsession is that co-addicts do not have to make choices for themselves or deal with their own issues and pain. The obsession with the addict becomes the organizing principle of their lives. Co-addicts are often filled with self-righteous impaired thinking and rage about how much they have invested in the relationship. They need to gain clarity about the rule of obsession over their lives, and to grieve over their loss of identity.

Third, co-addicts mistake control for security. In all relationships, there is a risk of being left alone. In healthy relationships, commitment and a history together transform this risk into a loving confidence that intimacy can occur without fear. The co-addict, however, feels compelled to fight against the possibility of abandonment. Co-addicts view the world through "if only" lenses: the relationship would survive if only the addict would change; the addict would change if only the co-addicts would be perfectly sexual, perfectly need fulfilling, or perfectly controlling. Changing the addict becomes their goal. An additional benefit is that by being "in charge" the co-addicts' inadequacies are never exposed. Ironically, however, gone forever is the chance for the real, loving relationship co-addicts so desperately want and think they are working for.

In some African forest regions, the native people catch monkeys by putting fruit in small wooden boxes with narrow slats on the sides. Monkeys are able to reach in and grab the fruit, but they are unable to pull the fruit through the openings. They refuse to let go of the fruit, however, and struggle with the box. Soon someone comes by and captures the monkeys. The monkeys are trapped by holding on too tight. This is an apt metaphor for the co-addict's plight. Co-addicts, out of intensity, obsession, and above all, the need to be in control, won't let go, and so they imprison themselves within the addictive system. Only through a complete acknowledgement of their own powerlessness—another commonality shared with the addict—will the co-addict find peace. That process will be explored in depth in the next chapter.

For helping professionals to assist co-addicts like Sarah and Herb, they must recognize first how co-addicts can be remarkably different and then identify what they have in common. Both the extreme differences and the common behavioral "corollaries" are equally important in treatment.

The Co-addictive System

The greatest commonality shared by co-addicts is the co-addictive system, which is like the addictive system and has the same shame-based set of core beliefs. On the basis of those beliefs, the co-addict's thinking also becomes impaired, with rationalization, denial, minimization, and blame getting the upper hand. This fundamental distortion of reality justifies the co-addictive extremes and behavioral corollaries described earlier, and the behavior results in further unmanageability, which proves the co-addict's basic life propositions. Thus the co-addictive system perpetuates itself just as the addictive system does.

The helping professional needs to know how these two systems link. The term "good fit" indicates the degree of compatibility between variables. Clinicians will find the match or fit extremely tight between co-addictive and addictive systems. Belief systems run parallel and reinforce one another. For example, if the addict justifies acting out because of the sexual unresponsiveness of the spouse, and if the spouse blames herself or himself for the addict's actions because of personal sexual inadequacy, they agree on the cause of the problem. Because of the mutuality of behavior, even unmanageability is shared. Sarah's lying to the neighbors and her financial overextension in response to George's increasing unreliability illustrate how unmanageability compounds unmanageability between the two systems.

Another level of fit or match is reached when children are involved. Because children are clearly tuned in to the extremes and interaction of their parents and are forming their own beliefs and behavior patterns, the match of the parents becomes the family of origin of the next generation of addicts and co-addicts. In the case of child abuse, children are subsumed in the pathological systems of their parents.

Another matter of fit in co-addictive relationships is the issue of concurrent addictions. When the co-addict enables the alcoholism of his or her spouse as a way to curb sexual addiction, the match becomes more convoluted but just as tight a fit. Consider what happens when addictions are distributed among family members. When the husband is a sexual addict and the wife is chemically dependent, they become co-addicts to each other's dependencies. When the wife's morbid obesity is a central issue in her husband's sexual addiction, it could be a co-addictive response to his sexual pressure, or it could be compulsive overeating in response to pain, or both. Unique problems emerge when two sex addicts marry each other. Within the context of co-addiction, multiple dependencies escalate exponentially the complexity and the "good fit" of co-addictive and addictive systems.

The Etiology of the Core Beliefs and the Addictive System

Thus far, we have observed the growth of the addictive system as a pathology, the significant relationship of the family of origin and co-addictive systems to the addictive system's evolution, and the powerful role of core beliefs as they represent the addict's shame, the resulting faulty logic, and ultimately compulsive behavior. Figure 6-2 traces the development of those core beliefs. To summarize, the addict starts with self-perceptions that reflect family extremes, including both dependency and intimacy issues. In addition, sexual experience, including child abuse and sexual and cultural messages, combine to create negative conclusions about self. Catalytic events and environments in the initiation phase of the addictive system transform those self-perceptions into the core beliefs which drive the addictive system. These core beliefs are sustained by co-addictive systems, which most commonly echo the lessons of those early childhood experiences, and the addictive system which confirms the beliefs as true.

How can these beliefs be replaced with affirmations of worth, lovability, and trust? How can the system be disrupted? In the next chapter we proceed to the problem—and opportunity—of recovery.

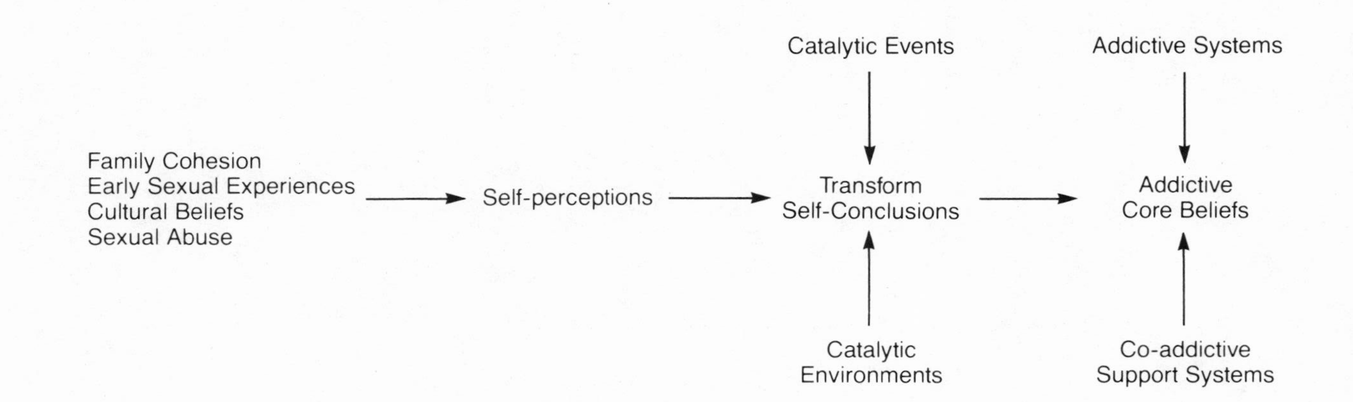
Etiology of Core Beliefs
Family Cohesion
Early Sexual Experiences
Cultural Beliefs
Sexual Abuse
Self-perceptions
Catalytic Events
Transform
Self-Conclusions
Catalytic
Environments
Addictive Systems
Addictive
Core Beliefs
Co-addictive
Support Systems

Figure 6-2

7

The Twelve Steps and the Beginning of Recovery

The majority of offender therapists believe that deviant sex is much like alcoholism: it can be controlled but not cured.

Kathleen Fisher
American Psychological Association Monitor, May 1984

Now about sex. Many of us needed an overhauling there.

Alcoholics Anonymous, "The Big Book," 1939

Millions of people have received help through the Twelve Steps of Alcoholics Anonymous, and not all of them have been alcoholics. Groups like Gamblers Anonymous, Overeaters Anonymous, and Emotions Anonymous have demonstrated how the Twelve Steps can be adapted to break through the core beliefs of people with other types of compulsive disorders. Now there are groups for sexual addicts and their families.

They go by different names: Sexaholics Anonymous, Sex and Love Addicts Anonymous, Sexual Addicts Anonymous, and Sexual Abuse Anonymous. They are not unified, at least, not at this time, and they are active all over this country and in Europe. What these groups have in common is that they have extended the Twelve Steps of Alcoholics Anonymous to sexual addicts. A desire to support professionals in working with their clients who are members of these anonymous fellowships was one of the motivations for writing this book. Figure 7-1 lists the original Twelve Steps of Alcoholics Anonymous and figure 7-2 the Twelve Steps as adapted for sexual addiction.

Working the steps entails becoming actively involved in a therapeutic process compatible with professional therapy. However, the twelfth step adds an important dimension that professionals need to recognize: the value of the shared, common experience. The twelfth step says, "Having had a spiritual awakening as a result of these steps, we tried to carry this message to others and to practice these principles in all our affairs." Fellow addicts can get through to the addict in ways that professional helpers cannot, and it has much to do with the addicts' shared core beliefs—not the professional's ability or skills. The central role which the professional can play is the focus of the remaining chapters of this book. But first the professional needs to understand the primary importance of an ongoing Twelve Step program for the recovering sexual addict.

Twelve Step programs have been sharply criticized in some quarters of the professional community. They have been accused of "substituting one dependency for another" and "pushing religion" on their group. The criticism has been made that a professional is not present in these groups to guarantee the quality of therapy and to hold the addict accountable, especially in the case of sexual addiction. Critics of this persuasion suggest that these programs are too loose to supply the type of controls necessary. I believe this criticism says something about our professional anxiety about the issue. Critics usually fail to see that to discount observable recoveries as well as Twelve Step programs is to neglect possibly the most significant resource addicts and their families have in their recovery: their peers.

The Twelve Step programs themselves complicate this situation, partially out of an understandable commitment to the established traditions of the groups. One of these traditions establishes that the program must not affiliate with any organization; another requires that the program acquire new members through attraction, not promotion. These two traditions have served the programs well.

A few members of Twelve Step groups, however, interpret these standards to mean that cooperation with professional helpers such as therapists or pastors, or with hospital-based treatment programs, violates the traditions. Dedicated professionals may have found themselves frustrated in reaching what they see as the common goal—helping the addict. There are a number of ways for professionals and Twelve Step groups to collaborate, as we shall see in chapter 8. First, let's consider a story of how the addictive system responded to Twelve Step intervention in the case of Ruth.

While in treatment for alcoholism, Ruth was told by the hospital staff that her sexuality problem would take care of itself once she had established sobriety. After treatment, Ruth continued her contact with Alcoholics Anonymous and maintained sobriety, but her sexual behavior became even more extreme. She found herself regularly walking in dangerous neighborhoods as a way of being picked up. Only later, after getting into recovery from sexual addiction, did she appreciate that she had two addictions, that in fact she had used drugs and alcohol as a way to control her sexual compulsivity.

Ruth traced her sexual addiction back to when she was a toddler. A neighbor named Larry who lived across the alley befriended her when she was about two and a half. He had no children of his own and was devoted to her. Ruth in turn was grateful because she received from him the affection and attention that was lacking at home. However, Ruth paid a price. Larry sexually abused her from that early age until he died when she was seven. As a result of the sexual abuse, she suffered from vaginal swelling, bleeding, bladder infections, and nightmares. Somehow her family never connected her

The Twelve Steps of Alcoholics Anonymous

1. We admitted we were powerless over alcohol — that our lives had become unmanageable.
2. Came to believe that a Power greater than ourselves could restore us to sanity.
3. Made a decision to turn our will and our lives over to the care of God, *as we understood Him.*
4. Made a searching and fearless moral inventory of ourselves.
5. Admitted to God, to ourselves, and to another human being the exact nature of our wrongs.
6. Were entirely ready to have God remove all these defects of character.
7. Humbly asked Him to remove our shortcomings.
8. Made a list of all persons we had harmed, and became willing to make amends to them all.
9. Made direct amends to such people whenever possible, except when to do so would injure them or others.
10. Continued to take personal inventory and when we were wrong, promptly admitted it.
11. Sought through prayer and meditation to improve our conscious contact with God, *as we understood Him,* praying only for knowledge of His will for us and the power to carry that out.
12. Having had a spiritual awakening as the result of these steps, we tried to carry this message to alcoholics, and to practice these principles in all our affairs.

Figure 7-1

The Twelve Steps of Alcoholics Anonymous
Adapted for Sexual Addicts

1. We admitted we were powerless over our sexual addiction — that our lives had become unmanageable.
2. Came to believe that a Power greater than ourselves could restore us to sanity.
3. Made a decision to turn our will and our lives over to the care of God as we understood Him.
4. Made a searching and fearless moral inventory of ourselves.
5. Admitted to God, to ourselves, and to another human being the exact nature of our wrongs.
6. Were entirely ready to have God remove all these defects of character.
7. Humbly asked Him to remove our shortcomings.
8. Made a list of all persons we had harmed, and became willing to make amends to them all.
9. Made direct amends to such people wherever possible, except when to do so would injure them or others.
10. Continued to take personal inventory and when we were wrong promptly admitted it.
11. Sought through prayer and meditation to improve our conscious contact with God as we understood Him, praying only for knowledge of His will for us and the power to carry that out.
12. Having had a spiritual awakening as the result of these steps, we tried to carry this message to others and to practice these principles in all our affairs.

Figure 7-2

physical problems with Larry, and he had sworn Ruth to secrecy.

As she got older, Ruth only remembered Larry as a "father-like" figure. Not until after three months of sobriety did she start to remember the childhood rapes. Her memories were like a "camera out of focus." Sitting in a restaurant one night, she started writing about one of the experiences:

> A brown drape separates his bedroom from the dining room I enter. It's late autumn before snow and late afternoon. Dusk. I should be home for supper.
>
> He knows. He knows. I have to be home or they'll come looking. He knows. This time again there was blood. I've bled and he's gone to the dim bathroom to wash out the stains from our clothes. He is sorry and worried he can't help that it hurts me. He feels bad enough so I please won't cry. From here I can see him scrubbing furiously.
>
> He hasn't turned on the lights yet and the house is getting darker. Near me the console radio dial glows. The radio is talking grownup so I don't understand . . . jokes, weather, or bad news, I guess. I can listen to music anytime. I'm not to touch the dial.
>
> He had the gray flannel shirt on today. His pockets have smooth flaps. I like this shirt because when he sits me on his lap like he does there are no pocket buttons to hurt my face. I don't like pocket buttons sometimes.
>
> He is upset. With me? With us? I can't tell; it's all in a piece. He moves back and forth a few steps at a time in front of me . . . pacing, I think. I don't know.
>
> He takes away the padding he's made me wear—some bulky white thing I've had to wear like a diaper. My bleeding's stopped. He thanks God the bleeding has stopped.
>
> They're going to want me at home. He knows. He knows. And I want a cookie. But I mustn't ask like that. It's not polite. Besides they don't want him giving me anything so close to supper.

> He has wrung out my panties. I put them back on. If they ask, he says, tell them you wet. Nothing more. He insists. His eyebrows make a V, like seagull wings. But I'm all wet and it still stings so bad. He is waiting for my promise. His eyes stay on me. I understand. Nothing. I promise.
>
> His face gets smooth again and he picks me up, hugging me hard. I am his good little girl. I will be all right. They won't do anything to me. Everything will be fine. Don't be afraid, Baby. But he is afraid or maybe it is me. I can't tell anymore. It's all in a piece.
>
> He waves me away and good bye. I am late. Yardlights shine on the alley. I imagine crossing a scary, dark river. I chill myself with this pretend. They are eating. No place for me. Since I am not home on time, then I am not hungry, they guessed. Their worried looks like mad to me. I am to go to my room. I am to feel lucky I am not spanked. I cannot sit down anyway, especially sit still. But my stomach does not understand.
>
> The tear burns. It is hard to pee without crying. But if I cry Mama will hear. She would see the redness and be angry. She would demand to know what I did to get myself torn. It is not safe to cry. Not now. Maybe later.

In response to his own father's alcoholism, Ruth's father was a teetotaler. He was an autocratic, repressive man who enforced his will with physical abuse. In addition to the rigidity, the family was very enmeshed, allowing for little individuality. As in all rigid enmeshed families, asking for help, especially from outsiders, is strictly discouraged. For example, when Ruth's mother miscarried at home in her seventh month, she delivered the baby herself and then buried the fetus in the yard.

Ruth couldn't depend on her family or anyone else. She was raped by a group of boys at the age of ten and molested again when she was eleven by her girlfriend's father. She had already internalized the family rule: do not tell and do not ask for help.

Although she didn't trust others, as Ruth matured, sex became a source of comfort to her; to be exciting, however, it had to be without intimacy. She couldn't respond unless sex was violent or dangerous.

Consequently, when she married in her early twenties, being responsive to her husband was extremely difficult. She had already been involved with twenty men and knew that she was in trouble. Using fidelity in marriage as a control on her sexuality left her only one apparent, available option for coping with her pain: drugs and alcohol.

Ruth's marriage broke up under the stress of her chemical dependency when she was twenty-seven, and by the time she was thirty-five, she had been involved with more than three hundred men. She had a magic number: she tried to have eight relationships going at a time—never more nor less. With her work as an occupational therapist, her efforts to be a single parent to her son, and the conveyor belt of men in her life, her life became quite unmanageable.

Most of her sexual partners she met at singles bars and parties. Ruth found herself targeting her partners by walking into a room and deciding, "I am going home with him." After her chemical dependency treatment at the age of thirty-one, her behavior shifted to cruising in dangerous neighborhoods. She also started to pick up men at AA meetings. Her eye for partners who would be vulnerable to her became more acute. Her sexual activities also increased in their level of violence.

Sometimes Ruth used masturbation as a method of controlling her cruising. Then she developed serious infections from masturbating with objects to the point of injury. But she continued to masturbate anyway, consoling herself that it was safer than being in the streets. Another alternative was to play mistress, especially with older married men. As her addiction escalated, Ruth became more of an exhibitionist, both in terms of dress and emotions. She discovered the provocative quality of indiscreet revelations about herself as she discussed intimate sexual issues with strangers.

At one moment Ruth was the prowling predator; the next she was pursued by her own despair. The despair component of her addictive cycle was vicious, particularly on weekends when her son was gone and she had unstructured days. Before treatment, drugs helped her to cope, allowing her to spend the days in oblivion until her son returned. Drugs had been a way to keep the men out of her life. Without them she stepped once more on the conveyor belt that made men a faceless blur. Many times the choice between a weekend of oblivion and the sexual conveyor belt brought her to the point of suicide. When she got sober and free of drugs, her depression virtually immobilized her. Diagnosed as manic-depressive, Ruth was given Lithium as a way to survive her despair.

Not knowing what to do, Ruth asked Roy, an AA friend she respected, to talk with her about her life. One night in a meeting he had talked about how sexual compulsivity was like another addiction for him. During a long walk around a city park, Ruth shared much of her painful story. Roy told her about a group that used the Twelve Steps like AA only for sexual addicts. He was a member of this group himself and shared how his professional life as an attorney had almost ended because of his sexual addiction. Roy also knew about a group that was exclusively for women that met on Saturday mornings.

Ruth met two women from this group, and they spent two hours talking about their experiences. One, a social worker, talked about losing her job because her addiction had taken her to the point of being sexual with her adolescent clients. The other woman had become so powerless over her addiction that she approached men at work, stimulated them physically, and then found a place to have sex with them in her office building.

When Ruth finally attended a meeting, a lesbian woman talked about how her life had been careening out of control. At first Ruth worried about whether she could relate, but then the woman speaking said that, like Ruth, when she was treated for alcoholism, her counselor had assured her that her behavior would change once she was sober. Tears welled up in Ruth's eyes. She was home.

Ruth's journey has been described at length to serve as background for detailing how the Twelve Steps can help sexual addicts break their denial and gain hope that they can change. The remainder of this chapter focuses on each element of the addictive system, and how it relates to the Twelve Step process of recovery. The story of Ruth's recovery will provide context for theoretical discussion. But before proceeding to the addictive system, we need first to provide some brief background on the Twelve Steps.

An Amazing Intervention: The First Twelfth Step Call

When Dr. Bob and Bill W. walked into Akron's City Hospital in June of 1935 to call on Bill D., they made the first twelfth step call in the history of Alcoholics Anonymous. Like the two women who called on Ruth, Dr. Bob and Bill W. were carrying the message of hope for recovery as indicated in the twelfth step of their new program. The two message bearers were not doing this just to help Bill D.; they were convinced that they needed to reach out to fellow sufferers in order to recover themselves. So Bill D. first had to deal with the fact that these two men were not doctors on whom he would have to depend. These men depended on him; the notion that he was needed meant a great deal. Bill D. was to write later:

> Then she [his wife] told me that these two drunks she had been talking to had a plan whereby they thought they could quit drinking, and part of that plan was that

> they tell it to another drunk. This was going to help them to stay sober. All the other people that had talked to me wanted to help *me*, and my pride prevented me from listening to them, and caused only resentment on my part, but I felt as if I would be a real stinker if I did not listen to a couple of fellows for a short time, if that would cure *them*. She also told me that I could not pay them even if I wanted to and had the money, which I did not.[1]

The co-founders of AA had struck on one critical issue from those battling addiction: dependence on others. Almost any form of help will run into that critical core belief. Dr. Bob and Bill W. in effect had created a paradoxical intervention: they could enter the world of the addict in a way that others could not.

They also were able to bypass other core beliefs through sharing their own stories. They could accept Bill D. and see him as a valuable person because they had done the same things. They could care for him even though they knew the truth about him. Bill D. writes further about this experience:

> Before very long we began to relate some incidents of our drinking, and, naturally, pretty soon, I realized both of them knew what they were talking about because you can see things and smell things when you're drunk, that you can't other times and, if I had thought they didn't know what they were talking about, I wouldn't have been willing to talk to them at all. (*Alcoholics Anonymous*, p. 185)

For the first time in years Bill D. experienced the possibility of having an honest and intimate relationship with another person.

The Twelve Step Challenge to the Core Beliefs

The Twelve Steps challenge the addict's belief system and help to restructure the core belief that he or she is a bad and worthless person. Ruth's challenge began when she and Roy walked in the park. She found it both exhilarating and scary to know someone else who had struggled with the same issues but who was recovering. The exhilaration stemmed from not having to be alone and from discovering hope. The scary part came from her shameful feelings of inadequacy and her fear that she might fail at this too.

But as research has shown, the capacity to image a future reality has an enormous power to bring it into reality. That is why models are so important. For Ruth to meet people who had been in the same shape she was or worse, and to see them with years of recovery behind them, gave her real courage. And to learn that her success as a newcomer was vital to them in their continued progress felt very affirming.

The most powerful part of the experience for Ruth was listening to other members' stories. She learned about how the program worked as others talked of their struggles. In the language of Twelve Step fellowships, telling your story is a significant part of recovery. It helps to be accepted even though people know your secrets. Also, recovery is facilitated by learning from the experience of others, as well as by the common supportive bond between addicts who struggle together with a common illness in a nonsupportive world.

The stories told by members are healing metaphors of great power. Professionals appreciate the importance of metaphors, tales, and personal stories in treatment. Anecdotal therapy, as it is sometimes called, has the power to penetrate resistant self-destructive systems as few other therapeutic resources do. Through the works of leaders like Bandler and Grinder, Haley, and the expositors of Milton Erickson—one of the great therapeutic storytellers—an impressive literature on this topic has evolved.[2] Considering that knowledge, skill, and art go into constructing effective metaphors, the question might be asked: How does the self-help nonprofessional group use metaphors so effectively? In his book *Therapeutic Metaphors*, David Gordon helps us understand when he writes,

"Those components which combine to create an effective therapeutic metaphor are components which very often occur as the natural and unconscious result of storytelling."[3]

A further question to be asked is how do stories work when sex addicts are involved in such diverse types of activities? True, they share the same addiction, but how does a woman like Ruth whose addiction involved men relate to a lesbian whose behavior involved women? Gordon again has a suggestive comment:

> The most important requirement for an effective metaphor is that it meet the client at his model of the world. That does not mean that the content of the metaphor is necessarily the same as that of the client's situation. "Meeting the client at his model of the world" means that the metaphor preserves the structure of the client's problematic situation. That is, the significant factors in the metaphor are the client's interpersonal relationships and patterns of coping within the context of the "problem." The context itself is not important. (Gordon, p. 24)

Stories can be about diverse problems yet reveal a common struggle.

Addicts arrive at the doorstep of a Twelve Step program convinced they are unique in their badness, telling themselves, "No one has been as bad or as out of control as I have. No one would accept me or care for me." Being accepted in the fellowship, they learn through the stories that they have an illness which in fact is common. What has been shrouded in agonizing secrecy for years becomes openly talked about. In working the first step, addicts admit that they, too—like all these other people—have become powerless over their illness. With the fourth step, in which they do a thorough moral inventory of their own lives, the good with the bad, and the fifth step, in which that inventory is shared with another person, they can join the human community again. Ernest Kurtz, one of the most astute observers of the Twelve Step experience for alcoholics, describes the program as "uniquely a therapy for shame . . . the dynamic underlying its fifth step and its practice of story-telling . . . drive home to the alcoholic his unexceptional ordinariness."[4] The same is true for the sexual addict.

With the secrecy and shame of the core beliefs alleviated by the program, the ability to incorporate new core beliefs is born. Other interventions in the addictive system contribute to the preparation of the new beliefs. Few have more significance than how the program helps addicts with their impaired thinking.

Reclaiming Reality through the Twelve Step Program

A major focus of all Twelve Step programs is restoring the addict "to sanity." Translated, this phrase means that the program helps the addict sift through all the distortions, denial, rationalizations, and other defenses to reclaim reality. Ruth, for example, set herself apart from the other women in a meeting, suggesting that she was more a weekend addict than a daily one. Her comment was greeted by knowing and gentle smiles which Ruth found irritating. Later her sponsor, a member of the group Ruth chose to teach her about the program and provide support, explained that Ruth's weekend notion did not fit the facts of her story, and the group had noticed the discrepancy.

Further, the sponsor continued, it is common, especially for a new member, to claim some specialness which separates her from everyone else in the program. The knowing smiles Ruth received meant that each person remembered her own moments of addictive grandiosity. Ruth started to feel ashamed, but her sponsor pointed out that Ruth's comment was a gift. Whenever a member struggles, the other members benefit; they are reminded of their common vulnerability.

As in Ruth's case, the group intervenes in the addict's impaired thinking on two levels: feedback and meaning.

From the thinking systemic perspective, the homeostatic balance of the addictive system is disrupted by the Twelve Step fellowship. First, the addict experiences the paradox of being cared for even when people know all there is to know. So the addict's most fundamental expectation no longer fits. With that primitive logic disrupted, the impaired thinking coming out of the faulty beliefs then becomes vulnerable to feedback. Discrepancies and distortions are shattered as group members hold a mirror to the addict's behavior.

For the addict who has kept his addictive side secret for so long, such exposure would be devastating were it not for the care of others in the program. Also, recovering people quickly realize that their honesty paradoxically helps others as well as themselves. Kurtz writes about this paradox as it works for alcoholics:

> A.A. members learn deeply, then, the mutuality between honesty with self and honesty with others: the necessity of avoiding self-deception if they are to be honest with others, and at the same time the necessity of honesty with others if they are to avoid self-deception. Living this paradoxical insight, indeed, is one of the most profound yet also most clear messages of A.A. as both fellowship and program. (Kurtz, p. 61)

The same process prevails for sexual addicts in Twelve Step fellowships. Being accountable and holding each other accountable transforms the life of isolated secrecy and shame into one of meaningful common commitment. A special bond is created when a group shares a common painful struggle. Deep loyalties are forged. The argument that a professional needs to be present to ensure accountability pales before the reality of what goes on in these groups. That is not to say that all groups are equally successful in presenting reality to the addict, nor that professionals are unimportant. The point is that the presence of a professional would be counterproductive to the group's most fundamental processes.

Some professionals are concerned that members of Twelve Step programs may simply switch one dependency for another, their assumption being that dependency is bad and independence good. A further assumption is that dependence on a group for a sense of reality is bad. For addicts who struggle with dependency issues the group provides a mirror for monitoring self-recovery, and a new family which can be depended on for its insight. This new family is a more open system than the addicts' real families, and addicts can experience relationships they can rely on to promote openness and recovery.

Also, support from others helps a person to develop a capacity to affirm from within, that is, *to be independent*. Dependency and independence are thus indispensable to each other. Kurtz writes of their "mutuality":

> To speak of a mutuality between human dependence and human independence, then, is to point out not only that both are necessary within human experience, but also that each becomes fully human and thus humanizing only by connection with the other . . . the mutuality between dependence and independence furnishes another example of the paradox of the necessity of both, the impossibility of either, that inheres in the human condition as essentially limited. . . . (Kurtz, p. 62)

Part of the professional concern about dependency stems from the addiction model's insistence that the illness can be arrested but not cured. Critics challenge the notion that once an addict, always an addict. They especially take issue with the corollary that the Twelve Step program is something the addict attends for life because they are never "cured."

The addictive system is incredibly powerful. Specialists in the treatment of sex offenders recognize that two to three years of therapy are not enough. In a review of sex offender treatment programs in the *American Psychological Association Monitor,* J. Clayton Stewart points out that most experts in the field agree that the behavior "may be as unshakable as alcoholism."[5] Thus, both research and clinical experience suggest that, for all practical purposes, the illness should be considered a lifetime affliction and be treated as such.

In terms of impaired thinking, the delusional power of the addictive system can cast its shadow with uncanny ease, even upon someone with several years of "sobriety"—no compulsive sexual behavior—and healthy, affirming sexuality. But then the impelling force of the twelfth step—carrying the message to others—brings experienced members of the program in contact with people who are in extreme stages of addiction. This contact reminds addicts how it was for them. With each new member the addict renews a commitment to recovery, and each new member benefits from meeting people whose lives have changed through the program. Hope exists; the old and the new give life to each other's recovery. That was the learning that Dr. Bob and Bill W. passed on in Bill D.'s hospital room so many years ago.

In place of the unrealistic impaired thinking, the Twelve Step group member possesses a new reality: caring relationships which will not disappear even in the most honest exchanges. The experience can be exhilarating.

Grief as Part of Recovery

The support of the group is always vital, but perhaps it is most critical when addicts in recovery go through a profound grief process, as all of them do. For the sexual addict, sex has been the primary relationship—the main source of nurturing in life. The end of that relationship is like a death. The addict who stops the addictive cycle, which gave meaning and direction to life, suffers a very real loss. For example, the following signs of grief may be noticed as patients start their recovery:

—confusion about how to act and what to do

—feelings of alienation

—fantasies about how things could have been different

—sadness over unfulfilled expectations and a wasted life

—desire for a quick fix

—feelings of exposure and vulnerability

—failure to take care of self

—uncontrollable emotions

—dark thoughts about death, including suicide

—sudden accident-prone behavior

—fear that the pain will not go away

Severe grief reactions are caused by many types of losses or major changes such as death of a spouse or child, divorce, loss of job, or change of residence. In all of these situations the signs of grief and patterns are predictable. This same process occurs for the addict in recovery.

The Twelve Step program helps addicts through their grieving process; it disrupts preoccupation and obsession with sex and supports grieving over the loss of the pathological relationship. To make the connections explicit, let's explore each stage of the grief process as it affects the addict, focusing on the help Twelve Step programs offer.

With all losses, bereaved people initially deny the reality and isolate themselves. They resent people who urge them to accept their loss, who would rob them of their denial. Living in denial and isolation, addicts in particular deny the impact addiction has on their lives. Concerned friends, relatives, and professional helpers who make an effort to confront that denial often find extremely defensive behavior.

The *first step* of the Twelve Steps helps with the denial and isolation in several ways. Addicts admit that they are powerless over the addiction and that their lives have become unmanageable. Usually they do a methodical inventory of all the ways the addiction proved more powerful, including all those events they would have done anything to avoid but were powerless to stop. Throughout the inventory, addicts note how life had become unmanageable and intolerable with the addiction. The process helps them own their loss. They admit (powerlessness) and surrender (unmanageability) to the illness and acknowledge their need for help.

Once they have acknowledged a loss, most grieving persons become very angry. When a loved one has died, they feel angry with God, angry with the deceased, and angry with themselves for not having done more. Sometimes the anger is punctuated with moments when the bereaved bargains with God ("If only you change it, Lord, I will . . . ") or continues to deny ("Maybe a terrible mistake has been made . . . "). Usually they experience alarm, or panic which reflects the terror of facing life without the loved one.

Addicts, too, become angry. They feel angry at God for letting this happen, anger at the addiction, anger for loss of the addiction, and anger at themselves for not having done something sooner. Bargaining and denial ("Maybe I am only a partial addict . . . " or, in Ruth's case, "I'm more a weekend addict") give relief to the pain. By taking the *second and third steps*, addicts make a significant act of trust, acknowledging a higher power who can help them regain sanity. They then can turn their lives over to their Higher Power. This leap of trust requires acceptance of the fundamental dependency of the human condition. The addict can then make meaning out of the experience. Like Viktor Frankl's experience in the concentration camp, suffering has meaning in a spiritual context.

Those who suffer losses, and pass through the stages of denial and anger, come to accept themselves through letting go of the loved one. For addicts, however, letting go does not repair all the damage the addiction has done to the self-concept. The enormity of the addictive patterns and the self-degradation overwhelm the addict. Steps four and five help the addict bypass shame and gain self-acceptance. *Step four* asks addicts to make a thorough inventory of personal strengths and weaknesses, including all the ways they have not lived up to personal values. This careful look at themselves may cause sadness and remorse.

Step five invites the addicts to share their inventory with another person. In sexual addiction programs, this is usually a chaplain or pastor, although it may be another member of the fellowship. The experience of relating all that history to someone else exposes the recovering person at an extreme level of vulnerability. Being so exposed, and yet being affirmed and accepted, creates healing of the highest order. The spiritual skills of the clergy may play a key role in self-forgiveness and self-acceptance. In effect, the addicts can feel restored to the human community. Often great joy and relief occur after the fifth step has been taken.

As in all grief, the struggle does not subside with self-acceptance. Bereaved persons have moments during which they intensely search for the lost relationship. Addicts experience pangs of loss when their sadness and their desire for the old way returns. This is a time for "slips," loss of courage, euphoric recall, and testing limits. Once again the program provides a framework to help with this hanging on of grief. *Steps six and seven* ask addicts to be ready to let go of the defects of character which could bring back the active addictive life. Again, part of letting go requires a trust in a Higher Power and trust in the existence of a healing process.

With steps six and seven, the program participants identify their addictive "friends"—those beliefs, defenses, attitudes, behaviors, and other issues that supported the addiction when it flourished. For example, the addict may see how self-pity serves as a gateway back into the addiction. Since self-pity was very much part of the addiction, self-pity in recovery simply adds to the grief reactions. Now addicts must learn to stop giving in to these so-called old "friends of the addict."

As the grieving process evolves, a new sense of identity emerges. With restored confidence, the bereaved seek reconciliation with people they had pushed away. For addicts, the renewal of identity takes concrete form in terms of celebrating their progress. Marking anniversaries (e.g., three months, six months, one year, ten years) becomes extremely important.

Building on this renewed sense of self, the addicts' shame no longer prevents reconciliation with friends and family. With *steps eight and nine*, the addicts list those people who have been harmed and make amends, hopefully to heal the breach in the relationship. Making these direct efforts brings comfort through further restoration of self and, in some cases, forgiveness.

All who suffer great losses reach a point where they must establish their renewed identity and recognize that life goes on. It is not true, however, that when grief subsides, pain goes away entirely. In effect, although the sadness never leaves, it is transformed becoming incorporated into our beings as part of that suffering that brings wisdom and depth of feeling to all of us. One simply learns to adjust life in order to carry the suffering.

Step ten encourages a daily effort to take stock of one's life using the principles of the first nine steps. *Step eleven* suggests that spiritual progress results from a daily effort to improve conscious contact with a Higher Power. *Step twelve* asks addicts to tell other addicts about the power of the program. They pass on what they have received.

These last three steps help the addicts integrate the program principles into daily life, and the program thus becomes an intervening system which disrupts the addictive system and provides ongoing support for the lifelong process of surviving the loss. In effect, the addict joins a community based on healing principles validated over time. The Twelve Steps consolidate these common principles into a discipline for living daily with suffering and loss. Although their simplicity misleads the unknowing, these steps require great courage and can result in profound human experiences.

Table 7-3 summarizes the impact of the Twelve Steps on the loss of the addictive relationship.

Sex addicts are particularly vulnerable to using preoccupation with addictive behavior as a way to cope with the sorrow of loss and the sadness of life. Also, unlike alcoholics or compulsive gamblers, sex addicts cannot avoid their sexuality, so the compelling forces which were a part of the addiction will always be an integral part of their lives. Consequently, the tendency toward grief remains immediate, and the Twelve Step program becomes even more vital as a path to return to sanity.

Co-addicts use the Twelve Steps as well. They have experienced the loss of a loved one to the addiction. They, too, have a need to cut through their denial, replace anger with trust, alleviate their shame, and renew their sense of identity. The processes are the same since the addictive and co-addictive systems parallel each other so closely.

This "simple" program reaches far and touches many. Emotions Anonymous fellowships abound. Chaplains use the program in oncology and hospice programs for the terminally ill and their families. Divorce meditation professionals have discovered the program's healing power. Based on the commonality of human experience, the Twelve Steps can be for everyone.

The Healing Power of Rituals

When Ruth had been in her Twelve Step group for about six weeks, she had a particularly rough week both at work and at home, but by the time she reported the experience in her group, she was doing much better. Group members asked her why she had not called when she was in trouble. When she stumbled for an answer, they gently suggested she needed to make "rehearsal phone calls." They explained how easy it is for an addict to report a crisis after the crisis is over.

The Loss of the Addictive Relationship

Typical Grief Reactions to Loss of Loved One	Typical Grief Reactions of Addict to Loss of Addictive Relationship	Steps	Therapeutic Tasks
Denial and isolation. Blame for those who press for acceptance.	Denial and isolation. Defensive around behavior.	1	Admission (powerlessness) and surrender (unmanageability)—acknowledge need for program.
Anger. Bargaining. Alarm reactions.	Anger and rage about loss of addiction. Slips into denial about being addict to prevent loss. Efforts to bargain — the "partial" addict. Terror at life without addiction — "Will I die"?	2,3	Trust, mistrust issues worked through, including accepting Higher Power.
Acceptance of self.	Struggle to get past enormity of addictive patterns and self-degradation.	4,5	Bypass shame; self-acceptance.
Search for the lost relationships. Pangs of loss.	Time for slips, loss of courage, euphoric recall, testing limits.	6,7	Identify the "friends of the addict."
Emerging new identity. Reconciliation.	Pride in progress; anniversaries and straight time important.	8,9	Comfort with new sense of self. Reconciliation with old/new friends. Restoration and forgiveness.
Establish and maintain continuity.	Integration into lifestyle and behavior.	10,11 12	Establish network for new identity.

Figure 7-3

Asking for help at the moment of crisis, however, is difficult for addicts who normally handle things by themselves and use their addiction to get them through. To make a phone call feels inconvenient or perhaps like an imposition on others. The resistance lies in the addict's unwillingness to rely (to be dependent) on others. So the group's prescription for Ruth was to make a commitment to make rehearsal phone calls. In other words, Ruth could call and say, "There is no crisis. This is just for practice."

The group was doing more than teaching about the use of the phone to maintain contact with other members between group meetings. As part of the oral tradition of the group, they were passing on a problem-solving ritual and having fun with it at the same time. At many levels, the old rituals of the addictive system are replaced, as the Twelve Step program supplies new rituals through group membership, sponsorship, meetings, readings, and slogans. Sponsors formally pass on group traditions. Extensive reading and daily reflection are encouraged. The result is a mosaic of rituals which teach, solve problems, and provide coping strategies.

Some professionals have been put off by what they misperceive as a loose federation working for self-help using seemingly glib aphorisms and slogans to solve complex problems. They further believe that self-help groups certainly do not provide the level of accountability necessary to deal with difficult-to-treat groups like exhibitionists and rapists. Finally, they believe that talk-oriented therapies do not provide the essential skills training, such as relapse prevention skills, that recovering people need.

These criticisms call forth several responses. First, most Twelve Step groups are democratic yet highly structured communities. To play on the title of Bandler and Grinder's therapeutic classic *The Structure of Magic*, the magic of structure also exists. Consider the structured process of a Twelve Step program as a proven recipe which can answer the needs of a particular group—whether made up of alcoholics, sex addicts, or overeaters, for example. Like any recipe, if followed carefully the results are predictable. In that sense, the Twelve Step communities are part of a genre of leaderless group formulas which are highly structured. To dismiss Twelve Step communities because of their lack of structure not only reflects inaccurate information but dismisses an important resource for the client.

Second, in the past decade evidence has accumulated about the healing power of rituals. Michael Harner, for example, stirred up considerable interest in healing rituals with his book *The Way of the Shaman.*[6] He documents the healing power of rituals in primitive communities and details the common processes in training that tribal witch doctors experience, whether in the Australian outback, Northern Siberia, or South America. Simply stated, his point is that modern Western medicine has abandoned forms of healing at a psychobiological level that are extremely potent. At the top of Harner's list are rituals.

Dutch psychotherapist Onno van der Hart's book *Rituals in Psychotherapy: Transition and Continuity* is a veritable catalog of models from anthropological as well as clinical settings for healing rituals. He describes, for example, how rituals are significant in dysfunctional systems such as disengaged or enmeshed systems. He pinpoints rituals as significant in overcoming grief and transition and as important problem-solving strategies. He suggests that rituals can alter affective and cognitive structures in ways that no amount of information or teaching can. In fact, he writes:

> . . . many aspects of the problem to be solved do not have to be considered at all in the treatment. They are indirectly influenced. Therapeutic rituals also have the advantage that they—because of their condensed symbols—are active at the same time in many ways. . . . Psychotherapists in our society do not work . . . ecologically. . . . Still, they are confronted with problems that they cannot solve with their usual strategies. No matter how

> difficult and labor intensive this may be, they will just have to work more ecologically—possibly via complex rituals—and integrally approach the ecosystems involved.[7]

A Twelve Step program with its multi-layered rituals is one ecosystem that the therapist can support as part of the treatment plan. Ritualization is already an integral part of the addictive system so replacement of ritual is a vital treatment goal. Ruth's rehearsal phone calls helped make her part of the healing process of the group. Making the calls also gave her the opportunity to lean on others and risk vulnerability, thus helping her to approach some of her most basic doubts and fears.

Coping with Anxiety: Behavior and Existential Reality

In the case of chemical addictions such as alcoholism, recovering persons recognize the strength of the pathological system and the recursive nature of systems in general, and they make a commitment to "sobriety." Some years ago a considerable amount of excitement was generated by research on so-called controlled drinking. Those research efforts were seriously challenged and are now in some disrepute, but the controversy continues. The fact remains: alcoholics simply fare better if they stop completely. The illnesses are too strong, the impaired thinking too deep, and the risks much too high to even take the first drink—which AA has maintained for more than fifty years.

On the other hand, people must eat to survive and they carry their sexuality within them wherever they go, making recovery a different issue for them. Clients with concurrent addictions like sex and chemicals frequently tell therapists that overcoming sex addiction is more difficult. Determining a "sobriety" is harder. Also, the source of supply is within and one only has to dip into preoccupation to access it.

When sex addicts join a Twelve Step group, they are asked to define the specific behaviors over which they are powerless. However, at first many obstacles may stand in their way. Some addicts enter a de-escalation phase in which they see all sex as the enemy, and the Twelve Step group and the church as allies in a war against their urges. Such warfare simply intensifies the struggle the addict has had for years, with no fundamental change in the addictive system. The task of the group then becomes to help new members affirm the essential goodness of their sexuality and to accept as fundamental their illness which renders them powerless.

Other addicts come with only tentative commitments. Their addiction is so strong and their trust so low they do not see joining the group as a viable alternative. Some have not suffered severe enough consequences, or their delusion prevents them from seeing the prices being paid. In these cases, their impaired thinking results in denial and bargaining. So the exhibitionist who admits to the problem of exposing may balk at including affairs or massage parlors. In fact, he may reason that the only successful way to stay off the street is prostitution. The group's experience and feedback serve to help these addicts regain reality.

The first requirement for the recovering sex addict must be a realistic picture of the sexual behaviors that have damaged him- or herself and others. The inventory of the first step develops that picture. At first, stopping these behaviors constitutes the sexual addict's definition of sobriety. A deepened understanding of sobriety develops as addicts mature in the program. Steps four and five with the moral inventory and steps eight and nine with amends-making expand the addict's awareness of the extent of addictive behavior and its harm. Every group member can add to or modify the list of what is unacceptable behavior to him or her. Then the member tells the group about the list and tries to keep the commitment. If the group member cannot stay sexually sober, he or she is asked to seek help from the group.

At first some Twelve Step groups took a position that the only acceptable form of sexual behavior in "sobriety" is sex within marriage. For some, that standard worked well. That stance, however, which excluded large numbers of the addicted population such as gay and lesbian persons, has been revised considerably to reflect the plurality of lifestyles in our culture. A group's process for determining sobriety needs to be taken into consideration when a therapist recommends a Twelve Step group.

Along with sexual sobriety is the group's support of enriching, healthy sexuality. Most addicts have had little sexual experience that was rewarding or life-enhancing. In fact, many addicts talk about "normal" sex as being boring or uninteresting. Sex without risk, degradation, exploitation, or ritualization pales by comparison. In order to retain sexuality that is honest—not secret or abusive—requires a total refocus on the part of the addict. Fantasy life must undergo drastic change. Here is an example of an area in which professional support can dramatically improve chances of recovery, as we shall see in the remaining chapters.

Co-addicts, too, benefit from the Twelve Steps. Like the addicts, they must determine the set of behaviors which imprisoned them in the addictive system. As they continue to work the steps, their awareness also expands about how the self-destructive behaviors permeated their whole life. Also, they must explore what they are going to replace their co-addictive relationship with—which may mean a refocus of their sexuality as well. Co-addicts used their obsessive relationship with the addict to cope with anxiety. The program's recipe works for them as well.

In many ways, the Twelve Steps become more than an individual process. They form a curriculum for recovery which takes the addict's or co-addict's own experience within the context of group experience and teaches basic strategies to return one's life to normal. As part of the instruction, the addict can draw on the oral tradition of the group, which contains years of experience with successful strategies for behavioral change. The people who have been successful serve as live models and coaches.

Behind the process and the curriculum is a philosophy and a psychology. Alcoholics Anonymous evolved under the influence of William James, Carl Jung, and Dr. William Duncan Silkworth and the Oxford Group, as well as others. Because of its existential orientation and its broad social influence, some scholars like Ernest Kurtz regard the Twelve Step philosophy as "a movement of unique intellectual significance." That history and philosophy has been well described in other places.[8] For our purposes, we need to recognize how the Twelve Steps provide a basic philosophy of life which helps with personal anxiety.

Spirituality and the Twelve Steps

Some professionals may reject the Twelve Step approach because they look upon it as a religious program. Twelve Step programs, however, do not promote religion *per se*, although they do ask participants to define on their own terms a spiritual discipline that reflects their own values. As we said earlier, addicts need a discipline that makes meaning out of their recovery. In that sense, these programs simply reflect a growing consensus among mental health professionals about uses of spirituality in countering anxiety.

The best statement of this position from a mental health point of view is Ernest Becker's Pulitzer Prize winning book, *The Denial of Death*. Becker argues that one difference between human beings and animals lies in the human capacity to imagine all possibilities. But with every talent comes a liability. Our tragic flaw is that we imagine that we are more than we are. We make ourselves into gods. In our exuberance we fail to maintain reality about our limitations. We can imagine living forever, act as if we will, and deny our own deaths. We are literally, in Becker's often quoted phrase,

"Gods who shit." In our minds we can participate in divinity because we can conceptualize infinity; our bodies, however, retain their limits. We will die, although we go to extraordinary lengths to deny that fact.[9]

According to Becker, accepting our fundamental limitations is critical to health. That acceptance leads to some form of faith:

> One goes through it all to arrive at faith, the faith that one's very creatureliness has some meaning to a Creator; that despite one's true insignificance, weakness, death, one's existence has meaning in some ultimate sense because it exists within an eternal and infinite scheme of things brought about and maintained to some kind of design by some creative force. (Becker, p. 90)

Steeped in denial about their ability to control their own destiny, addicts represent in a tragic form our most basic struggle. But here is where the Twelve Step programs help. Kurtz writes about AA:

> The fundamental and first message of Alcoholics Anonymous to its members is that they are not infinite, not absolute, not God. Every alcoholic's problem had first been, according to this insight, claiming God-like powers, especially that of control. But the alcoholic at least, the message insists, is not in control even of himself: and the first step towards recovery from alcoholism must be the admission and acceptance of this fact that is so blatantly obvious to others but so tenaciously denied by the obsessive-compulsive drinker. (Becker, p. 42)

Sex addicts receive the same message. Professionals need to remember that addicts struggle with issues of dependency. In fact, sexual addicts have a special struggle. When perceptive observers comment about our most fundamental distortions of death, they see a connection with delusional sexuality. Earlier in this book we noted French historian Phillipe Aries' observation that with the eighteenth-century shift of our attitudes toward death came our fears of unmanageable sexuality. Becker's writings also point out the link between denial of death and sexual compulsivity and perversion. Sex becomes a way to shield the self from the realities of daily limits. He comments, "No wonder people dedicate themselves so all-consumingly to it, often from childhood on in the form of secret masturbations that represent a protest and a triumph of the personal self." (Becker, p. 45)

With the Twelve Steps, new coping behaviors supported by a spiritual discipline replace sexual behavior as a mechanism for managing anxiety. This spiritual discipline includes faith in a Higher Power—whether it be God, goodness, the support of a group, or other. Thus, the addicts have a source greater than themselves to draw upon at all times. The essence of the program's philosophy appears in the famous Serenity Prayer: "God grant me the serenity to accept the things I cannot change, the courage to change the things I can, and the wisdom to know the difference."

Healthy Shame and Guilt: Path out of Despair

The Twelve Step program makes an additional contribution to recovery: it restores healthy shame and guilt with the support of a caring fellowship. Despair, the downside of dramatic mood shifts which characterize addictive systems, stems from an unhealthy shame-and-guilt cycle that immobilizes the addict in hopelessness. To understand how healthy shame and guilt can return, we need to look at how they relate to other elements of the addictive system.

The development of the core beliefs as a shame-based system has been outlined. Addicts feel so bad about themselves that they do not trust that anyone can forgive them. Thus, guilt can never be acted upon. No apology, no forgiveness, and no reconciliation can occur. As a result, the addict becomes progressively even more isolated. In healthy persons, shame serves as a guide to appropriate behavior. We are embarrassed when we act inappropriately. Guilt helps us to know when we have harmed others. We wish to make it up to them when we have done something wrong. Both shame and guilt are fundamental to healthy functioning in human beings; both become distorted by the addictive system.

When an addict's thinking is impaired due to negative core beliefs, the addict acts without considering the reality of the situation, and in that sense, there is true insanity. The addict thinks and acts without guilt (guiltless) and without shame (shameless) in the preoccupation and acting-out stages of the addictive cycle. The addict's total value system becomes compromised. This is why addicts have been described as psychopathic. Most addicts, however, have well-integrated value systems, but abandon them when the addictive cycle begins. Addicts often have the experience of looking back and literally being stunned with disbelief at what they have done.

Usually, immediately after sexually acting out, addicts experience reality and then feel despair. They talk about this moment as one in which they desperately wish to get out of the situation they are in. The only thing that apparently can help them is preoccupation and the generation of another cycle of the addiction, which only intensifies the downward spiral they are already in. That despair becomes more intense as the unmanageability of the addiction escalates. Eventually, there are undeniable consequences—brushes with the authorities, personal danger or injury, confrontations with friends and family, violation of basic personal values—and the addict is confronted with full force by the consequences of his or her compulsive behavior, becoming filled with shame and guilt. Being shameful and guilt-ridden validates further for the addict the primitive logic of the core beliefs.

Consequently, the life of the addict alternates between being shameless and guiltless and being shameful and guilt-ridden. Healthy shame can never guide behavior in the shameless/shameful extremes. Similarly, healthy guilt transforms into guiltless and guilt-ridden extremes. Addicts cannot face themselves or others as a result.

The Twelve Step group breaks through the despair of recycling extremes of shame and guilt. Sharing experiences with others who have lived the Jekyll/Hyde life and have returned to normal creates hope. The steps provide a structure for alleviating excessive guilt and shame. First, the moral connotations are removed by accepting the illness and its power of course, the addict is still accountable for the consequences of his or her behavior. However, no longer is the behavior a matter of choice and will power. Further, each step progressively reinstates the conscience as a viable part of the addict's life right through the making of appropriate amends where possible. Finally, the program restores a positive sense of self to sustain the vitality of healthy shame and guilt.

Second-Order Change: Reframing Unmanageability

Throughout this book a steady theme has emerged about change: Systems are recursive and, as a result often what looks like change is really not, as in the example of a woman who marries the same kind of alcoholic three times. The husbands change but the system does not. The de-escalation phase of the addictive system may look like change but is just an extension of the same tortuous path the addict has already traveled. The rigid disengaged spouse who goes to even more rigid and disengaged extremes succeeds only in intensifying addictive behavior. The more things change, the more they remain the same.

In their book, *Change: Principles of Problem Formation and Problem Resolution,* Paul Watzlawick, John Weakland, and Richard Fisch use a systems approach which describes change in terms of different levels or "orders" of change.[10] First-order change usually involves going to the opposite level of intensity or increasing the intensity: if cold, apply heat. When it comes to systems, however, applying a counteractive measure only makes the problem worse. The solution is part of the problem. When the spouse applies pressure to the addict, for example, the pressure results in more of the same. Such situations then call for second-order change, in which a radical—and quite often paradoxical—solution can disrupt the system.

When life becomes unmanageable due to compulsive sexual behavior, addicts typically attempt to solve their problem by controlling their behavior. But the more they try to control it, the more out of control they become. So they try harder. The more they fail, the worse they feel. The attempts to stop merely escalate the addiction, but do not bring it under control. Life becomes even more unmanageable. With more and more negative consequences, the addict feels even more shameful.

The addict's efforts to control are also a solution which becomes part of the problem. Controlling the addiction is a first-order change solution which brings only more drinking for alcoholics and self-management for sexual addicts. Addicted sex offenders in prison have met with only limited success because they continue the first-order change efforts in prison that perpetuate addiction. Change occurs at the second-order level when the addict stops the efforts to control and admits to being powerless. The Twelve Steps disrupt the efforts to control and reframe unmanageability as part of powerlessness. Only at that point in addictive systems is there significant change.

The same paradoxical principle of powerlessness applies for co-addicts. Imagine a couple who use an electric blanket in winter. Somehow their controls get mixed up. She has his and he has hers. He gets cold, so he turns up the heat; she becomes warm, so turns down hers. He gets even colder, so jams his control to high; she turns off hers. What they need to be comfortable is to regulate their own sides. So it is with addicts and co-addicts. The more the sex addict turns up the heat, the more his or her partner will turn down the other side. Co-addicts, too, are powerless over the addict. They need to take responsibility for themselves and their own behavior. And again that is what the Twelve Steps help family members to do.

Twelve Steps as One Path to Recovery

The emphasis here on the strengths of Twelve Step programs may present an optional treatment method to professionals who have not had experience with the Twelve Step approach. Perhaps the greatest strength of these programs lies in their ecological approach, which intervenes at every level of the addictive system. To summarize, the Twelve Steps:

—challenge the addict's belief system and help to restructure the core beliefs

—help the addict sift through all the distortions, denial, rationalizations, and other defenses to reclaim reality

—support grieving the loss of the "pathological relationship"

—supply new rituals through group membership, sponsorship, meetings, readings, and slogans

—provide new coping behaviors supported by a spiritual discipline to replace sexual behavior as a mechanism for managing anxiety

—restore healthy shame and guilt with the support of a caring fellowship

—disrupt the addict's efforts to control and reframe their unmanageability as part of powerlessness

Twelve Step programs may have their limits, but used in partnership with the professional community, many of those weaknesses can be transformed into strengths.

8
Assessment

The elevator door opened. It was not she. It was the elevator operator. He was wearing street clothes and a hat. He went directly to where Sears stood and embraced him. Sears put his head against the man's shoulder. The stranger's embrace seemed to comprehend that newfound province of loneliness that had frightened Sears. . . . The stranger whose name he hadn't learned, took him downstairs to a small room off the lobby, where he undressed Sears and undressed himself. Sears' next stop, of course, was a psychiatrist.

John Cheever
Oh What a Paradise It Seems

When psychiatrists, psychologists, and sometimes those most closely related are trying to assess the addict's problem, probably the last thing suspected is sexual addiction, for it is hidden from view behind closed doors, in darkened rooms, where the addict leads a second life.

Jacques Devereaux led two lives. Officially, Devereaux (a pseudonym) was a top-notch language specialist for French intelligence, but he was also a Soviet counterspy for over fourteen years, passing critical information to Russian agents. Devereaux's counterespionage only came to light when his sexual unmanageability could no longer be hidden. He confessed to his wife that he had committed a series of sexual assaults, showing her a file of 2,500 index cards cataloging details of the lives of young girls living in their district. A short time later, he was picked up by French police for child molesting. It was then that she found his spy kit under their bed, complete with a powerful short-wave radio.

Like Jacques Devereaux, many addicts admit they have a problem only when their lives have become too unmanageable, and often, this admission is forced upon them. Consider the grandfather who took his grandchildren one by one on camping and fishing trips and in the process was sexual with them. When six out of the ten grandchildren compared notes and discovered they had experienced the same thing, they told their parents.

Or consider the minister's son who worked as a teacher. When one little girl told her parents that her teacher had asked to take a picture of her holding her dress up, they reported him. In his room the arresting officers found over a thousand photographs of students.

Sometimes the unmanageability takes unusual turns. Standing on a street corner, a father and his adolescent daughter had an argument over a birthday present. The angry daughter turned to a passing police officer and reported her incestuous father for his sexual abuse.

A parishioner saw his parish priest in the same massage parlor he was using and called the bishop.

A husband found a shirt that did not belong to him in his closet. The shirt of one of his wife's lovers had gotten mixed in with her clothes on a recent business trip.

In some ways, these are the optimum conditions under which people seek help. Unmanageability is the therapist's ally. Severe consequences—including loss of marriage, disease, unwanted pregnancy, arrest, or court order—provide leverage to help the addict break through the addictive cycle. Many times the unmanageability causes the addict to move into the de-escalation phase of the addiction. Addicts often seek help earnestly at this point. Those who criticize the addiction concept as a way to minimize the seriousness of sexually abusive behavior ignore the fact that facing severe personal losses or legal penalties is one of the things that motivates people to seek help. A similar pattern has been seen in efforts to combat alcoholism and drunk driving; stiffer penalties assist in intervening in the illness.

Assessment is much more difficult when unmanageability is hidden or controlled. For example, when a therapist working with a married couple is told that one or the other is having an active affair, the tendency is to see that as caused by a troubled marriage, rather than the tip of the iceberg of addiction. Similarly, therapists often have to struggle with the effective collaboration of an entire family who want to protect the secret of addiction.

Among the most difficult situations for professional helpers are ones involving dramatic issues that obscure the addiction, including suicide attempts—common in sexual addiction or concurrent addictions like alcoholism, gambling, or family violence.

In assessment and intervention in sexual addiction, the first step is to acknowledge the strength of the addictive system.

The Strength of the Addictive System

Sex addiction derives its strength from five basic aspects. Understanding these can help any professional helper assess the illness:

1. *The addiction in origin is multivariate versus singular.* Earlier chapters explored the complex etiology of the illness. One isolated cause cannot be singled out. Rather, a constellation of factors emerges: catalytic events and environments; childhood experiences of extreme family dynamics; co-addictive systems which feed the compulsive behavior. In some cases, why the addict developed negative core beliefs and turned to sex for relief from anxiety will never be known. Moreover, the literature on medical and psychological decision-making indicates that practitioners often do not follow

an established procedure for making diagnostic decisions. Instead, they may be heavily influenced by specific cases, such as their first case, their most spectacular case, or their most recent case. If a therapist has successfully diagnosed an addict with a certain history and a certain type of family, the risk is that the therapist will use that case as a model and misdiagnose clients whose pathology is as severe but whose developmental process is quite different. A simple example would be an accurate assessment of the disorder in a man, but missing the same pathology in a woman, because outwardly her circumstances seem so different.

2. *The addiction is contingent versus progressive.* A characteristic which makes the addiction elusive is its contingent quality. The fact that it can be controlled, even for years, makes it hard to see any pattern which suggests that the individual has a problem controlling his or her sexuality. Further, the client may fervently believe that a true course has been set and old behaviors left behind. A careful assessment, taking into account factors elaborated at length in earlier chapters—such as the quality of obsession and preoccupation—can pin down evidence of the addiction's presence. Constant self-control is a time-consuming, misery-producing preoccupation. The addiction can simply remain untouched behind a wall of shame.

3. *The addiction is eurytopic rather than stenotopic.* Eurytopic means that a system can survive in many environments. Human beings are eurytopic; we can inhabit the North Pole and the Equator. Our adaptability is our strength. A tropical plant, however, is stenotopic, limited in its range. The sexual addiction can be found in many different environments. The assembly line factory worker whose addiction is in partial response to the stress of boredom and lack of meaning in his life shares a common illness with the executive whose addiction is in response to overextension and overcommitment. The sexual addiction can flourish in a rigid or a chaotic family environment, in a sexually permissive culture

or a sexually restrictive culture. In fact, one great strength of the addiction is that it derives energy from environmental extremes.

4. *The addiction is extensive in range, level, and intensity.* The addiction can take many forms. Within a specific level of addiction there is also a wide range of behaviors which can be the focus of the addictive cycle. In addition, an addict's behavior can transcend one, two, or all three levels of addictive behavior. The intensity of the behavior will vary with the phase of the addictive system. Contrast two exhibitionists both in the acute phase of the addiction. One started his exhibitionism and voyeurism at the age of thirteen and continues to the present. The other started also at thirteen but changed his behavior at the age of twenty-one and for the last seven years has focused on multiple relationships, prostitution, and pornographic videos. Both are in the acute phase. Both started by intense exposing. Some people might think that the latter exhibitionist overcame his problem. Others who are more knowledgeable would see that the illness simply changed its behavioral expression. Any assessment must take into account the addict's capacity to change sexual behaviors to match new conditions.

5. *The addiction is both multisystem and autonomous in nature.* The addictive system has the virulent capacity to perpetuate itself no matter what its environment. Its interdependency with other systems, however, is the source of its tremendous destructive power. Assessment of the addictive system must extend to these other systems which give the addiction its vitality and which can also be vital resources in healing. One way to help professionals diagnose and treat their clients is to visualize the addictive system as being interconnected with six other systems: The biological system, relationship networks, the family system, the work system, concurrent addictions, mental illnesses, and environmental systems. Figure 8-1 illustrates the interdependent relationship between these systems and the addictive system.

The Biological System

John sought his physician's help because he was having problems with frequent urination. His doctor recommended a cystoscopy, a surgical procedure to widen the urethra. John elected to have the procedure and when finished his physician invited him into his office to debrief. His doctor got straight to the point. He asked John if he had been under a great deal of stress lately and if the stress had been sexual in nature. John was stunned. In fact, he had maintained at least five relationships outside his marriage for over seven years.

With the birth of his second child, the last six months had been incredibly demanding. But the real crisis had come several months earlier when a lover had announced that she was pregnant and wanted to get an abortion. This situation created a severe crisis of conscience for John since he was a pro-life advocate. His self-despair was enormous. He initiated a new relationship on the very day of his lover's abortion.

When his doctor asked about what was going on, John felt totally vulnerable but scared enough by his recent physical ailment to be honest. After hearing his story, the doctor took from the desk drawer a series of pamphlets on sexual addiction developed by a local Twelve Step group. He asked John if he could ask one of the groups to call him to talk about his problem. John said yes, but as he left he felt as if he had made a mistake. When the group member called, John was still distrustful. Not until many months later was John able to call his physician and express his gratitude for what he termed "blowing the whistle" on him.

Physicians and allied health professionals can play a key role in helping sexual addicts get into treatment. Many addictive symptoms are biological, including:

—genital infections and disorders

—herpes, gonorrhea, and other venereal diseases

—AIDS, Aids Related Complex

Multi-System Support for Addiction

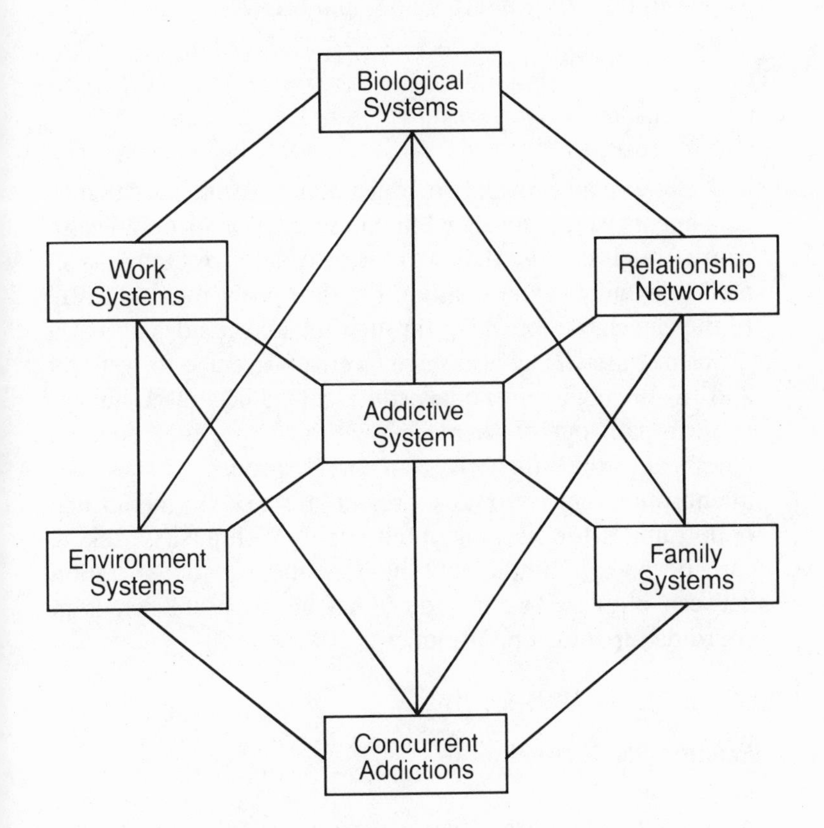

Figure 8-1

—unwanted pregnancies

—signs of physical abuse

—abnormal muscle tissue from prolonged sexual activity

—injuries to genitals, colon, and breasts

—malnutrition

—insomnia

Because addicts and co-addicts can present a wide range of ailments which can signal the presence of addiction, health professionals can use these indicators of addictive unmanageability to initiate an evaluation. Physical problems are helpful to the clinician in breaking through the addict's denial that a problem exists. They also serve to create leverage for referral and treatment. Professionals can assist addicts or co-addicts in their path out of shame by affirming that they have an illness and that there is a recovery process. Issues like malnutrition and insomnia present a series of therapeutic opportunities for teaching about coping with anxiety, taking care of oneself, and establishing boundaries. Cooperation between physical health and mental health professionals in coordinating these opportunities is critical.

Relationship Networks

All addicts suffer as they become extremely isolated with their problem. They create distance even from those who care the most, a distance which contributes to making the addiction a "closed" system, that is, one difficult to influence from the outside. Addiction thrives on isolation. Once the interpersonal system opens up, the power of the addiction wanes.

Further, most addicts have few, if any, healthy relationships. When a male addict has no close male friends, when he believes that he can only talk to a woman about his problems, and when he sexualizes all relationships with women, he limits his chances for intimacy and support. Again, he has no one to "depend" upon. The same process is true for women. Women who rely on sexual approval from men to feel good about themselves severely restrict their options for getting their emotional needs met. Addicts tend to invest emotional energy in eroticized relationships and neglect meaningful, nonsexual relationships.

If this narrow band of relationship options can be widened, the addictive system is disrupted. The local Twelve Step communities become a social intervention, since the addict joins a network of members committed to developing meaningful, nonsexual relationships. The group serves as a social testing ground where addicts can risk connecting with others who know the truth about them. Out of that experience comes trust in their capacity to maintain relationships. Men's and women's consciousness-raising groups can also add new dimensions to the addict's relationship life. The clinician can then build on these experiences therapeutically, starting with an assessment of what support networks already exist—or do not exist.

Negative support networks should also be part of the assessment process—memberships in swapping groups, sex rings, and nudist colonies, or any group in which the major bond is sexual behavior. Sometimes the distinction is subtle: for some people nudist colonies or nude beaches, for example, may be simply an expression of freedom and sun worship. For the exhibitionist they are not. For some people belonging to a hard-drinking and carousing group of business executives whose favorite pastime is hustling is just an expression of youthful enthusiasm. For the addicted member the enthusiasm masks desperation. In short, for some addicts, entering recovery may call for major alterations in lifestyle and friendships.

The Family System

We have already explored the many symptoms of addiction within the family system, including family behavioral extremes, co-addictive behavior, family isolation, and family rules and myths about sex. The family system demands special attention, given the power of the family of origin and the sustaining energy of the current co-addictive family system. The core beliefs of the addict originate with the family and are confirmed by the family, although the beliefs can be developed in various ways. As Tolstoy observed, "Happy families are all alike; every unhappy family is unhappy in its own way." The validity of that statement can be easily confirmed in sexual addiction.

Sixty-seven incest families were asked to take FACES I, an instrument developed by David Olson based on the circumplex model described earlier. These families were participating in a treatment program of the Family Renewal Center at Fairview Southdale Hospital, funded by the National Center for Child Abuse and Neglect. The principal investigator of that project, Miriam Ingebritson, creatively used the circumplex model as both a clinical and teaching tool for the families. The goal of giving FACES I was to establish empirical norms for differential diagnosis in addition to clinical rating scales and before clinical work began (see fig. 8-2).[1]

Therapists who work within a systems framework focus on transforming dysfunctional systems into resources for recovery—a principle that applies to sexual addiction as well. Family members can help by staging an intervention, citing examples of the addict's unmanageability and supplying data about the illness. More helpful yet are co-addicts who enter treatment for themselves. Recovery is optimum when both the addictive system, the co-addictive system, and their interconnecting relationships are disrupted. Fortunately, the growth of community programs for spouses like S-Anon and

Incest Family Member Ratings

Individual FACES Percentages for Total Sample

(Family Members; Total of 67 Families)

n = 209

ADAPTABILITY	Disengaged	Separated	Connected	Enmeshed	Raw Total
Chaotic	2.9 (6)	9.1 (19)	12.0 (25)	13.9 (29)	**37.8 (79)**
Flexible	4.8 (10)	3.8 (8)	5.7 (12)	8.0 (17)	**22.5 (47)**
Structure	7.7 (16)	7.2 (15)	6.2 (13)	1.0 (2)	**22.0 (46)**
Rigid	7.2 (15)	5.3 (11)	3.3 (7)	1.9 (4)	**17.7 (37)**
Column Total	**22.5 (47)**	**25.4 (53)**	**27.3 (57)**	**24.9 (52)**	**100.0 (209)**

Note: Numbers in parenthesis indicate raw scores.

Special thanks to Miriam Ingebritson, Fairview Community Hospitals, for use of this data.

Figure 8-2

COSA (Co-dependents to Sexual Addiction) provide professionals with additional resources to maximize recovery.

The Work System

Mannie was the technical genius of the company. His innovations had produced new products that had added several hundred million dollars to the company's annual revenues. His enthusiasm and charisma had earned him the title of the company's "spark plug." When news of his arrest for prostitution with young men came out in the papers, he was promptly fired in the interest of the corporate image. The employee assistance staff worked extremely hard to convince management to reverse their decision, arguing that Mannie had a treatable illness; that corporate policy was to help people so they could return to productive work; that Mannie was an irreplaceable resource; and that whatever public relations damage might be done had already been done. Unfortunately, the decision stood.

On the other hand, Tod worked for a company that promoted a supersexualized environment. As one visitor observed, "To walk into this place is a turn-on." Staff were selected for their attractiveness. Every Friday afternoon the marketing department had a beer party for clients, which was known for its seductive and erotic qualities. Office affairs were commonplace and an ongoing source of amusement. When Tod's long string of affairs extended into the office, it was in the spirit of "everyone is doing it." For Tod's secretary, however, her sexual relationship with Tod was deeply significant until she realized she was just one of a series. She resigned and her therapist urged her to file a sexual harassment suit. The company quickly settled, buying her off and covering for Tod. His supervisor cautioned him to "keep his peter out of the payroll."

These examples represent two extremes. The management of one company could not accept the illness, and the other aided the illness. Fortunately, some companies are now using their existing employee assistance programs to develop responses to sexual addiction, partly in response to the growing movement of comprehensive employee assistance efforts. Also, the same symptoms that forced business decision-makers to respond to the need for alcoholism treatment exist for sexual addiction as well—loss of productivity, lack of accountability, consumer and employee complaints, and employee financial stress. Finally, the experience of employee assistance professionals in the workplace is that addictions like alcoholism, compulsive overeating, and sexual addiction become silent partners to the so-called workaholic.

EAP counselors can help therapists in their assessment and intervention with the addict. Using data from the workplace, the counselor can refer employees to help and can use the company's support as leverage by making treatment a condition for further work. They can sponsor management in-service programs to create awareness among supervisors and they can work for broadening of corporate addiction policies. They can join the therapist in exploring the feasibility of a job change if it is in the interests of recovery. They can arrange for stress and time management seminars to help recovering people, whatever the addiction, to deal with anxiety in the workplace. Like other systems, the work system can be transformed from being part of the problem to part of the cure.

Concurrent Addictions/Mental Illnesses

Two other related types of systems add strength to the sexual addiction. First, there are other addiction systems, such as alcoholism or gambling, which are intact systems in their own right. These can interact with sexual addiction in a mutually supportive fashion. Using one dependency to justify the other is often a sign of such interaction. The sexual addict who is also alcoholic who rationalizes her behavior on the basis of having drunk too much has woven a mosaic of beliefs to support both behaviors. Or there is the sexual addict who compulsively gambles and sexually binges when he wins, because he deserves it, as well as when he loses, because he needs something to go right. Each addiction strengthens the other addiction.

Someday, when knowledge of addiction is more complete and research skills in treatment settings are more developed, helping professionals will look back and be able to account for the percentage of failures in the treatment of alcoholism that are due to overlooking interaction with other addictions. After the failure to use differential diagnoses with families, probably the next major factor in recidivism in alcoholism treatment is the counseling paradigm which sees alcoholism as the underlying source of all the addict's problems.

In assessment, the therapist's goal is to bring to light whatever mutually supportive addictive systems are interacting and to set treatment goals to disrupt them. Fortunately, from a case management perspective, the recovery programs for each addictive system also support one another. For example, learning from AA will generalize to SAA and vice versa. Treatment plans should maximize opportunities for that type of cross-referencing and cooperation.

Personality and emotional disorders can also support addictive patterns. Because of their despair, addicts have sometimes been misdiagnosed as depressed. When the addictive system is disrupted, however, the depression often disappears. In other cases, a depressive disorder may be found to exist—the pain of which feeds the addiction, which in turn prolongs the depression. This symbiotic interaction needs to be considered when mental health and addiction treatment plans are developed.

This consideration extends to families as well. The early conceptualization for family systems theory came chiefly from the therapists who saw the family's central role in schizophrenia. The famous "schizophrenic" family, i.e., a family that produces schizophrenics, opened up new modalities of treatment with much higher recovery rates for many types of mental illness. Clinical experience has shown that addiction and mental illness can be mutually reinforcing within a family context.[2]

Sometimes determining priorities for treatment tasks is difficult when sexual addiction interacts with other addictions, mental disorders, and family dynamics. For example, consider a family in which the father is physically violent with the mother, sexually abusive with two of his daughters, and chemically dependent as well. The mother is obese and physically abusive with the children. One child is chemically dependent, schizophrenic, and epileptic. What does the professional treat first?

In this case, setting treatment priorities is relatively easy. As a general rule, safety is always first, so the family violence is the first order of business. Next is detoxification, because until the chemically dependent persons are free of chemicals, therapy cannot proceed. Only then can the addiction issues be addressed and other issues be addressed. Priorities are not always so easily determined in assessment. For certain, the more complex the conditions, the more virulent the addiction can be. An effective assessment comes from a complete picture of all the toxic systems and conditions involved.

Environmental Systems

Charlie was a thirty-eight-year-old attorney of Hispanic origin whose family and ethnic ties were very deep. He liked to have anonymous sex with men. Because it was his perception that homosexuality is regarded with disdain in the "macho" Hispanic culture, Charlie felt ashamed about his behavior and was terrified at not being able to stop it. His greatest fear was that he might be gay. His next greatest fear was that he might be picked up by the police which would destroy his career and his place in the family as the "successful" son. Charlie's shame was so complete that he had to ask his wife to search for a therapist to help him.

Charlie was physically depleted when he met Frank, his new therapist. Two days before he came for the interview, he had had what he termed a "final fling." In that time he had been sexual with five different men, none of whom he knew, and virtually had not slept for days. He walked into Frank's office raw and vulnerable to the point of having no boundaries. When he told his story he gave long detailed rationalizations for his behavior.

After listening patiently, Frank quietly talked to Charlie about his "addiction," pointed out that all the concerns and issues such as whether Charlie was gay, or whether his conflicts about his family and culture were real or imagined, would have to wait. The top priority was to get help for the addiction. Nothing could be worked through while the addiction was active. The therapist outlined his best guess about some of the therapeutic tasks Charlie would face as part of his treatment. Central to his recovery would be strengthening his cultural pride while abandoning debilitating myths. Also, Charlie would need to understand how being labeled "special" in his family was in many ways a real liability. Specialness was his family's way to control him and also give him permission to be irresponsible. He would come to understand how his family functioned as a "rigid-enmeshed" unit. His sexual behavior would be examined to determine whether it was an expression of sexual preference or an addictive expression of defiance, or both. The orchestrator of all these issues, however, was the addiction. Charlie needed a thorough assessment, treatment, and a Twelve Step group.

Frank used an ecological approach to the addiction. The environment that surrounded Charlie's addiction provided a strong foundation for its support. The Hispanic culture and Charlie's link with his family were key to the belief system which supplied direction to Charlie's addiction.

Throughout this book the ecology of the addiction has been implicit. It has been underlined how difficult choosing a new sexual lifestyle can be in a culture that, for example, supports a seven-billion-dollar-a-year pornography industry. It has been noted how ethnic subcultures can be vital factors. Therapists need to see the addiction as the center of a series of overlapping patterns, like concentric waves on disturbed waters. But just a "snapshot" of an addiction's ecology is not enough. Bradford Keeney, Director of Research for the Ackerman Institute for Family Therapy in New York, writes about the importance of seeing ecological patterns over time:

> In addition to reducing or magnifying the territorial or spatial events upon which phenomena occur, one can change the time frame wherein events are observed in order to detect pattern. An example of this approach is given by the cultural anthropologist Hall . . . who describes the use of film technology in a research project of one of his students:
>
> > Using an abandoned car as a blind, he photographed children dancing and skipping in a school playground during their lunch hour. At first, they looked like so many kids each doing his own thing. After a while, we noticed that one little girl was moving more than the rest. Careful study revealed that she covered the entire playground. Following procedures laid down for my students, this young man viewed the film over and over at different speeds. Gradually, he perceived that the whole group was moving in synchrony to a definite rhythm. The most active child, the one who moved the most, was the director, the orchestrator of the playground rhythm!
>
> The point . . . is to illustrate that certain forms of synchronic patterns of phenomena are detectable to the observer only through manipulating their representation in space and time.[3]

To make a diagnosis or an assessment means that the therapist or helping professional becomes an ecological pattern seeker. The search for patterns starts with the addictive system itself.

Assessment of the Addictive System

The ecology principle extends to assessing patterns of sexual behavior. Historically, clinicians have used behavior categories such as "exhibitionist," "voyeur" or "rapist" as diagnostic labels without relating one kind of sexual behavior. In part, such labels stem from a problem orientation. Therapists have been trained to focus on the presenting issue. In a systems framework, illness is a *series of systems whose functioning or growth is impaired*. In sexual addiction, the illness usually appears as a patterned set of behaviors. For example, the exhibitionist may also compulsively masturbate, use pornography, and visit massage parlors.

In one study, two groups of sex addicts and one group of sex offenders were asked to respond to a survey which in part listed the thirteen behaviors we have used in describing levels one, two, and three of the addiction. After a brief description of the behavior, each respondent indicated whether (1) they had no experience with the behavior; (2) they had experienced the behavior but with no problems related to it; or (3) they had problems because of the behavior. Figure 8-3 summarizes the problem behaviors of each population.

Of the three groups, one was composed of 142 members of Sexual Addicts Anonymous in Minneapolis and St. Paul. Note that most of the problematic behavior fell in the Level One category. Such a finding makes sense, given that this was a community group as opposed to a clinical or prison population. Even so, note that Level Two and Level Three behaviors were reported.

Problem Behaviors of Separate Populations

(By levels of addiction)

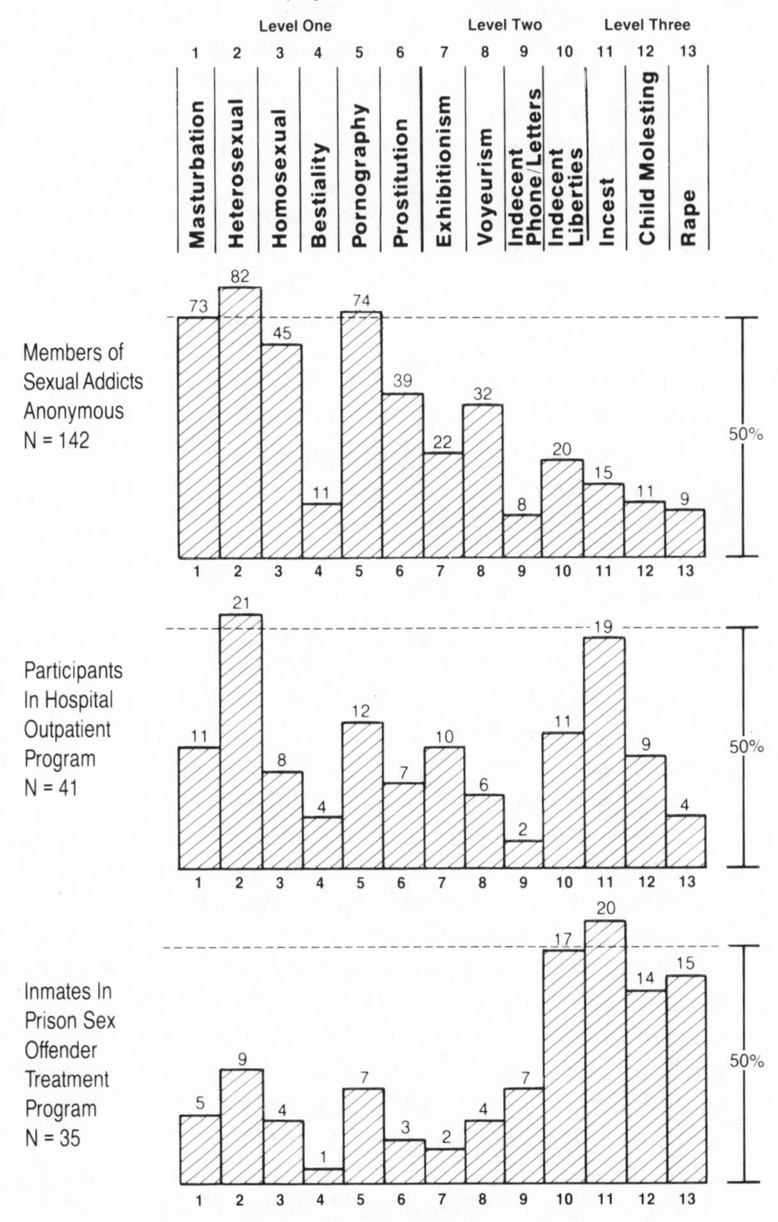

Bars indicate the numbers of people who responded that the behavior was a problem.

Figure 8-3

Another group consisted of 41 participants in a hospital-based outpatient sexual addiction treatment program, the other group of 35 sex offenders from two separate state prison rehabilitation programs (Minnesota and Georgia). The outpatient program members reported behaviors throughout all three levels, whereas there is a clear predominance of Level Three behavior in the prison group. That the prison group reported more Level Three behavior fits the group context. Note, however, that numbers of Level One and Two behaviors were reported as well.

Obviously, these are self-reported results and are subject to under- and over-reporting. Yet the results strongly suggest that the addicts and offenders in this study experienced more than one problem behavior. In fact, in all three groups, the average participant had three problem behaviors. A few reported only one, and some as many as six, but the average is three. The data support a long-used clinical maxim for working with sexual addicts called the "rule of threes." Therapists should look for three behaviors or more in their initial assessments. Remember that addicts may not see a behavior as a problem until they have entered recovery.

A chi-square analysis was performed to see what behaviors were typically associated with each other. Figure 8-4 shows which behaviors were most likely to be found with other behaviors at a .05 level of significance. (An asterisk indicates a behavior at the .01 level; two asterisks indicate a relationship at the .001 level. Each list can serve as a "shopping list" of possible behavior configurations.)

For the professional, assessment means studying the overlapping patterns of sexual behavior that would seem to fit within an addictive cycle. For example, indecent liberties emerged as having particularly strong associations with a number of behaviors in all three levels of addiction. Faced with a client who reports taking indecent liberties, a therapist should start searching for related behaviors.

A further analysis of correlations between behaviors revealed a series of "linked pairs" in which one behavior's presence was highly correlated with the presence of another. They include:

		r
1.	Masturbation-heterosexual relationships	.30
2.	Pornography-prostitution	.36
3.	Exhibitionism-voyeurism	.40
4.	Obscene phone/letters-rape	.38
5.	Indecent liberties-child molesting	.31
6.	Incest-child molesting	.44

Such correlations raise significant questions. For example, what is the connection between pornography and prostitution? In *Pornography and Silence*, Susan Griffin describes the connection eloquently as the expression of deeply held cultural beliefs about women. Similarly, neurolinguistic programming researchers tell us that human beings access information through primary sense modes such as seeing, hearing, and touching. Does that mean exhibitionist-voyeurs are addicts whose primary access mode of stimulation is visual? Do obscene letters and indecent liberties collapse fundamental personal boundaries and serve as gateways to child molestation and rape?

Before researching these and the many other questions these data generate, we will need to develop a common form to study behavioral patterns of addicts. The format and content we used were clearly inadequate for the level of research that yet needs to be done. For example, note the few associations that occur under homosexuality. Since the form did not list the wide range of sexual behavior practiced by homosexuals, consequently possible addictive patterns did not emerge. Similarly, the form was specifically designed for men. Later in this chapter we discuss how women can exhibit

Sexual Addiction Behavior Patterns

Level One Presenting Behavior	*Level One Associated Behavior*	*Level Two Associated Behavior*	*Level Three Associated Behavior*
Masturbation	Heterosexual Bestiality **Pornography *Prostitution	*Exhibitionism *Voyeurism	Incest
Heterosexual	Masturbation Homosexual *Bestiality	Exhibitionism Voyeurism *Indecent liberties	Incest *Rape
Homosexual	*Prostitution Heterosexual		*Rape
Bestiality	Masturbation Heterosexual *Pornography	*Exhibitionism *Indecent phone/letters **Indecent liberties	**Incest
Pornography	**Masturbation *Bestiality **Prostitution	*Voyeurism	Child Molestation
Prostitution	*Masturbation *Homosexual **Pornography	Exhibitionism Voyeurism *Indecent phone/letters	

Figure 8-4

By Presenting Behavior

Level Two Presenting Behavior	*Level One Associated Behavior*	*Level Two Associated Behavior*	*Level Three Associated Behavior*
Exhibitionism	*Masturbation *Heterosexual *Bestiality Prostitution	**Voyeurism Indecent phone/letters *Indecent liberties	
Voyeurism	*Masturbation Heterosexual *Pornography Prostitution	**Exhibitionism Indecent liberties	
Indecent phone/letters	*Bestiality *Prostitution	Exhibitionism **Indecent liberties	**Rape
Indecent liberties	*Heterosexual **Bestiality	*Exhibitionism *Voyeurism **Indecent phone/letters	**Incest **Child Molestation **Rape

Level Three Presenting Behavior	*Level One Associated Behavior*	*Level Two Associated Behavior*	*Level Three Associated Behavior*
Incest	Masturbation Heterosexual	**Indecent liberties	**Child Molestation **Rape
Child Molestation	*Pornography	**Indecent liberties	**Incest Rape
Rape	*Homosexual	**Indecent liberties **Indecent phone/letters	**Incest Child Molestation

All entries are significant at the .05 level.
** indicates significance at the .01 level.*
*** indicates significance at the .001 level.*

Figure 8-4 (cont.)

themselves, although the cultural context is different than for men. Also, American women are culturally sanctioned to be more blatantly intrusive physically with men than men can be with women.

The data, however, make a point. To use singular categories such as "exhibitionist" excludes a range of addictive behavior. I emphasize this point because it is critically related to recovery. If an exhibitionist whose behavior includes extensive prostitution and pornography use is involved in treatment which focuses on exhibiting behavior only, as opposed to the larger addictive pattern, the chances for recovery remain slim.

Whenever therapists suspect the presence of addiction, their first assessment priority is to *determine the extent of patterned sexual behavior*. Many therapists ask clients to fill out forms or use an autobiographical or journal approach. Homework assignments like these facilitate data-gathering while minimizing the use of treatment time. Most clients embark on this journey with some enthusiasm because it is a high-interest assignment. It also avoids power struggles over whether the client is an addict or not. After all, all the therapist has asked for is a sexual history.

Some clients will do a less than adequate job of detailing their sexual activities out of fear, overextension, and other factors. A calendar approach can sometimes be effective in these cases. Starting with the most recent complete week, work backwards a week at a time. A laborious process at best, but three to four months of carefully cataloged behavior teaches the client what you are looking for and indicates the importance you, as the therapist, place on the activity. In most cases, some relevant fact emerges which builds enthusiasm for continuing. Asking the client to go to this much effort is warranted, given the significance of the data. And if addictive patterns do emerge, the data help toward intervention in the system, and the client is well prepared for initiating step work and treatment.

Therapists must have an eye for changes in behavior patterns in terms of the client's increasing sexual activity within the range of a given level, of new sexual behavior at a new level, and changes in intensity and frequency of existing behaviors. Beyond behavior, the rest of the addictive system—preoccupation, ritualization, and despair—provides important evidence of the addiction's presence. Professionals do not have to rely on behavior alone.

The Ideal Scenario

The helping professional must *determine the priority obsession modes.* The level of preoccupation as well as its content are significant clues to the existence of the addiction. The metaphor of Gollum's shadow applies here since preoccupation may exist while behavior is being controlled. There are a number of ways to identify preoccupation. When they say that sex is all they can think about and that they want relief, exploring the obsessional part of their addiction is not difficult. But, it is still important to pursue the priorities of their preoccupational life. What do they think about? What or who do they use for stimulation? How do they fantasize? What are some favorite fantasies? What are fantasies they would be ashamed of if people knew? When they find preoccupation exciting, what do they imagine might happen? How much time is spent just seeking sexual stimulation to think about it?

It is extremely important to make the addict's "ideal scenarios" explicit early. These scenarios often hold the key to understanding addictive behavior patterns that did not emerge as part of the sexual history. They will reveal dysfunctional beliefs and impaired thinking. Usually they are related somehow to catalytic events and catalytic environments.

Not always is preoccupation obvious to therapist or addict. Some subtle clues will help the alert therapist. Note that in our culture sex is often referred to in the language of drug addiction. Strip shows are sometimes called "pain relievers" and massage parlors advertise "tension relief." Sex is referred to as a "fix," as primarily medicinal and mood-altering as opposed to personal and life-enhancing. Does the client refer to being "hooked" on a specific form of sex? Or does the client think about sex in times of stress as a way to get through the crisis? One sign of preoccupation is thinking about sex as a form of "relief" or medicine. For example, Martha, a character in Lawrence Sanders' best-selling novel *The Seduction of Peter S.*, talks of sex as "the thinking woman's Valium."[4]

Another subtle but important clue is what happens to the client's preoccupation when there is no immediate access to sex. Does the preoccupation escalate when there is a lack of opportunity? A male addict might talk, for example, of his dislike of events in which there are "no ladies present."

Another, often not as subtle, indicator is simply the amount of time the addict puts into preoccupation. A client might complain about thinking about sex all the time and about seeing every person from a sexual point of view. Another not so subtle characteristic is predatory viewing. Most people notice someone who is attractive and certainly are aware of their own attractions. They can enjoy and delight in that part of themselves and then move on. Many addicts report compulsively looking with almost a voracious anxiety lest they miss the slightest sexual nuance. More than being casual gawkers, they use a desperate scan that is not unlike the way alcoholics gulp their drinks.

Addicts in the de-escalation phase who obsess about eliminating sex are suffering from a negative form of preoccupation. Still desperate and anxious, they pursue any form of public sexuality with almost hunt-like zeal. Part of their determination stems from the need to make a public stand to cover the shame of their private lives. Another part rests in the addict's ever present dysfunctional belief that sex is the enemy. Finally, addicts in de-escalation betray their compulsivity when their anti-sex efforts take over their lives. Their preoccupation is like the compulsive nonsexuality that occurs in many co-addicts. Both try to obliterate the sexual feelings which have been so painful.

Therapists who have a great deal of experience with this illness often report amazement at how closely preoccupation and ritualization are tied together. Rituals enhance and support the addict's obsessions. Going to the bar to scan the prospects there exemplifies the melding of the two activities. Sometimes this interdependence makes assessment difficult. When an addict obsesses about cross-dressing and when he actually does cross dress they become extensions of the same stimulation theme. To *identify specific rituals* is another central task of the assessment, but it may simply mean that the therapist sees how the ideal scenario gets played out. The female addict who uses costumes as part of her seduction scenes, or the male addict who selects only certain types of pornography for masturbation, are relying on a script embedded in their obsessive thoughts.

To assess the origins of that script, the therapist needs to *determine the catalytic events and the catalytic environments* on which the addict's total belief system rests. Usually a common story line weaves its way through the various experiences. The helping professional, as a "pattern seeker," notes the connection between the emerging story line and the ideal scenario played out in ritual and obsession.

Consider the five-year-old boy whose first sexual experience occurred when a group of older girls asked him to show them his penis. He found the experience intensely pleasurable and felt profoundly rejected when the girls lost interest and did not want to play anymore. Shortly thereafter he exhibited himself to some playmates. He left the fly on his pants open and got initial interest on the part of his friends. Again however, they lost interest, and he felt deeply rejected and disappointed.

As an adult, he found himself repeating the same pattern of intense pleasure at exposing and then the wrenching shame when rejected. He pursued the eternal hope of the five-year-old that someone would stay and look. As part of the assessment, therapists always need to *check for life-threatening depression* which may be part of any addict's despair. When rejection and shame are built into the ideal scenario, the addict is particularly vulnerable to suicidal feelings. In the case of this exhibitionist, it was the suicidal depression that brought him to treatment. He saw no other way out.

Therapists routinely attempt to *elicit rationalizations and distortions of reality* when conducting their assessments. The effort is to gather data, not to confront, because the therapist seeks to enter the addict's world to understand the organization of the addict's impaired thinking. Again the idealized scenario can be determined from how the defenses support the script. The addiction might manifest itself in a quest for the ideal life partner, and the addict might eventually find each new person merely human—and profoundly disappointing. For this addict, interactions with strangers can take on "cosmic meaning" if it means they go to bed together. The therapist may be tempted to point out that cosmic meaning does not happen three times a day to most people. At the assessment stage, however, the therapist simply stays with understanding the scenario which impels the client on a constant quest for yet another person with whom life would be better.

Sometimes addictive behavior and impaired thinking are in reaction to a favorite scenario. If the scenario involves violence or severe consequences, the addiction may transform into another behavior in a "precautionary acting out" pattern. The exhibitionist described earlier used massage parlors because his exhibitionism was so painful. His rationale was, "I do this so I will not be out on the street which is so humiliating. At least, in the parlors, women will stay if I pay them." He discovered that it was only a variation of the theme since he ended up with the same feelings.

Perhaps the best test of the presence of addiction is its unmanageability. The therapist makes a thorough effort to *search for "out of control" behavior.* Chaos which results from the addict's pursuit of the addiction scenario provides many clues to the internal conflict that the addict experiences due to distorted priorities. Perhaps the surest sign is that the addict repeatedly makes efforts to stop and fails, despite the obvious consequences of the behavior. Sometimes these efforts to control take the form of dramatic changes—changing jobs, location, and even spouses—but to no avail. Tapping into the desire to quit is key to the assessment and also recovery. If it is an addiction, this desire is there even if buried under layers of shame and impaired thinking.

An instrument which can help the therapist tap into that desire to quit is the Sexual Addiction Screening Test which is covered in the next section. Before proceeding, we need to summarize the key steps the therapist takes in doing a good assessment. These are listed in the order discussed, but may occur in different orders, of course, in work with different clients. The key steps to assessment are:

—determine the extent of sexual behavior or co-addictive behavior

—determine priority obsession modes

—identify specific rituals

—determine catalytic events and catalytic environments

—check for life-threatening depression

—elicit rationalizations and distortions of reality

—search for evidence of "out of control" behavior

The Sexual Addiction Screening Test

A wealth of literature exists on the usefulness of screening instruments to assist in diagnosing alcoholism. Paper and pencil tests have their limits, but historically these *have* proved valuable as adjuncts to the therapist's assessment process. This kind of tool has been developed for sex addiction, called the Sexual Addiction Screening Test or SAST, the development of which proved to be a difficult task for several reasons. The anonymity issues of Twelve Step communities made it difficult to find sufficient numbers of sexual addicts willing to be part of samples for validity and reliability studies. Developed over a period of three years, the SAST shows promise as a useful assessment instrument.

Initially, fifty items were selected from a list of over one hundred items on the basis of apparent validity by a group of clinicians, both in private practice and hospitals. The questionnaire was then given to a sample of 73 addicts who were either members of Sexual Addicts Anonymous (SAA) in Minneapolis or were in outpatient treatment for their illness. The next step was to select 24 highly discriminatory items and extract oblique factors. Ninety percent of the variance ($r = .74$) stemmed from awareness that personal sexual behavior was a problem or out of control, and that help was needed. In this early study, we assumed a 10:1 nonaddict to addict ratio in the population to discriminate. Only seven variables added to the discrimination ability of the evolving instrument. These were largely unrelated to meaningful clusters or factors which had emerged.

Out of the 50 items, 25 were selected on the basis of the above analysis and clinical judgment (fig. 8-5). This revised instrument was given to a new group of addicts from SAA and compared with the convenience sample of nonaddicted men gathered in the earlier study.[5] The internal consistency of the instrument as measured by Cronbach's alpha for 191 male addicts was .92; for 67 nonaddict men was .85; and for 258 men in the total sample was .95.

Figures 8-6 and 8-7 show the distribution of the scoring patterns of the respondents. They can be summarized as follows:

SAST Score Range	Nonaddict	Addict
0-4	89.3%	10.7%
5-8	89.6%	10.4%
9-12	77.2%	22.8%
13+	3.5%	96.5%

Over the score of 13, the SAST shows a promising ability to discriminate addicts from nonaddicts. A smoothed graph illustrates the relationship of the scores between the populations, but not sample size (see fig. 8-8).

The SAST has only one well-defined factor which accounts for 50 percent of the variance. No other factor accounted for more than 6 percent. Apparently the SAST taps into the desire to stop because of life unmanageability and powerlessness over sexual behavior. At this point, all that can be said of this early stage instrument is that it is an assessment tool to support clinical judgment. Within that context the SAST can indicate presence of addiction. It may also provide a vehicle to talk with clients showing how their high scores relate to the scores of other addicts.

Some caveats are in order. First, no relationship exists between the SAST and specific types of behaviors. No significant differences were found between the scores of Level One, Level Two, or Level Three addicts. So the instrument cannot be used as a predictor of dangerousness. The focus of the instrument is the addictive system and not specific levels of behavior.

Second, great care must be taken with homosexual clients—or perhaps any client whose behavior would have heavy cultural sanctions—because these people have experiences and feelings in some ways parallel to those of addicts in terms of secrecy and shame, and yet are not addicts themselves. More work needs to be done to establish validity of the instrument with special populations.

The Sexual Addiction Screening Test (SAST)

The Sexual Addiction Screening Test (SAST) is designed to assist in the assessment of sexually compulsive or "addictive" behavior. Developed in cooperation with hospitals, treatment programs, private therapists, and community groups, the SAST provides a profile of responses which help to discriminate between addictive and nonaddictive behavior. To complete the test, answer each question by placing a check in the appropriate yes/no column.

YES	NO	
☐	☐	**1.** Were you sexually abused as a child or adolescent?
☐	☐	**2.** Have you subscribed or regularly purchased sexually explicit magazines like *Playboy* or *Penthouse?*
☐	☐	**3.** Did your parents have trouble with sexual behavior?
☐	☐	**4.** Do you often find yourself preoccupied with sexual thoughts?
☐	☐	**5.** Do you feel that your sexual behavior is not normal?
☐	☐	**6.** Does your spouse [or significant other(s)] ever worry or complain about your sexual behavior?
☐	☐	**7.** Do you have trouble stopping your sexual behavior when you know it is inappropriate?
☐	☐	**8.** Do you ever feel bad about your sexual behavior?
☐	☐	**9.** Has your sexual behavior ever created problems for you or your family?
☐	☐	**10.** Have you ever sought help for sexual behavior you did not like?
☐	☐	**11.** Have you ever worried about people finding out about your sexual activities?

Figure 8-5

SAST (cont.)

YES	NO	
☐	☐	**12.** Has anyone been hurt emotionally because of your sexual behavior?
☐	☐	**13.** Are any of your sexual activities against the law?
☐	☐	**14.** Have you made promises to yourself to quit some aspect of your sexual behavior?
☐	☐	**15.** Have you made efforts to quit a type of sexual activity and failed?
☐	☐	**16.** Do you have to hide some of your sexual behavior from others?
☐	☐	**17.** Have you attempted to stop some parts of your sexual activity?
☐	☐	**18.** Have you ever felt degraded by your sexual behavior?
☐	☐	**19.** Has sex been a way for you to escape your problems?
☐	☐	**20.** When you have sex, do you feel depressed afterwards?
☐	☐	**21.** Have you felt the need to discontinue a certain form of sexual activity?
☐	☐	**22.** Has your sexual activity interfered with your family life?
☐	☐	**23.** Have you been sexual with minors?
☐	☐	**24.** Do you feel controlled by your sexual desire?
☐	☐	**25.** Do you ever think your sexual desire is stronger than you are?

Figure 8-5 **(cont.)**

Relative Distributions of Addict and Nonaddict SAST Scores

Score	Observed # of cases Addict	"Smoothed" % of cases Addict	Observed # of cases Nonaddict	"Smoothed" % of cases Nonaddict
0	8	10.6	1	1.0
1	9	11.8	3	1.0
2	6	12.5	3	1.0
3	5	12.4	4	1.0
4	11	11.7	3	1.0
5	6	9.8	1	1.0
6	5	7.4	1	1.0
7	1	5.8	0	1.0
8	5	5.0	4	1.0
9	0	3.2	1	1.0
10	2	2.5	0	1.0
11	3	2.0	3	1.2
12	3	1.7	3	1.5
13	0	1.0	0	1.8
14	0	.3	6	2.1
15	0	.2	2	2.7
16	0	.2	8	3.4
17	0	.2	7	4.7
18	0	.2	13	6.7
19	0	.2	21	8.8
20	0	.2	20	10.8
21	0	.2	21	11.6
22	2	.2	24	11.6
23	0	.2	18	10.2
24	0	.2	17	7.8
25	0	.2	7	4.1
Total	**66**	**99.9%**	**191**	**100.0%**

"Smoothing" was done as an "eyeball" fit so percents added graphically to 100% and so that the % of cases in the "tails" of the distributions was preserved.

Subjects included were men only.

Figure 8-6

Third, the SAST simply does not address the needs of women. Female addicts did take the instrument, but with very poor reliability results. The reasons why this happened are supposition at this point. However, a number of efforts are now under way to develop a screening instrument with items appropriate to women.

This instrument is included in this book as an invitation. Despite its early stage of development, we hope clinicians will find it useful in their work. Second, researchers may expand the instrument's data base and further comment on its usefulness. Or perhaps they may find special applications to further our knowledge about the illness and its relationship to our culture. The most important purpose for including the SAST, however, is to demonstrate that sexual addiction, despite severe difficulties in data collection at this time, is a viable area for serious researchers.

The Assessment of Sex Addiction in Women

In a series of interviews with groups of female addicts, recovering women were asked how a therapist could recognize the addiction's presence in women. Some of the issues raised are unique to women. Many issues, however, involve shared characteristics with men and differ only in frequency, or intensity, or maybe nuance. The most important information from these interviews clearly indicates that therapists need to be aware of cultural and professional biases which interfere with accurate assessment of sex addiction in women.

First, a fundamentally different context exists for the behavior of women. Exhibitionism, for example, is more culturally sanctioned for women. Media hype and women's magazines participate in a value system which shares common values with *Playboy* and *Penthouse* or even hardcore pornography. It is a more routine occurrence for a woman's body to be displayed as an object, although the feminist movement has made more people sensitive to this issue. However, a

Percentages of Addict and Nonaddict Respondents For a Given SAST Score

SCORE (# of questions answered yes)	NONADDICT (%)	ADDICT %
0	91.4	8.6
1	92.2	7.8
2	92.6	7.4
3	92.5	7.5
4	92.1	7.9
5	90.7	9.3
6	88.1	11.9
7	85.3	14.7
8	83.3	16.7
9	76.2	23.8
10	71.4	28.6
11	62.5	37.5
12	53.1	46.9
13	35.7	64.3
14	12.5	87.5
15	6.9	93.1
16	5.6	94.4
17	4.1	95.9
18	2.9	97.1
19	2.2	97.8
20	1.8	98.2
21	1.7	98.3
22	1.7	98.3
23	1.9	98.1
24	2.5	97.5
25	4.6	95.4

These percentages assume:

1. The smoothing of curves is reasonable.
2. Equal numbers of people being tested will be addicts and non-addicts.

SAST Score Range	Nonaddict:	Addict:
0-4	89.3%	10.7%
5-8	89.6%	10.4%
9-12	77.2%	22.8%
13+	3.5%	96.5%

Figure 8-7

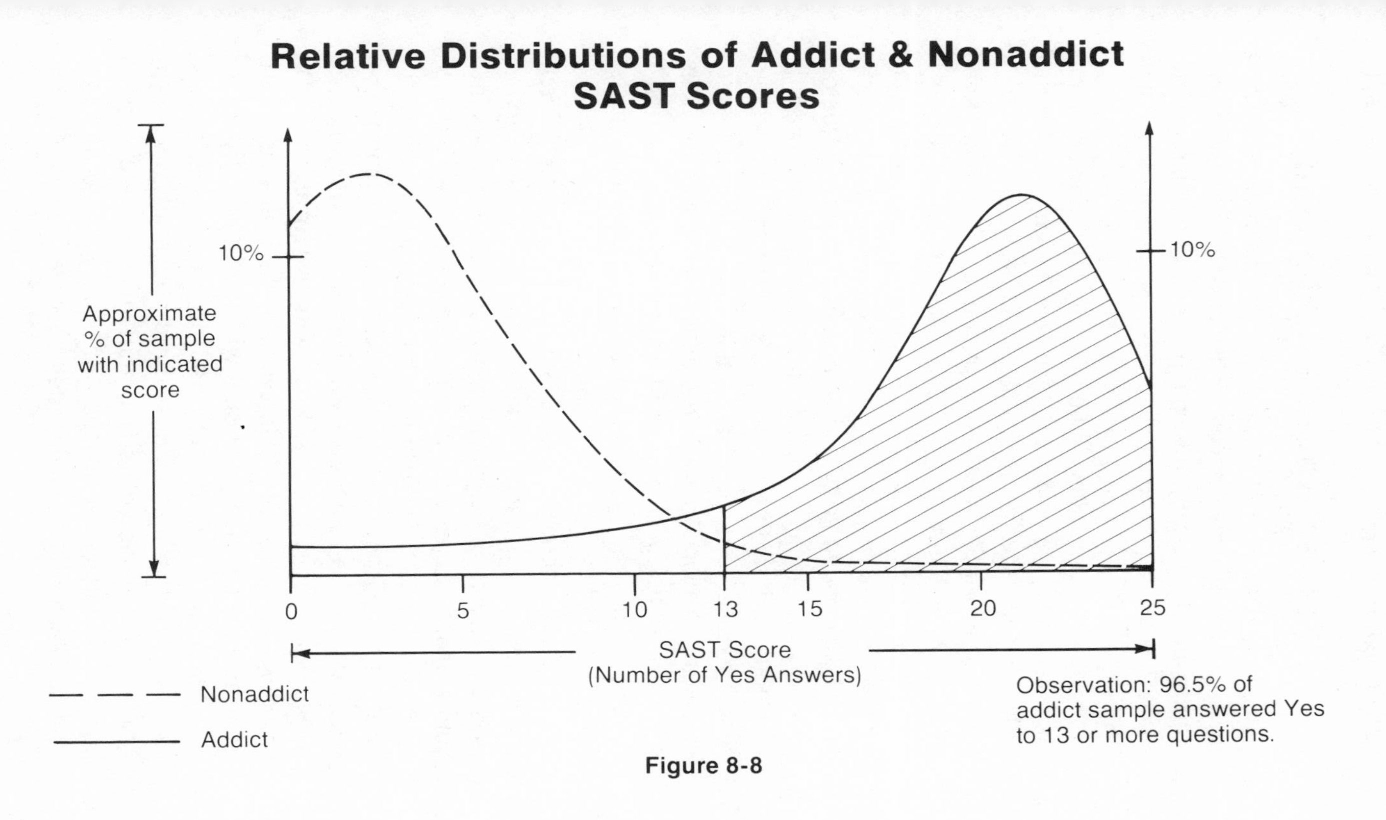
Relative Distributions of Addict & Nonaddict
SAST Scores
Approximate
% of sample
with indicated
score
10%
10%
0
5
10
13
15
20
25
SAST Score
(Number of Yes Answers)
Nonaddict
Addict
Observation: 96.5% of
addict sample answered Yes
to 13 or more questions.

Figure 8-8

female addict might make exhibiting herself part of a seductive scenario, in contrast to the popular conception of a male exhibitionist as someone who lurks in the bushes. So, women aren't typically thought of as "exhibitionists," and when they do exhibit themselves it is viewed as an acceptable behavior.

Second, women have little difficulty attracting attention. As one addict remarked, "Men are so easy." Another followed with, "What men did not understand was that I was in control—that I could be punishing, objectifying, and demeaning with impunity." The power of the seduction is part of the high, or as addicts called it, "the Mata Hari syndrome." The woman addict who goes to a party primarily to find someone to go to bed with shares the same predatory style as many addict men, yet there is less risk of refusal or rejection. Intrinsic to the seduction scenario was the frequent shocked reaction of men who would say, "But you look so innocent." Yet one of the most difficult obstacles for many educated professional women in accepting their addiction is to admit to behavior based on what they perceived as "male" values.

Cultural attitudes about sexual abuse are clearly different toward men than women. Consider the movie *The Summer of '42*. Here is a poignant, even romantic story about a young man's initiation into adulthood. The viewer feels sympathy for the new widow who has just learned of the death of her pilot husband. She reaches out for comfort to a young lad who is infatuated with her. Reverse the story and imagine the public reaction to a twenty-seven-year-old man spending the night with a fifteen-year-old high school girl. Somehow the poignancy vanishes with a shift of perspective.

Many male addicts find it difficult to see themselves as victims of sexual abuse. For a thirteen-year-old to have his first sexual experience with a thirty-nine-year-old aunt is abusive. Yet an adolescent male most likely will see this as a "score." Similarly, female addicts relate how long their behavior went unnoticed because of their sex. Cultural attitudes preclude women as being exploitive. The "guardians of morality" do not victimize children or use men sexually.

In addition, women can operate with greater ambivalence around contextual behavioral cues. They can be more intrusive with touch than men can, or indiscriminately flirtatious or teasing without consequences. Many female addicts report that this latitude, combined with the notion of being a "liberated woman," was a deadly part of their denial. Operating with that standard, wherein many cultural norms have not changed, proved to be a potent combination. Telling themselves that what they are doing "should be completely fine" did not obscure in most women the feeling that there was "something wrong." But as one woman observed, "It was the only place I felt like I had power."

The irony is that for women, like men, no safety exists in the addiction. The consequences, especially in terms of victimization, are different. Women put their physical safety at risk for sexual attention. When women do this, the energy of fear combines with sexual energy and intensifies the experience. Being in jeopardy for the sexual high requires ignoring or misinterpreting internal signs that serve as guides to most of us. While this statement can be made about men, the incidence of physical injury among men who ignore warning signs would probably be less. Tragically, being a victim is a familiar role to female addicts, partly because of our culture and partly because of childhood experiences. Psychologist Charlotte Kasel's extensive interviews with female addicts prompted her to write her manuscript, "Women and Sexual Addiction":

> I believe that sexual addiction or coaddiction is frequently the baseline addiction for women who were sexually abused or exploited as children. That is, it is the core addiction underlying food, alcohol, work, drugs, shopping, and cleaning addictions.[6]

Further confirmation of Kasel's observation can be found in the conversations of many female addicts who talk of their co-addiction as the starting place for their addiction. One woman talked about how she started her sexual acting out behavior as a co-addictive response to her husband's sexual addiction. But as she quipped, "Once started, why stop?"

For the clinician, the assessment of women requires special awareness. Catalytic events, for example, may include such factors as the start of menstruation. Special needs such as post-abortion counseling exist. But most important for female addicts is their need for therapists to recognize that despite the various shades of differences, the addiction exists for them as well. Yet many therapists who are also caught up in traditional cultural attitudes find the concept of addicted women too much of a leap. In fact, when a woman clearly suffers with sexually excessive behavior, she stands out clinically. In his 1978 classic statement about the problem of sexual dependency, Jim Orford writes:

> Many writers on the subject . . . have commented on the apparent greater clinical incidence of nymphomania than of male variants . . . despite evidence from surveys that males indulge in a greater amount of pre- and extramarital sexual behavior with a larger number of partners. Thus the social reaction is different, and the individual herself as a recipient of society's attitude reflects this in her own reaction to her own behavior.[7]

The shame of being a sex addict exists. But double shame exists in being a female addict. To help women, therapists must acknowledge and understand those problems unique to women due to culture and gender. Like all addicts, recovering women initially need support to acknowledge their illness. Once the problem is acknowledged, then intervention and treatment of the addictive system is in order. That is the topic of our next and final chapter.

9
Intervention and Treatment

It all started in the early 1800's with Sylvester Graham, a self-styled doctor who recommended no sex for men before age 30, and only once a month thereafter. To cool sexual urges he prescribed a bland diet featuring such health foods as a special whole wheat Graham bread and cold cereals. He opened boarding houses serving this diet.

The Kellogg family got its start in breakfast cereals in 1876 when John Harvey Kellogg became superintendent of a Seventh Day Adventist health resort in Battle Creek, Michigan. He manufactured a cold cereal which he claimed would keep children from falling prey to the sin of "self-pollution," a euphemism for masturbation.

"Medical Self-Care"
Winter 1982

We have come a long way since the days of colorful figures like Graham and Kellogg, in the excerpt above. We now begin with the premise that sex is "good," not a "moral problem." One primary goal of treatment is to help the addict reclaim a healthy and vibrant sexuality. In fact, one of the foremost obstacles to that goal in therapy is overcoming all the negative and moralistic myths which have entrapped the addict's belief system. The concept of sexual addiction is not a contemporary version of nineteenth-century moralism.

Treatment goals become clearer when sex addiction is compared with eating disorders. When patients enter treatment for compulsive overeating, they do not give up eating. Rather, they learn to eat different foods, to use different rituals, to monitor their feelings, and to change their attitudes and beliefs about eating. Food becomes positive and life-enhancing rather than self-destructive.

Of course, the purpose of treatment is not to create superficial change. The overweight person who compulsively diets only to regain the weight is all too familiar. Similarly, sex addicts who go into de-escalation (the sex addict's "diet") never lose their obsession and are extremely vulnerable to continuing the illness. The purpose of treatment must not be to push the addict into de-escalation, but rather to *bring about a profound shift of beliefs and behavior in which the obsession loses its power.*

Many who fear that sex addiction is a "sex-negative" concept assume that treatment is based on the abstinence model typically found in alcoholism and drug treatment programs. Chemical dependency treatment professionals rightly insist on the importance of abstinence. The psychobiology of sex and food, however, is different, and when these are the focus of compulsive illness, in many ways the addiction is harder to treat. Eating disorders have raised our consciousness about healthy eating, and understanding sex addiction will probably do the same for healthy sex. Critical now is a treatment model which can allow for change without abstinence and for a health orientation.

Addiction can be understood as one way that a system adapts to change. To illustrate systemic change, Fritjof Capra uses the example of acclimatization, citing the runner who trains at sea level and then attempts to run at a high altitude. The runner finds his or her system "rigid" and stretched to its limits trying to accommodate the changes in environment. The situation is quickly reversed when returning to sea level. The accommodation made for the moment (such as panting) is quickly abandoned. Capra writes, however,

> if the environmental change persists, the organism will go through a further process of adaptation. Complex physiological changes take place among the more stable components of the system to absorb the environmental impact and restore flexibility. . . . This form of adaptation is known as somatic change. Acclimatization, habit-forming, and addiction are special cases of this process.[1]

Another type of systemic change is achieved through *evolutionary* adaptation in which the change is much more difficult to reverse. Simply said, the further the ecological adaptation of the organism, the more difficult it is to reverse the adaptation. This provides a principle about reversibility which can be used to view addiction.

In the distribution curve presented in chapter 1, the two extreme subgroups—compulsively nonsexual and compulsively sexual—have acclimatized to a point where individuals have, so to speak, lost the power to reverse their "adaptation." When left unchecked, the adaptive response that led to compulsivity and addiction becomes embedded in the system. Many times adaptive responses are necessary for survival, for example, in the case of childhood sexual abuse. However, when the adaptive response develops into part of an established addiction, only a substantial environmental shift can help stop the self-destructive behavior. Most often, this change in environment is treatment. An intervening system of which the therapist is part helps the damaged system establish a new set of responses and behaviors which brings balance—not another extreme.

An Ecological Approach to Treatment

To understand the ecology of addiction, we first need to recognize the nature of all human systems. Bunny Dahl writes:

> When we visit a house or a building and see several rooms, only the mind can connect their simultaneous existence by some sort of inner imagery. So it is with living systems in dynamic interaction. Only by some inner imagery, some image of the senses, like the hearing of an orchestra . . . can we capture the idea of living systems! Thus living human systems are like a moving hologram again, constantly shifting planes and fields, there but not there. The only comprehension we can have of living, human systems is metaphoric, analogic, organismic, synesthetic.[2]

Throughout this book the many systems involved in sexual addiction have been emphasized, including work, family, physiology, culture, and environment. These are the "many rooms" that must be visualized when making a treatment plan. This vision of the illness requires what Palazzoli has termed a *transdisciplinary* effort on the part of professionals: professionals of different disciplines working together on a common problem, sharing a common body of knowledge of the systems involved. Thus the internist who checks for infectious diseases needs to share a common overriding view of sexual addiction with the chaplain and the family therapist. In fact, if they don't share the same view, their individual prescribed treatments very likely will work against each other.

Once the transdisciplinary vision is established, the components of the intervening system need to be specified. Some addicts can recover by simply participating in a Twelve Step group—especially a strong one with committed membership and accountability. In most cases, the additional help of a therapist is needed. If the addict is seeing a therapist who understands addiction as an adaptation to the addict's environment, the addictive system is easier to interrupt and acclimitization reversed. If that therapist can include the client in a group of sexual addicts, the healing environment further expands, and when the spouse and family are included, the potential for recovery is exponentially multiplied. In severe cases, a larger system may be necessary to create change. It may include an outpatient treatment program, or in the escalation or acute phases of the addiction, an inpatient facility. Whatever the components, the therapist's task is to design a treatment environment with "many rooms."

Having established the systemic philosophy that ought to fuel the therapist's efforts, the remainder of this chapter concentrates on the intervention and treatment of the addictive system. We shall start with the addict's beliefs.

The Addict's Beliefs

The novelist John Updike has created a number of characters who have been undone through their sexuality, none more engaging than the Reverend Tom Marshfield in *A Month of Sundays*. The clergyman's sexual exploits with members of his parish create such a scandal that the bishop sends him to a "vacation" residence in the desert for errant clergy. There the Reverend Marshfield remains obsessed and at one point writes:

> Be kind to me, poor Wasp stung by the new work-ethic of sufficient sex, sex as the exterior sign of interior grace, as the last sanctuary for violence, conquest, and rapture, in a world as docilely crammed as an elevator ascending after lunchtime.[3]

Updike reveals with skill and humor how the addict struggles with sex as the primary source of meaning, nurturing, and excitement in a world perceived as meaningless, empty, and boring. The "interior grace" of the Reverend Marshfield is no different than real-life clergy who struggle with addictive sex. Addicts in the clergy are actually typical examples of sexual addicts because: (1) they are pressured to be role models and the pillars of the community, which often demands hiding their flaws at all cost; (2) by occupation they are the interpreters of meaning at our most significant life events, including life and death; and (3) they especially feel the pressure of moralistic sexual proscriptions, for example, the celibacy requirements of the Catholic clergy.

Consider the case of Fred. When Fred began to work his first step of the Twelve Step program, he was appalled at how long his life had been unmanageable. His first public scrape had occurred when he was thirteen and was discovered peering into a neighbor's window. His minister father, severely embarrassed, took many opportunities to lecture him about self-control, and there was no doubt in Fred's mind what self-control meant. As he considered his life story, he reflected that even his choice of career was in part a reaction to early sexual experiences. He had been dating another minister's daughter, also a virgin, and the two of them attempted intercourse. Their inexpert efforts resulted in much pain and blood, and Fred was horrified although they never completed intercourse. Because of his shame over having "used" the woman and because of his sexual behavior, he decided to become a minister, thinking that such a career choice would help him deal with his "demon."

In seminary, Fred started to use pornography heavily. During a cleaning of the dormitory, his collection was discovered. When confronted by the dean, Fred broke down into frustrated tears. He explained to the dean how he had used his credit cards to charge the pornography and virtually all of his meager earnings went to pay off the debt. The dean contacted the local bank and a consolidation loan was arranged to ease Fred's financial burden. Although he promised he would not use pornography again, within three months Fred had charged all his cards up to their limits for pornography one more time.

Fred's next solution to his problem was to get married. He had been dating a young woman who was very much in love with him. They had been intensely sexual for about six months, during which he found his obsession less bothersome. Later, in treatment, it became clear to him that he had decided to marry her for three reasons. One, he thought that her sexual availability would cure his problem. Two, marrying her cured his shame about being sexual since married sex was okay. And three, she had a full-time job and could help him with his debts, which she thought were from school tuition and textbooks.

Marriage was not a cure, however. Within six months Fred was having two simultaneous affairs. And after graduation, parish life for Fred was the continuation of a theme. Counseling young women was an exciting way to begin new sexual relationships until the pastor discovered his problem and turned him over to the bishop. The matter was handled as an indiscretion, and Fred was reassigned. When his relationships with members of the congregation were discovered a second time, however, the bishop sent him to a specialist in counseling clergy. That is how Fred ended up in treatment for his sexual addiction.

Intervention started with Fred's therapist doing a sexual history as part of the assessment. He talked to Fred about his concerns over the possibility that Fred was an addict, stressing that addiction was an illness and that Fred was a good person who could not stop without help. Although angry, Fred agreed to read literature from a local Twelve Step community. He steadily resisted the idea of addiction, however, until one day when he came to a session and was confronted by four important people in his life: his wife, the pastor of a church he had served in, the dean of the seminary, and the bishop. His counselor asked him to simply hear what people had to say. Carefully, each person presented pieces of the story. The dean brought up the loan consolidation and reminded Fred of how he'd hurt a student with whom he'd had an affair. The pastor talked of the repercussions of his behavior in the parish. His wife told him she knew everything and was going to leave him. And the bishop concluded that if Fred did not accept help, he would not have a position in the ministry. All these comments were made with great concern and care. Fred agreed to commit to treatment.

Intervention starts when the counselor *affirms the client as a person, using the illness concept*. The illness concept helps affirm the personal worth of the addict, and such affirmation penetrates the primitive logic of core beliefs, opening the addict to new possibilities. Furthermore, realizing that one has an illness decreases the shame of being out of control; finding out that there are other addicts undermines the basic feelings of uniqueness and isolation.

The illness concept provides a foundation for treatment. Therapists can now *provide a process for restructuring belief systems*. The elements of that process can be quite varied, but include the following treatment goals:

—allowing the addict to hear the faulty beliefs of other addicts

—breaking through the addict's myths and rules through assignments and permission-giving

—expanding the addict's options for being nurtured, handling anxiety, and developing a lifestyle congruent with personal values

—challenging the addict's family roles and rules

—providing information about healthy sexuality

—uncovering multigenerational patterns

—giving spiritual assistance

Once in the treatment program, Fred was amazed at how much he knew about the addiction from his own experience. One day in his therapy group, a fellow patient described how she had joined the Marine Corps, hoping that the discipline would help her with her sexual behavior. At first Fred felt superior because he thought he had not made major life decisions on the basis of sex. He started to confront her because he felt that she was still deluding herself. But even as he talked it struck him how he had done the same. His decisions to marry and to go to seminary had been rooted in his addictive process. When the two of them finished talking, the entire group sat in stunned silence, realizing the enormity of the addiction. They had a feeling of fellowship as they recognized the prices they had paid for their illness. They were not bad people—wounded, battered maybe—but not bad.

Fred learned the following in treatment:

—Part of his powerlessness with his illness stemmed from his own family upbringing, especially his father's messages about sexual self-control as the key to being a good person.

—His family had many patterns of compulsive and addictive behavior, including alcoholism, sex, and gambling.

—Sex was not the enemy but a badly misused source of vitality that had become the only trusted source of nurturing.

—The more honest he was about his behavior, the more he was himself and the more people accepted him.

—Through recovery, he could feel peaceful, not driven.

Most important, Fred identified the faulty core beliefs he had as an addict and their role in governing the rest of his belief system. As part of his recovery, he learned to integrate the following core beliefs:

1. I am a worthwhile person deserving of pride.
2. I am loved and accepted by people who know me as I am.

3. My needs can be met if I let people know what I need.
4. Sex is but one expression of my need and care for others.

As a member of the clergy, Fred found that his addiction had called a halt to developing an ongoing spirituality. He needed to rethink all of his theological assumptions, and maybe even his career choice. In fact, he found that his religious training at one level was a help, but at another level his current thinking was a jumbled mass of contradictive assumptions. One day he told his counselor that he was having as much trouble as another person in his group who was aggressively atheist. His counselor mentioned Luzanov's oft-quoted comment that "disbelief was simply belief with a negative sign." No matter what their backgrounds, all addicts have to struggle with the source of meaning in their lives.

The process of confronting what gives life meaning can be enhanced by the use of the first three steps of the Twelve Steps during treatment. With the first step, the addict deeply acknowledges the presence of the illness—admits that he or she has become powerless and that life has become unmanageable. Then steps two and three ask, "Whom do you trust? What do you depend upon?" The intensity of that experience is deepened by the presence of those who are facing the same questions. A special bond develops among people who experience such an ordeal together. As old core beliefs are dismantled and new feelings of self-worth and meaningfulness emerge, the impaired thinking of the addictive system becomes exposed.

Impaired Thinking

Intervening in the addictive system often requires leverage and confrontation, particularly when impaired thinking prevents the addict from acknowledging the problem. No amount of logic or personal affirmation will dent the defense system of the addict in these cases. The therapist must *confront the gross defenses and work toward acceptance of the "illness."* Addicts in the escalation or acute phases of the addiction may prove extremely difficult, even though the addict has experienced severe consequences. The interventionist must always bear in mind that the addiction is in charge, not the person.

Fred's case again serves as a good example. Fred's behavior was causing his life, his marriage, and his career to unravel. Fred seemed blind to these consequences. He needed a strong dose of reality. His therapist therefore pulled together a group of significant people who were concerned about Fred. Fred was presented with the truth as observed by people who obviously cared for him. He had to deal with the fact that he stood to lose both career and marriage. Some therapists may shudder at such harsh measures, but as many employee assistance specialists and alcoholism professionals have long known, Fred would have lost his marriage and his career anyway. The intervention was simply making the existing reality explicit. At the time, Fred thought the intervention was the worst thing that ever happened to him, but later he came to see it as the beginning of a new life.

During treatment, Fred attended a series of sessions to help him identify his own defense mechanisms, including his great denial about the impact his illness had on others. The intervention had started that process. The dean of the seminary told Fred that a student Fred had been involved with had had to get an abortion and had become deeply depressed. The pastor reminded Fred of an eighteen-year-old from the young adults church group who still believed that Fred really loved her and not his wife. When his wife started to talk about her pain at his losing yet another job because of his involvement with a woman, Fred finally gave in. Treatment was a continuation of that process.

In treatment, Fred started to gain new insights:

—He used his ministry as a way of getting trust from potential sexual partners.

—He had as many as five and six sexual partners in a week, all of whom believed his lies about how much they meant to him.

—He was outraged with his wife when she talked with other attractive men, but felt she should accept his affairs and trust him.

—What he valued the most—his ministry, his honesty, and his marriage—was compromised by his illness.

The treatment process must *develop feedback mechanisms that keep reality in focus.* The therapist and the therapy group and/or the Twelve Step group serve as a standard reality test for the addict entering recovery. Other less direct measures, such as the use of hypnosis, the re-creation of experiences, or intensive journal or autobiographical writing also support the reclaiming of reality. Whatever the feedback mechanism, two critical elements must emerge for the patient: (1) that the "insanity" of the addiction stemmed from the addict's loss of touch with what he or she was doing, and (2) that the addict often does not recognize the loss of reality—or in the words of the "Big Book" of AA, the addiction is "cunning, baffling and powerful."

Reality may be lost or obscurred in one of three ways. First, there may be instances where reality is honestly not perceived. Many addicts in treatment report a loss of memory or a loss of contact with here and now events due to a combination of factors including obsessions, overextension, exhaustion, or anxiety. Addicts in rapid escalation phases or acute phases of the addiction often display symptoms of not having been present when something significant was going on. For example, as honestly as he searched, Fred could not remember a particular series of events that had occurred at the parish where he last served.

Second, addicts misperceive or distort reality. In treatment Fred was asked to list examples of his delusional thinking, things he believed to be true when he was acting out. At the top of his list, he said that he had believed that his sexual involvement with parishioners was an extension of his ministry. He prepared elaborate rationalizations about his behavior in case he was challenged. In treatment, he reclaimed what really happened: having sex with those women had little, if anything, to do with his ministry, except that his ministry provided a convenient way to meet them and gain their trust quickly.

Another type of reality distortion comes from the addict's faulty beliefs. If the addict starts with dysfunctional beliefs (such as the belief that women have to be seduced in order to enjoy sex), the thought processes will have to be faulty as well (i.e., seduction is the only way to get needs met).

Third, addicts ignore or deny reality. They sometimes see and then ignore clearly the risks they are taking. When addicts compulsively ignore disastrous experiences and repeat them, they feel even more despair. They see what is happening, but cannot stop it. Fred saw that for him changing parishes was moving from a bad situation to one that was worse.

In order to recover, addicts have to make a commitment to face reality. No other option exists. Their capacity to delude themselves is so great, they have to commit to a process which keeps them from the old delusional patterns. In recovery, addicts recognize the ongoing need for feedback. Treatment based on a Twelve Step approach helps addicts prepare for membership in a Twelve Step group in the community. The ongoing need for feedback can be met in these groups since in them they commit to a process which:

—daily asks them to recognize their defenses and set them aside

—requires regular, quality sharing with others about what is happening in their lives so that damaging addictive secrets are not re-nurtured

—supports the quick identification of delusional thinking and the immediate admission of those errors to others

—integrates feedback loops and reality checks into a lifestyle

Preoccupation

The symbol of Trace's addiction was his van. He joked in treatment about his van as a "four wheel trance." All he had to do was step into it, and he began to obsess about women. The van's height allowed him to gaze down at women in cars next to him, checking for shorts, hiked skirts, or blouses in disarray. The windows had mirrored glass through which he could see out, but people could not see in. Trace's habit was to park the vehicle by beaches and sit in back watching and masturbating. He hoped for bikini-clad teenagers to primp in the mirrored glass, and this occasionally happened.

The beds in the rear, where Trace had affairs with married women, were the most important feature. He preferred married women because there was little likelihood of emotional entanglements, and because they would not want to be discovered either. The van became a place where these sexual liaisons could take place with little risk of discovery, unlike a hotel room or the workplace.

So, when Trace drove, his obsession took over. In treatment he needed to understand the many contexts for his preoccupation, including the important role of driving. He could even document numbers of accidents and near misses resulting from his sexual obsession. He recalled one incident in which he had been masturbating while driving and hit a young girl on a bike.

The girl was shaken up, but not injured. However, Trace would never forget that moment when he was trying to zip his pants before anyone saw him and his absolute panic about what he might have done to the girl. When he drove away after the police report was taken, he vowed that it would never happen again. When he was only two blocks away, however, a young woman pulled up next to him with her skirt mid-thigh. He was off in his obsession again.

Trace's wife Laura shared the problem of obsession in her own way. She constantly reacted to his behavior, accusing him of affairs and demanding accountability for his time. Her detective work was successful, and helped prove to Trace that he had a problem. On a hunch one day she followed him to a massage parlor, walked in and caught him. From her perspective, being right and having proof vindicated her actions.

Her therapist, however, helped her see that while her actions had created the leverage that got him into treatment, her own preoccupation took much of her waking hours. She literally had given herself away in the worry that she would be hurt. As time went on, her self-righteousness gave way to a profound realization at how much she had:

—organized her life around her distrust of him

—given up significant parts of her life to maintain vigilance

—used her obsessive behavior to avoid her own loneliness and other problems

—spent as much time and effort on sex as he had

In treatment Trace and Laura came to understand the *role preoccupation plays in addiction and co-addiction.*

Ending preoccupation presents recovering addicts with one of the greatest challenges of recovery. A helpful strategy for therapists to teach about preoccupation is the concept of the addictive personality shift. The therapist actually extends the Jekyll and Hyde experience of the addict by asking the addict to think as if he were two people—his true self and his addict. The therapist asks the client to describe what his addict is like. For example, some questions might be:

—How does your addict use thinking about sex as a way to avoid the problems in life?

—What does your addict do to start the cycle all over again?

—What does your addict do when you are successful? When you fail?

—What does your addict want to do to keep you from getting help?

—How will your addict make you distrust me as your therapist?

—What kind of feelings do you have about your addict?

—What tricks will your addict use to gain control?

With such questions, the therapist introduces the concept of the addict as an alternate ego. The client may refer to "my addict" as a way to talk about the addiction. This is not an artificial construct. Every addict knows the moment when the addict is in charge. The therapist simply provides a vehicle for the client to talk about the internal reality of addiction. The strategy accomplishes many important therapeutic objectives:

—It helps patients gain perspective on their illness while bypassing the shame.

—It allows a lot of information about the addiction to come out which is useful for patient and therapist alike.

—It supplies a concrete way to talk about an illness of powerlessness.

—It makes more objective the patient's efforts to plan for relapse prevention.

—It provides a format to acknowledge the subtlety of obsessive preoccupation.

Treatment efforts must help addicts replace preoccupation as a way to cope. Addicts have to *develop new coping strategies to deal with anxiety.* When Trace and Laura entered treatment, one of their first therapeutic tasks was to learn to recognize when the addictive and co-addictive personalities took over. For example, one of the characteristics of Trace's "addict" was to have no limits. As a social worker he was constantly overextended in efforts to save the world. In addition, as a rather high-ranking government employee, he was caught up in the drama of office politics. In fact, the never-ending crises of his work world served as a constant excuse for his "addict" to take over.

Trace said he used to feel he was like a "big tit to the world" on which clients and the government sucked. He learned that his victim stance and his chronic physical depletion made the world of the van a safe harbor where he could lose himself. His feelings of grandiosity were rooted in self-pity. Recognizing that he did not have to live that way, Trace learned that when he felt sorry for himself, his addictive personality was about to take over. A parallel feeling that he learned to distrust was his excitement at being the hero/martyr.

Feeling self-righteous was Laura's best clue to her co-addictive personality shift. She discovered how the intensity of vengeance and feeling superior obscured her own pain. An exercise that was particularly helpful in her treatment is called the tension line. Initially developed by family violence specialists, the exercise simply asked Laura and other co-addict participants in treatment to list "signals" that they knew meant they were "over the line." These signals became danger signs which demanded immediate action, such as calling a sponsor. At the top of Laura's list was when she found herself "insisting that she was right," that she could do no wrong. Her therapist was helpful in distinguishing between obsession and legitimate anger. Obsession is not being in touch with yourself but focusing instead on the faults of someone else. Legitimate anger starts with an acknowledgement of one's own part, focuses on problems and behavior, and seeks an opportunity to make things better. Obsession finds new things to remain angry about.

Her therapist and group also pushed Laura to make her list more concrete by specifying other behaviors that were other signals of being over the line, including:

—watching to see if Trace was looking at other women

—saying things in front of the children to discredit Trace

—trying to accomplish too many things in a day, resulting in such physical depletion that she was depressed, critical of everyone around her, and having extreme, desperate fantasies

—setting up "tests of fidelity" to check out Trace's commitment, love, or sexual interest

Laura was also confronted on her "reverse" preoccupation. When really desperate, she would start to obsess about her own body. This was not personal pride in looking good. This was a constant and often despairing self-appraisal about whether she was attractive or not. Laura was actually quite thin, but saw herself as very overweight. She would anguish about being "fat." When her therapist used the word "anorexic," Laura protested. But as many learn, what upsets us the most, especially in therapy, may be the most important thing we need to look at. At first, being referred to an eating disorders program came as a crushing blow to her, but with help she could see the significant connections among her obsessive preoccupations.

Laura received help in being specific about what she could do when her tension line was crossed. She could:

—call her sponsor or other people in her group who could give her perspective and distance from her preoccupation

—read from her daily meditation books

—when on the verge of angry tirades, ask herself how she is hurting

—agree to not talk about significant issues after a certain time in the evening to avoid nonproductive fights

—learn to set big issues aside and to agree on times to work on them

—insist on quality time with Trace as an ongoing connection to support conflict resolution, as opposed to using a fight as a way to be involved with Trace

—have "automatic" ways to nurture herself such as taking a long bath or reading a good novel

—give herself the gift of time for periodic regeneration

Laura needed to learn to be gentle with herself. By allowing herself the limits of being human, her preoccupation would not take over her life. In fact, she discovered some curious human paradoxes: fidelity to oneself is the best way to be faithful to others. To acknowledge personal limits generates an understanding of others' limits. To be honest with oneself allows for greater realism with others. To be loving of oneself releases new caring energy for others. To nurture oneself creates new reservoirs of support for others. And, of course, to do these things encourages others to be forgiving, realistic, honest, loving, and nurturing.

One sign of recovery from crippling obsession is a clear *awareness of personal limits*. Addiction in many ways is like the denial of death mentioned in chapter 6. In preoccupation, the addict and co-addict search for the ideal, the perfect, and the infinite. That search in itself becomes a "solution." Trace's van and Laura's anorexic behavior were ways to avoid the limits of being human. Therapy is intended to help people rediscover their human limitations.

Ritualization

As part of intervention, therapists must frequently *place injunctions on addicts' rituals*. Some may experience discomfort about taking responsibility for client behavior. When this is necessary, it helps to remember that by definition this illness renders its victims powerless. The way a recovering addict who is powerless assumes responsibility will be addressed later. But in the beginning, a nonnegotiable contract that serves as a condition to further treatment may be in the client's best interest.

To illustrate, acute phase exhibitionists who cruise the parking lots of shopping malls may be told that shopping malls are off-limits. If they need to go shopping, they must go with someone, preferably someone who knows about their illness. Because their addiction included ritualistic cruising, a shopping trip contains so many cues to initiate the addiction cycle that even entering the parking lot at an early stage of recovery may invite another episode. A valid comparison would be for a newly recovering alcoholic to go to his or her favorite bar alone. The cues that fuel the urge to drink may be overwhelming at that early stage of sobriety.

Stopping the rituals becomes one key to preventing relapse. Identifying those rituals, as we noted earlier, requires that both the therapist and the addict understand together the "scenario" of the addiction. What goes into the ritualization? How does it support the mood-alterating quality of the experience? One technique for ritual identification is guided imagery. The therapist asks the addict to relax and to share a series of fantasies about the addictive behavior. Whatever is used as part of the ritualization of the story line—clothing, dressing, undressing, cross-dressing, bathing, cars, bars, hotels, specific cities, conferences, work situations, drug use, animals, films, music, magazines, pornography—is cataloged as a potential ritual cue for the addiction.

Another strategy calls for the addict to make a complete list of all the high risk situations he or she has been in, where there is a high probability that the sexual behavior will occur—and look for the common elements. Once identified, the injunctions on the rituals must be:

—clear, unambiguous, and comprehensive (all shopping malls, not just the local one)

—nonpunitive (the client understands that the spirit of the injunction is to help, not judge)

—flexible to accommodate the inevitable complications (the emergency run to the shopping mall for medicine for a sick child)

—time limited (the client understands this injunction is temporary until sufficient involvement with a recovery program can support a return to normal behavior)

If the client fails to observe the injunction, several options are open to the therapist. The addict may be required to attend more meetings of the local Twelve Step program per week. Another option is added therapy sessions each week until a new balance is established. Or both. Inpatient programs for sexual dependency are available in some locations and so become another option. One good argument for inpatient treatment would be that a particular addict cannot stay straight on an outpatient basis, so the period of time spent at a treatment center serves as a foundation on which sobriety can be built.

Both therapist and client need to strive even at this early stage to remember the guiding principle: treatment is not the end goal. A major factor in recidivism is the client's belief that treatment will be the cure. Treatment simply launches recovery. Similarly, the therapist needs to remember his or her own limited role: to *create life-enhancing rituals* to replace destructive addictive rituals. One of the shortest paths to a proven set of healthy rituals is the Twelve Step program and group. Therapy then amplifies a Twelve Step process that the person will practice for life. The Twelve Step community will exist long after therapy is over. Therapy works on two levels: it takes patients through a process, and it also prepares them for a process.

The ecological approach to addiction becomes useful here. Therapists actually help clients prepare for participation in a new culture. Thus, therapists need to understand the Twelve Step culture since that community will have the greatest long-term impact on the addict's recovery, not a therapist's professional skills. If the reader has little experience with the Twelve Steps, reading the "Big Book" would be a good way to start. In addition, the references in this book, especially the work of Ernest Kurtz, provide an excellent introduction.

The internal structure of the Twelve Steps themselves becomes significant as we understand how new rituals are acquired in this program. Three tasks are accomplished within the steps: intervention, recovery, and systems maintenance. Also, each contributes healthy rituals to strengthen a recovery program.

Intervention

The first five of the Twelve Steps (see figs. 7-1 and 7-2) focus on stopping self-destructive behaviors and returning to a balanced life. These steps work toward arresting the growth of the addictive system and neutralizing its impact. The new member learns about participating in the group's rituals. Usually a sponsor works with the newcomer, talking about how the program has worked in his or her life. A "straight date" is established to mark the beginning of sexual sobriety. As early as a month after beginning, recovering persons start to receive symbols of their progress. Medallions, meditation books, or special gifts celebrate their achievement. They also learn about the twelve traditions which govern the group process.

Recovery

Steps six through nine initiate a rebuilding process using a systematic review of self (defects of character) and relationships (restoration through amends). This proactive phase of the Twelve Steps establishes personal responsibility patterns through self-inventories and structured efforts to renew significant relationships damaged by the addictive process. The member may choose to incorporate daily readings and meditations on program principles, as well as record days, weeks, and months of sexual sobriety as evidence of progress and commitment.

Systems Maintenance

Principles to help a system renew itself exist in all systems. Just as the addictive system has its recursive loops, so does the Twelve Step program. Steps ten, eleven, and twelve convert the program into an ongoing process. The tenth step asks for a daily effort which routinely cycles all the step work, thus deepening and intensifying the learning experience. Some professionals have heard a veteran AA member give a meditation on one specific word from one of the steps, such as the word "admitted" or "ready." After years of participation in the program, a member may find that one word can evoke or recall the richness of the group experience.

The program asks veteran members to become sponsors to others and to reach out to new members. They participate in the transmission of rituals and become witnesses themselves to other addicts' progress. This process reminds the recovering addict what life used to be like and why the program is important.

Professionals may ask, "How long does an addict have to belong to a Twelve Step group?" As in all addictions, the possibility of relapse remains as long as the recovering person lives, and as noted earlier, this illness is a particularly strong, embedded system. The ecology of the addiction requires us to remember the adaptational premise of systems in change. The more somatic the change (toward evolutionary change), the less reversible it becomes. Addiction exists within a band of change in which the behavior can be stopped but the system maintains for every addict; the Twelve Step program with all of its rituals stands in between the addict and the old behavior (fig. 9-1).[4]

Remembering that relapse is always a possibility is key to relapse prevention. Therapists fail in their mission if they see treatment as the end goal as opposed to an introduction to a process with all of its attendant healing rituals. The question then emerges, "How can therapists help with the Twelve Step process?" First, they can encourage the addict to work the Twelve Steps. Also, therapists can accelerate the healing process by assisting the family as a unit to support the impact of the individual's step work, as well as introduce new rituals which:

—nurture oneself

—involve having fun and leisure

—center around family life

—enhance committed relationships

A veteran of a Twelve Step program asked, "If addicts are powerless, what are they responsible for?" Probably the response is: "To work the program." Participating fully in the program is what the addict can do to prevent relapse. A sure sign of recovery is when the recovering person *perceives the ongoing rituals as a symbol of new life.*

The Twelve Steps and Recovery

Systemic Tasks	Steps	Rituals
Intervention: Stopping self-destructive behavior and return to balance. (reactive)	1. We admitted we were powerless over our sexual addiction—that our lives had become unmanageable. 2. Came to believe that a Power greater than ourselves could restore us to sanity. 3. Made a decision to turn our will and our lives over to the care of God as we understood Him. 4. Made a searching and fearless moral inventory of ourselves.	• participation in group rituals • sponsor initiates member into program tasks, rules and procedures • "straight date" established • early symbols of progress • participation in Twelve "traditions"
Recovery: Rebuilding process using systematic review of self and relationships. (proactive)	5. Admitted to God, to ourselves, and to another human being the exact nature of our wrongs. 6. Were entirely ready to have God remove all these defects of character. 7. Humbly asked Him to remove our shortcomings. 8. Made a list of all persons we had harmed, and became willing to make amends to them all. 9. Made direct amends to such people wherever possible, except when to do so would injure them or others.	• annualized events mark program commitment • self responsibility patterns established through program "inventories" • structured efforts to renew relationships • daily readings and meditations and program principles
Systems Maintenance: Nourishing growth of Twelve step process. (integrative)	10. Continued to take personal inventory and when we were wrong promptly admitted it. 11. Sought through prayer and meditation to improve our conscious contact with God as we understood Him, praying only for knowledge of His will for us and the power to carry that out. 12. Having had a spiritual awakening as a result of these steps, we tried to carry the message to others and to practice these principles in all our affairs.	• recycling of all step work to deepen and renew learning • becomes sponsor to others • reaches out to new members

Figure 9-1

Sexual Behavior

Therapists need to set specific limits on the sexual behavior of their addict clients. A working definition of abstinence needs to be in place while the addict initiates the recovery process in which he or she will determine what sobriety means. For example, if the client has six ongoing "serious" sexual relationships, the therapist might recommend that all sexual behavior with these partners cease until the client can sort out his/her feelings. At the least, the casual partners need to be dropped and some decisions made about what can be salvaged from the other relationships. Often the clearest path to recovery is simply to suspend all sexual relationships. But if a committed relationship is involved, then that partner needs to be informed and also involved in therapy because sooner or later he or she must deal with the illness. There can be mitigating circumstances about informing significant others, and that is a subjective therapeutic decision. The point remains that for recovery to begin the therapist often has to *set contractual limits with clients.*

An important treatment strategy that may come out of this initial contractual understanding is the celibacy contract. The therapist asks the client to commit to a period of celibacy, usually twelve weeks long. This is not an unusual practice. For years sexologists have helped people with sexual dysfunction by introducing periods of desensitization as a way of initiating new sexual behavior. Like fasting, it can be a cleansing experience. In that sense, the celibacy contract becomes a trial or "ordeal" by which the client becomes transformed. Jay Haley's recent book *Ordeal Therapy* argues effectively that the ordeal represents more than a therapeutic strategy. In effect, it may be the "real cause of change in all of contemporary therapy."[5]

For the sex addict, celibacy has specific benefits. First, the contract makes explicit the power of the destructive addictive pattern. For someone who has used sex to avoid suffering for most of a lifetime, life without it is terrifying. Addicts learn, however, that they can survive without sex and with the help of others. Alone they are powerless; with support there is a new life. During the painful period of withdrawal, support is indispensable.

Therapy gives the addict a chance to learn functional ways to cope. Celibacy (including no sex with spouse and no masturbation) means that addicts are no longer able to use sex to deal with difficult feelings. They are then fully open to the therapeutic process because the pain is not deadened and the addict has to rely on new methods to survive. Also, celibacy accelerates learning in treatment in many of the paradoxical ways that all ordeals do. For years the addict has struggled to be in control. With the help of others who admit they are powerless, the addict finds that the addiction's power diminishes.

Celibacy also facilitates and/or develops awareness. Early memories become more accessible. Blocked memories of sexual experiences return (another of celibacy's ironies). Celibacy generates a great deal of insight which affects internal beliefs and impaired thinking. Therapists may prescribe intense journal writing or autobiography work to help clients develop consciousness of their addiction. Consider the following extracts from the writing of three recovering women:

> Sally:
>
> Celibacy was one tool I've used to make clear which relationships were potentially ok and which were not—instead of finding out by getting "horizontal"! Early on in the program, celibacy had an additional benefit for me: It cleared out some of the unmanageability with which I came into the program. It also gave me a chance to break the habit of self-destructive sexual behavior long enough to feel what I needed to feel and change what I needed to change in my life.

This period of celibacy, a cooling off period in every sense of the word, helped reassure myself that I could relate to men I dated by getting to know them (new idea!) and be appreciated (or not) for who I am; I could also judge men in the same way. A bonus during my celibacy period was the discovery that magically I was no longer drawing the same kind of man.

Joyce:

When entering the program, I chose to be celibate for a time because I'd been acting out by being sexual indiscriminately and putting my life in danger. I then became aware of the extent to which I gave men ambiguous messages about my sexual intentions. I needed to stop flirting in order to be safe and communicate clearly.

Rene:

My search for abstinence began with my identification of the immediate, life-threatening actions I was doing when I came into the program. I was pursuing partners who were violent. I was being sexual with my pets. I was involved in sexual acts against myself. These included cutting, burning, whipping and violently masturbating. As I began to see what I was doing to myself, I realized that I was also isolating myself from other people. Getting a sponsor in S.A.A. and going to meetings helped me break through my isolation.

I also had to get the objects I was using to hurt myself out of my home. For a time, I had to practice total celibacy. I abstained from dating, masturbation, isolation, and going to places where I had gone to find partners. When I went out socially, I talked with women in the program and went with people with whom I felt safe. At the time I had no boundaries around other people, my perspective was limited, and I had no sense of my own values. I needed to question every motive and action. I began to learn that violence and gentleness are incompatible and to practice being gentle with myself.[6]

A recovering person faces two central tasks during the celibacy phase. First, the addict must develop a network of relationships which do not have the sexual component as core. Married addicts will have the additional task of clarifying sex behavior within their relationship. Celibacy aids that process and provides a concrete basis for the honesty necessary to be clear to themselves and vulnerable about their needs with others. The period of celibacy can be an intensely spiritual time which adds meaning to the building of relationships. The spirituality stems from the concrete expression of self-limitation. Historically, celibacy has been observed as an adulthood ritual to foster spirituality and community and to mark significant change.[7] So celibacy is an especially appropriate context for the relationship tasks facing addicts at the beginning of recovery.

With celibacy as the context, therapists can work toward the other main task which is to help establish sobriety. As in eating disorders, the task for the client is to learn how to eat differently. As opposed to using sex as a solution or as medicine, sex becomes a way to celebrate relationship and life. Celibacy should not be like a diet which only becomes a period of deprivation and which achieves no significant change in the obsession. Treatment must not create sexual teetotalers who are ever restless with their sexuality. Celibacy becomes a way to renew their healthy sexuality. Professionals can assist that process by:

—helping deal with questions of normalcy

—pinpointing self-destructive escalators of sexual excitement

—teaching about sexual intimacy

—supplying good sex information

—working toward new sexual imagery

—underlining the differences between degrading and enriching sex

Out of celibacy emerges a rebirthing process. Addicts whose recovery spans many years describe three phases, or plateaus, in recovery. The first year or two, addicts need to focus on stopping the progress of the addictive system. To borrow from the world of AA, the old phrase "nothing major for the first year" appears to apply to sex addicts as well. This means that major life decisions such as divorce, new jobs, or any significant undertakings that would jeopardize the solid establishment of recovery should be postponed.

In the initial excitement of getting relief from the clutches of the addiction, addicts often impulsively attempt to reorganize everything. However, this is really a time to slow down, establish new patterns, and let the new process work. Six weeks in recovery does not mean that now is the time to enter medical school, decide on whether the marriage is workable, or pursue a career in sexual addiction counseling. Sexual addiction is a serious illness, and while the initial relief may seem like a rejuvenation, "Easy does it" and "One day at a time" are good rules to follow.

Similarly, the client needs to understand that stopping the compulsive behavior does not signify a total transformation in his/her sexuality. Trust of self and others develops only over time; the process may take years. However, after a period of time in treatment, some addicts go through something like a new adolescence and appear to re-emerge with a new sexual identity. They may sense a new innocence and experience themselves in ways they never have before.

This emerging identity re-focuses the sexual experience. Nonaddictive sex becomes enriching. Consider this statement from Chris:

> Before my recovery women used to be unreal. My obsession and fantasy allowed only perfection. Any flaw detracted from the experience. Also I used sex as a way to deal with frustration in life. Some people played sports for relief. I screwed. Now it does not have to be perfect, and it isn't a way to get through. My wife, for example,

has a scar which I cherish because she earned it giving birth to our child. I play with her because of who we are together.

The rediscovery of healthy, nonaddictive sex is absolutely essential for the recovering person. With the hospital-based treatment programs, special resources, and with more and more sexual addicts achieving years of recovery, professionals now have an opportunity to study how and why some people have been able to reclaim their nonaddictive sexual selves more successfully than others. That knowledge can be gathered and translated into clinical practice.

Those who help addicts with a celibacy contract also need to consider the co-addict's role, first telling him or her about the contract and its purpose. The co-addict predictably becomes intensely sexually attracted to the addict who becomes celibate, and so needs to know at the outset that to seduce the addict would be self-defeating and a source of despair.

Co-addicts need to accept the celibacy period for the sake of their own recoveries because they also embark on a pilgrimage seeking their own sexual identity. In the shadow of the addict's sexual obsession, the co-addict may have neglected his/her own sexual issues. Honestly facing one's own sexuality becomes the co-addict's major task. As the addict and co-addict each proceed to establish a new sexual identity, their relationship will be tested. Very likely their recovery will grow at different rates as they advance in therapy, which means the relationship may be severely tested. At this point, professional help may be the only way to heal past scars and bridge the discrepancies the couple discover in their relationship.

The challenge of integrating the needs of both addict and co-addict, in fact, may be a significant deficit in Twelve Step programs, especially in the program for sexual addiction which concentrates on individual recovery with no emphasis on the recovery of the relationship. Of course, the effort needed to arrest the addiction is largely individual, but once that groundwork is laid, a couple finds themselves facing one another with no structure to assist in reintegrating the immense changes that have occurred in each of them. In other words, at this time there is no formalized Twelve Step process for couples to work together. In the future, Twelve Step communities may create a specialized support group to help with the relationships of recovering people.

Initiation to the Twelve Step community must come immediately after intervention. As soon as the illness is acknowledged, the professional must *connect the client and family members with Twelve Step sponsors. The reason is despair.*

Addicts struggle to keep the "high" going in their lives because to stop brings overwhelming despair and pain. So when they do stop and experience the vulnerability of others knowing the truth about them, they need an immediate safety net. In the Twelve Step group, they have the immediate support of others who have experienced the same thing. Addiction initiates and deepens shame—the basis for despair—and there is no hope for people who in their isolation are convinced of their own unworthiness. Gershen Kaufman describes the recovery process in a shame based illness:

> Internalized shame needs to be returned to its interpersonal origins. The self that feels irreparably and unspeakably defective needs to feel restored with the rest of humanity. The self that feels alienated, defeated, lacking in dignity or worth needs to feel whole, worthwhile and valued from within.[8]

A partnership between professional and Twelve Step community can help with that.

As noted above, the partnership needs to be immediate. Revealing the addiction and breaking the isolation and secrecy is a profound relief. For some addicts, however, the shame is so great that they face the ultimate break in the interpersonal bridge: suicide. The sense of vulnerability becomes so great, and the hopelessness becomes so overwhelming that suicide seems the only option. Many Twelve Step groups have learned that even sharing a first step in an established community where the addict feels truly cared for can lead to real despair, so a professional therapist can be a vital safety net.

The partnership further assists addicts in laying the foundations of recovery. And the biggest obstacle to that recovery will continue to be the despair. Remembering that the self-perpetuating momentum of the addiction stems from addict's efforts to stave off the pain of the despair, recovery will always be in jeopardy. "Slips" are always possible. The professional/self-help partnership needs to *establish a relapse prevention plan*.

Slips

Addicts have slips for many reasons, some of which may be found in limitations of the Twelve Step communities themselves. For instance, some groups do not have members with many years of recovery to serve as models for new members. One way to compensate for this would be for new groups to make contacts with established groups in other cities on a continuous basis until the stability of a new group is achieved. Also, professionals can encourage this contact with the other Twelve Step communities and national service offices.

Another factor is that the recovering addict simply may not be "working the program." In that case, it is appropriate for a professional person to ask clients how they are using the group:

—Are they attending meetings regularly?

—Do they have a sponsor and, more importantly, are they working intensively with the sponsor to learn about the program?

—Are they reading program literature and finding more information about their illness?

—Are they doing the daily readings and meditations on program principles?

—Are they actively working on a step?

—If in a committed relationship, is the partner in a Twelve Step co-addict group?

Defining Sobriety

Another major problem area for recovering people is the difficulty in establishing an adequate definition of sobriety. If neither the group nor the professionals involved have carefully and systematically helped the addict to think through and create a personal definition of sobriety, then relapse is almost inevitable. An example of the most common source of slips in this category is continuing the behaviors that are part of the addictive cycle, but for some reason are not included in the sobriety definition. These behaviors then become cues for repeating behaviors that are in the excluded list.

A major factor in recidivism has been that the addict simply hasn't had enough support. In the early days of AA, slips were fairly common. Hospital-based programs using the Twelve Step program originated in response to the addict's need for additional support in the early stages of recovery. Outpatient and inpatient therapeutic communities offer a level of support not possible in the self-help communities themselves, in addition to the medical factors which need attention.

The health agency's responsibility does not end with the discharge plan. Professionals need to construct a way to continue to monitor and support the recovery. The nature of sexual addiction is such that professional skills and knowledge may be needed even more after recovery has begun. Assisting a couple with their new, nonaddictive sexual relationship is one example, or assisting the addict when the hospital-based program assigns tasks as part of its follow-up program. Similarly, continuity must exist in the Twelve Step group. Even the most veteran member needs to be working on a continuing basis. The process does not stop.

That brings us to a fundamental task with which professionals can assist addicts: the *establishment of a relapse prevention plan.* Failure to do so is tantamount to a slip.

Two steps precede plan development. First, addicts need to understand the consequences of a slip. A strategy which helps is to ask the addict to prepare a "Consequences Analysis."[9] Although addicts need a clear image of the positive aspects—both immediate and long-term—of maintaining changes in their sexual behavior, they also need to picture the immediate and long-term negative consequences of a slip. Completing a form as simple as the format below would help:

	Immediate	Long-term
Positive Consequences of Recovery		
Negative Consequences of a Slip		

After completing the analysis, addicts can be asked to write letters to themselves to hold in reserve for reading when they are struggling in their recovery. They can also write certain sentences and phrases from the letter on a 3″ × 5″ card to keep in a wallet or purse for what we will call "last ditch" strategies.

These activities involve a process that builds on what professionals have learned about imaging and the psychology of expectations. There is a whole body of literature documenting how a person's belief about what is possible affects what he or she is actually able to do. Teacher education, management, stress reduction, and even sports medicine routinely integrate imaging as an ingredient to achievement. Similarly, with the help of professionals and veteran program members, addicts will be able to develop a vision of what a recovery can be. The consequences analysis is the first step toward that end.

In the second task preceding the prevention plan, addicts thoroughly review their own addictive system, with special attention to their addictive cycle. A pattern of behavior, thoughts, and feelings is common to the addiction but unique for each addict. Within that exhaustive inventory the addict must pinpoint:

—specific stressors likely to lead to acting out

—high risk environments

—entitlement scenarios in which the addict would feel deserving (entitled) to act out

—previous efforts to stop which may or may not have been successful

—cycles and seasons which are predictable

—delusional thought patterns which have supported acting out

With this knowledge as a base, the addict can proceed with a prevention plan.

The Prevention Plan

A prevention plan prepares the addict for what must be done before a slip (i.e., to prevent one), during a slip, and after a slip has occurred. Preparing for all three maximizes the chances for a successful recovery. Of course, the primary orientation of the plan is to prevent a slip, which requires anticipating all the slip-inducing possibilities and rehearsing for them. In place then should be a series of action steps which serve as escape routes, so that when a potentially seductive situation occurs, the addict can go on automatic pilot, as has been rehearsed. The process for the addict is to:

1. identify concrete "signs" that a slip is possible based on the consequences analysis and the addicts' knowledge of patterns in their addictive system (e.g., overload at work often precedes acting out)
2. specify immediate behavioral action steps that will prevent a slip (e.g., call sponsor or group member or therapist)
3. practice regularly as in a "fire drill" those action steps (e.g., regular phone contact with sponsor and group members)

The action steps in number 2 should be staged to match each phase of the addictive system and the addictive cycle. In other words, as the patterned sequence of events unfolds, a plan should exist at each phase, including last ditch strategies such as pulling the $3'' \times 5''$ cue card out of the wallet.

A number of support strategies can be integrated into the basic prevention plan. For example, some people have found it helpful to establish a secondary sobriety to support the recovery. The addict selects a behavior that is related but not essential to the recovery. If drinking too much coffee is related to overextension at work, then the addict may choose to give up the coffee as a symbol of commitment to recovery. What addicts discover is that if they suddenly find themselves abandoning their secondary sobriety, it is a certain sign that sexual sobriety may be in jeopardy as well.

Some professionals may respond that giving up something else would mean too much deprivation for the addict. Paradoxically, what happens is that it helps dilute the obsession and enhances feelings of success about how life is changing. Professionals must caution addicts, however, against selecting something that might create an overload. The goal is to have a symbol which is a sacrifice, but not a burden. Also, the secondary sobriety could have a time limit, for example, for the duration of the celibacy contract. The secondary sobriety can always be invoked when times are difficult and addicts need to reaffirm their commitment to the recovery.

Every prevention plan must nurture the addicts. Rewards need to be built in; the goal is to avoid feeling deprived. A survey of the many ways addicts have not been good to themselves because of the addiction needs to be made. Specific, concrete behavioral steps to self-nurturing must be part of the action plan, including hobbies, leisure, and family. Being good to one's body is of primary importance, and professionals who do not integrate a physical fitness program into the recovery plan neglect a force for healing. Physical exercise can do more for coping with anxiety than many of our best therapeutic strategies. Part of overcoming the inertia of the addictive system is a proactive physical program.

In part, prevention is an attitude. In high school and college, when you get in good physical shape and participate in athletics, you are said to be "in training." Training, a discipline one observes in preparation for the stress of competition, is a lifestyle really geared to excellence. The recovering person can also anticipate being under stressful challenge. The recovery plan is simply an outline of the training program that needs to be observed for success.

Even with the best of preparation, setbacks can occur, so these must also be planned for. The prevention plan anticipates what should happen if the addict starts to slip, on the premise that to start a slip does not mean you have to finish. So preparation involves the addict identifying all the choice points during the slip with appropriate action steps for stopping.

Similarly, the professional can help plan the steps to be taken if a slip occurs. The goal is to not give permission for a slip, but to underline the costs of a major setback and how to contain the damage. The risk is that when addicts slip, they can return to their most destructive, repetitive pattern within a matter of days. It helps to understand the pattern as a spiral which can work for addicts in one way (recovery) and destroy them in another (addiction). If the despair over a slip seizes the addict, isolation and secrecy will bring the addict down. If, however, the addict has a post-slip plan, being honest and seeking help can prevent further loss.

The addict needs to tell others about the plan. Sharing it with sponsors, group members, friends, and significant others gathers support for the recovery and involves them in the preparation process. A sure sign of recovery is that the addict *no longer has a secret life*. The Jekyll and Hyde existence is set aside—not left behind, for it will always be there, but set aside. And with that there is hope, not despair.

Unmanageability

As noted earlier, when Gollum, the mythical Tolkien figure, placed the magic ring on his finger, he became invisible except for his shadow. Since only the shadow of sexual addiction is visible, unmanageability becomes singularly important in treatment. In their impaired thinking, addicts believe they can do things others cannot, and that no one will notice. This does not mean they are psychopathic, rather to use Becker's title for their illness—they deny their death in denying their own limits. And one of the first places that the lack of limitation shows is in the unmanageability of life.

The therapist can start intervention into the addictive system by using evidence of *unmanageability as leverage to get the addict to seek help*. There is an old AA adage about being "sick and tired of being sick and tired." The same applies for many sex addicts. For some it is dramatic, such as the addict who first discovered he had AIDS and then discovered he had given his wife the same illness. For them, the recovery program is a spiritual path to dealing with the tragic impact of the addiction. For other addicts, the consequences of addiction show up as chronic, gnawing problems that aren't apparent to others, as in the case of a brilliant career woman who had thirty urinary tract infections in five years. It is this evidence of unmanageability the therapist uses to show addicts they need help.

Keeping life manageable and in balance continues to be an arena for recovery. When addicts first start a recovery program, they find so much relief that they feel a rush of excitement about life starting over. This enthusiasm often results in attempting plans not sustainable in an early recovery. However, to the degree that is possible addicts need to keep their lives simple. To addicts who have been careening out of control this may seem an insulting statement about their ability to handle life. Simplicity may even be boring by contrast. To embrace a simple life becomes, however, the learning ground in which addicts—as well as co-addicts—come to terms with limits—human limits. And in this, their therapists can help by *developing a recovery plan to support manageability*.

Alcoholism research shows us some important parallels. In an outstanding synthesis of recent research on alcoholism treatment evaluation, two leaders in systems research, Rudolf Moos and John Finney, pinpoint many of the key factors in recidivism for alcoholics. Their summary underlines work, family, and stressful life events as major factors in relapse. For example, in one study they report:

> The extra treatment factors accounted for an increment of between 7% and 27% of the variance in treatment outcome (depending on the specific criterion), compared with between 4% and 20% accounted for by patient-related and treatment-related factors. In short, the inclusion of extra treatment factors in the model more than

> doubled the explained variance in treatment outcome. These findings suggest that alcoholism treatment may be more effective when oriented toward patient's ongoing life circumstances.[10]

Since at this point we do not have a rich literature of outcome studies in sexual addiction to draw upon, we can only infer from parallel illnesses that the same factors would prevail. If so, therapists can help in the recovery plan by:

—minimizing major life changes that would add stress to the addict's life

—developing a financial plan to support recovery

—supporting work goals that would enhance recovery

—specifying appropriate boundaries, goals, and rules for the first year of recovery

—mobilizing family support for minimum change

Minimizing other changes in an addict's life does not mean that nothing is happening. The addict is going through massive change in arresting the addiction, and to add even more to the risk of a relapse. Scott Peck, in *The Road Less Traveled*, discusses this striving for simplicity during periods of great change as "bracketing." In short, bracketing is putting part of your life in parentheses, so as not to distract from the "sentence" or period of focus you are in. He writes:

> Bracketing is essentially the act of balancing the need for stability and assertion of the self with the need for new knowledge and greater understanding by temporarily giving up one's self—putting one's self aside, so to speak—so as to make room for the incorporation of new material into the self.[11]

Rather than setting off on great new adventures which may jeopardize sobriety, the addict learns from simplicity and from approaching life a day at a time.

In effect, a sign of recovery is when *manageability reflects acceptance of self and others.* Addicts and co-addicts in recovery learn that many things are unplanned and beyond their control and that these will always happen. By focusing on simplicity, a new order and peace emerge. People who have been in recovery a long time talk easily of the real differences in their lives.

Chris, for example, has been in a recovery program for eight years. He remembers the years when simply getting into a car meant that he might act out. He felt in constant jeopardy because of the unmanageability of his acting out. He did everything including shock therapy to stop, but with no success. When he did start his recovery, the first two years were extremely difficult because every street corner, every alley, and every campus where young women walked would tempt him. He cannot remember when those urges subsided, but they did. Now the most he feels is an occasional twinge—just enough to let him know his illness is still there. Yet he rarely thinks about it. The feeling he has about his recovery is literally a joy and an affirmation that he is on the right track.

For people like Chris, recovery and manageability are symbols of self-acceptance. The primitive logic of the addictive core beliefs relied on unmanageability for confirmation. However, recovery becomes validated by a lifestyle that starts with recognizing personal limits. Addicts come to know acceptance.

Through recovery, addicts come to know acceptance. In many ways, that is what this whole book has been about—the addicts' need for acceptance by themselves and by others. Paul Tillich's words, while meant for all of us, especially apply to addicts and their co-addicts:

> It strikes us when we feel that our separation is deeper than usual because we have violated another life, a life which we loved or from which we were estranged. It strikes us when year after year, the longed for perfection

of life does not appear, when the old compulsions reign within us as they have for decades, when despair destroys all joy and courage. Sometimes at that moment a wave of light breaks through our darkness, and it is as though a voice were saying "You are accepted!"[12]

Those of us who help start by voicing our acceptance.

Summary of Treatment Processes

	ASSESSMENT	INTERVENTION
BELIEF SYSTEM	Determine catalytic events and catalytic environments.	Affirm person using illness concept.
IMPAIRED THINKING	Elicit rationalizations and distortions of reality.	Confront gross defenses and work towards acceptance of "illness."
PREOCCUPATION	Determine priority obsession modes.	Teach role preoccupation plays in addiction and co-addiction.
RITUALS	Identify specific rituals.	Place injunctions on rituals.
BEHAVIOR	Determine extent of pattern of sexual behavior.	Set contractual limits.
DESPAIR	Check for life-threatening depression.	Connect client and family members with Twelve Step sponsors.
UNMANAGEABILITY	Search for evidence of "out of control" behavior.	Use unmanageability as leverage to commit to help.

Figure 9-2

Summary of Treatment Processes (cont.)

TWELVE STEPS	TREATMENT	RECOVERY
Challenge core beliefs and restore with new ones.	Provide process for restructuring belief systems.	Integrates new core beliefs.
Confront impaired thinking.	Develop feedback mechanisms to keep reality in focus.	Recognizes ongoing need for feedback.
Support grieving of loss of "pathological" relationship.	Develop new coping strategies to deal with anxiety.	Has awareness of personal limits.
Supply new rituals through sponsors, meetings and readings.	Create life enhancing rituals.	Perceives new rituals as passage to new phase of life.
Provide new coping behaviors.	Assist in establishing sobriety.	No longer sees sex as the enemy.
Restore healthy shame and guilt.	Establish relapse prevention strategies.	Has no secret life.
Initiate second order change to disrupt system.	Develop recovery plan to support manageability.	Manageability reflects acceptance of self and need for others.

Figure 9-2 (cont.)

Chapter Notes

Chapter 1 Sexual Addiction: An Overview

1. Patrick Carnes, Ph.D., *Out of the Shadows : Understanding Sexual Addiction* (Minneapolis: CompCare Publishers, 1983), 4.

2. John Cheever, *Oh What A Paradise It Seems* (New York: Ballantine Books, 1982), 18.

3. See Patrick J. Carnes, Ph.D., "Progress in Sexual Addiction: An Addiction Perspective," *SIECUS Report,* 14, no. 6 (July 1986): 4-6. See also, in the same issue, Eli Coleman, Ph.D., "Sexual Compulsion vs. Sexual Addiction: The Debate Continues," 7-10.

Chapter 2 Sexual Addiction: Obstacles to Understanding

1. Howard A. Liddle, "On the Problems of Eclecticism: A Call for Epistemologic Clarification and Human-Scale Theories," *Family Process,* 21 (1982): 243-250, p. 250.

2. John Bancroft, "Hormones and Sexual Behavior," *Psychological Medicine,* 7 (1977): 553-556, p. 555. Also H.R. Johnson, et al., "Effects of Testosterone on Body Image and Behavior in Klinefelter's Syndrome: A Pilot Study," *Developmental Medicine and Child Neurology*, 12 (1970): 454-460; Alan Cooper, "A Placebo-Controlled Trial of the Antiandrogen Cyproterone Acetate in Deviant Hypersexuality," *Comprehensive Psychiatry,* 22 (1981): 458-465; Thomas Frawley, "Physical and Psychological Sexual Effects of Hyperadrenocorticalism," *Medical Aspects of Human Sexuality*, 7 (1973): 38-57; R.B. Greenblatt, et al., "Endocrinology of Sexual Behavior," *Medical Aspects of Human Sexuality*, 6 (1972): 110-131; R. Rada, R. Kellner, and W. Winslow, "Plasma Testosterone and Aggressive Behavior," *Psychosomatics*, 17 (1976): 138-142; R. Rada, ed., *Clinical Aspects of the Rapist* (New York: Grune and Stratton, 1978).

3. George Barnard, C. Holzer, H. Vera, "A Comparison of Alcoholics and Non-Alcoholics Charged With Rape," *Bulletin of the American Academy of Psychiatric Law*, 8: 432-439. A good summary of alcohol research by offender category is in Timothy J.

Farrell, et al., *Alcohol and Sexuality: An Annotated Bibliography on Alcohol Use. Alcoholism, and Human Sexual Behavior* (Phoenix, AZ: The Oryx Press, 1983).

4. Richard Solomon, "The Opponent-Process Theory of Acquired Motivation: The Costs of Pleasure and the Benefits of Pain," *American Psychologist*, 35: 691-712. Solomon is not alone in speculating about a physiological base for addiction. For example, some researchers point to the body's stress reaction as a metabolic basis for a "high." For a good summary of this position, including interviews, see Richard Lyons, "Stress Addiction," *New York Times*, 26 July, 1982, p. C-1.

5. H. Milkman, S.E. Weiner, and S. Sunderwirth, "Addiction Relapse," *Advances in Alcohol and Substance Abuse*, 3 (1-2) (Fall-Winter 1983): 119-134.

6. C. David Blair and Richard Lanyon, "Exhibitionism: Etiology and Treatment," *Psychological Bulletin*, 89 (1981): 439-463.

7. Arthur Smukler and Douglas Scheibel, "Personality Characteristics of Exhibitionists," *Diseases of the Nervous System*, 36 (1975): 600-603, p. 602. Other examples of psychometric efforts to categorize sex offenders are: James Armentrout and Allen Hauer, "MMPI's of Rapists of Adults, Rapists of Children, and Non-Rapist Sex Offenders," *Journal of Clinical Psychology*, 34 (1978): 330-332; Fritz Henn, Marijan Herjanic, and Robert Vandepearl, "Forensic Psychiatry: Profiles of Two Types of Sex Offenders," *American Journal of Psychiatry*, 133 (1976): 694-696. For an excellent annotated source see: Joan Scherer Brewer and Rod Wright, *Sex Research: Bibliographies from the Institute for Sex Research* (Phoenix, AZ: The Oryx Press, 1983).

8. See Robert Spitzer, et al., *DSM-III (Diagnostic and Statistical Manual of Mental Disorders) Case Book* (Washington, D.C.: The American Psychiatric Association, 1981).

9. Jim Orford, "Hypersexuality: Implications for a Theory of Dependence," *British Journal of Addiction,* 73: 299-310, p. 308.

10. William Miller, *The Addictive Behaviors* (Elmsford, New York: Pergamon Press, 1980), 3.

11. For a discussion of culture and sex behavior see Marvin Opler, "Sex Mores and Social Conceptions of Deviance," in H. Resnik and M. Wolfgang, eds., *Sexual Behaviors: Social, Clinical, and Legal Aspects* (Boston: Little Brown and Co., 1972).

12. From the introduction of J. Paul de River, *The Sexual Criminal* (Springfield, Illinois: Charles Thomas, 1950), p. xiii.

13. Phillipe Aries, *The Hour of Our Death* (New York: Alfred A. Knopf, 1981), 405-406.

14. Peter Gay, *The Bourgeois Experience: Victoria to Freud* (New York: Oxford University Press, 1984), vol. 1, Education of the Senses.

15. Kate Millet, *Sexual Politics* (Garden City, NY: Doubleday, 1970). Susan Brownmiller, *Against Our Will: Men, Women, and Rape* (New York: Simon and Schuster, 1975).

16. Helen Block Lewis, *Psychic War in Men and Women* (New York: New York University Press, 1976).

17. Richard Michael and Doris Zumpe, "Sexual Violence in the United States and the Role of Season," *American Journal of Psychiatry*, 140: 883-886. See also S. Brodsky, "Sexual Assault: Perspectives on Prevention and Assailants," in M. Walker and S. Brodsky, eds., *Sexual Assault: The Victim and the Rapist* (Lexington: Lexington Press, 1976).

18. Thomas Jackson and William Ferguson, "Attribution of Blame in Incest," *American Journal of Community Psychology*, 11: 313-322.

19. Peter Steinglass, "Experimenting with Family Treatment Approaches to Alcoholism, 1950-1975: A Review," *Family Process*, 15: 97-123, p. 118.

20. Salvador Minuchin, Bernise Rosman, and Lester Baker, *Psychosomatic Families* (Boston: Harvard University Press, 1978), 76.

21. Claudette Cummings, Judith Gordon, and Alan Marlatt, "Relapse: Prevention and Prediction," in William Miller, ed., *The Addictive Behaviors* (New York: Pergamon Press, 1980), 306-307.

Chapter 3 The Beginning of the Addiction System

1. The work of Jim Orford is quoted from "Hypersexuality: Implications for a Theory of Dependence," *British Journal of Addiction*, 73: 299-310. All future references to this work in this chapter will be cited by author and page number within the chapter's text.

2. For an overview of this concept see Alan Gurman and David Kniskern, eds., *Handbook of Family Therapy* (New York: Brunner/Mazel, Inc., 1981). For an excellent collection of papers showing one pioneering therapist's conceptual journey to this concept see Carl Whitaker, *From Psyche to System*, John R. Neill and David P. Kniskern, eds., (New York: Guilford Press, 1982).

3. Milton Eber, "Don Juanism: A Disorder of the Self," *Bulletin of the Menninger Clinic*, 45 (4): 307-316.

4. Bradford P. Keeney, "What Is an Epistemology of Family Therapy?" *Family Process*, 21: 153-168, p. 161.

5. Anthony Thompson, "Emotional and Sexual Components of Extramarital Relations," *Journal of Marriage and the Family*, 46: 35-41.

6. Joseph H. Delaney and Marc Stiegler, "Valentina," *Analog*, May 1984: 109.

7. For a complete discussion of the compulsivity issue, see Eli Coleman, "Sexual Compulsion vs. Sexual Addiction: The Debate Continues," *SIECUS Report*, 14, no. 6: 7-10.

8. Professionals in the field of chemical dependency will quickly recognize the influence of the work of Mary and Robert MacAuliffe, *The Essentials of Chemical Dependency* (Minneapolis: American Chemical Dependency Society, 1975).

9. Perhaps the best description from an addict's point of view of the withdrawal experience is in chapter 5 of *Sex and Love Addicts Anonymous*, the Augustine Fellowship, Sex and Love Addicts Anonymous, Fellowship Wide Services, Inc. (Boston, 1986).

Chapter 4 Growth of the Addictive System

1. More elaboration on the three levels of addiction can be found in *Out of the Shadows.*

2. Susan Griffin, *Pornography and Silence: Culture's Revenge Against Nature* (New York: Harper and Row, 1981), 16.

3. A. Nicholas Groth and Murray L. Cohen, "Aggressive Sexual Offenders: Diagnosis and Treatment," *Community Mental Health Target Populations,* Ann Wolbert Burgess and Aaron Lazare, eds. (Englewood Cliffs, New Jersey; Prentice-Hall, 1976).

Chapter 5 The Addict's Family and Beliefs

1. A new stage has been reached in a field when pioneers have their works collected and published to show the progression of thought and when new works appear which synthesize existing theory to a whole new level of conceptualization. A work from each genre which can serve the initiate who wants to understand the role of homeostasis in the family is: John R. Neill and David Kniskern, eds., *From Psyche to System: the Evolving Therapy of Carl Whitaker* (New York: The Guilford Press, 1982) and Bunny S. Dahl, *From the Inside Out and Other Metaphors* (New York: Brunner/Mazel, 1983).

2. D.H. Olson, D. Sprenkle, and C. Russell, "Circumplex Model of Marital and Family Systems I: Cohesion and Adaptability Dimensions, Family Types and Clinical Application," *Family Process*, 18: 3-28.

3. D.H. Olson, H.I. McCubbin, et al., *Families: What Makes Them Work* (Beverly Hills: Sage Publications, 1983).

4. D.H. Olson, C. Russell, and D. Sprenkle, "Circumplex Model of Marital and Family Systems VI: Theoretical Update," *Family Process*, 22: 69-83.

5. The work of Gershen Kaufman is quoted from "The Meaning of Shame: Toward a Self-Affirming Identity,"Journal of Counseling Psychology, 31: 568-573, p. 569. Future reference to this work will be cited by author and page number within the chapter's text.

6. Alayne Yates, "Children Eroticized by Incest," *American Journal of Psychiatry*, 139: 482-485, p. 483.

7. Michael J. Martin and James Walters, "Familial Correlates of Selected Types of Child Abuse and Neglect," *Journal of Marriage and the Family*, 44: 267-276.

8. See also Karin Meiselman, *Incest* (Washington: Jossey-Bass, 1978).

9. There is a growing literature documenting the impact of childhood sexual abuse which goes far beyond the purposes of this book. The importance here is to underline another variable in how sexual shame evolves in the addictive family. For a collection of readings, see B. Jones, L. Jenstrom, and K. MacFarlane, *Sexual Abuse of Children*, U.S. Department of Health and Human Services, DHHS Publication No. (OHDS) 78-30161. Also Wendy Maltz and Beverly Holman, *Incest and Sexuality: A Guide to Understanding and Healing,* (Lexington, Mass.: Lexington Books, 1987).

10. For further information on Faces II write: Family Social Science, University of Minnesota, 290 McNeal Hall, St. Paul, Minnesota, 55108.

11. R.O. Nelson, "A Study of the Role of Sex Offenders' Marriages in the Commission of Their Sex Offenses," Ph.D. diss., University of Minnesota, 1980, order no. 74-10,555, and J. Bastani and D. Kentsmith, "Psychotherapy with Wives of Sexual Deviants," *American Journal of Psychotherapy*, 34: 21-25.

Chapter 7 The Twelve Steps and the Beginning of Recovery

1. *Alcoholics Anonymous* (New York: Alcoholics Anonymous World Services, Inc., 1976), 185. The proceding quotation, also from this work, will be cited by title and page number within the chapter's text.

2. See Richard Bandler and John Grinder, *Patterns of the Hypnotic Techniques of Milton H. Erickson, M.D.* (Cupertino, California: META Publications, 1975); Jay Haley, *Uncommon Therapy* (New York: W.W. Norton and Co., 1973); and Sidney

Rosen, ed., *My Voice Will Go With You* (New York: W.W. Norton and Co., 1982).

3. The work of David Gordon is quoted from *Therapeutic Metaphors* (Cupertino, California: META Publications, 1978), 24. All future references to this work will be cited by author and page number within the chapter's text.

4. The work of Ernest Kurtz is quoted from "Why A.A. Works," *Journal of Studies on Alcohol*, 43: 38-80, p. 65. All future references to this work will be cited by author and page number within the chapter's text.

5. J. Clayton Stewart, "Peer Counseling, Follow-up Help Sex Offenders," *American Psychological Association Monitor*, 15: 22-24, p. 22.

6. Michael Harner, *The Way of the Shaman* (San Francisco: Harper and Row, 1980).

7. Onno van der Hart, *Rituals in Psychotherapy: Transition and Continuity* (New York: Irvington Publishers, Inc., 1978), 73-74.

8. See *Alcoholics Anonymous Comes of Age* (New York, Alcoholics Anonymous World Services, Inc., 1980).

9. The work of Ernest Becker is quoted from *The Denial of Death* (New York: The Free Press, 1973). All future references to this work will be cited by author and page number from within the chapter's text.

10. Paul Watzlawick, John Weakland, and Richard Fisch, *Change: Principles of Problem Formation and Problem Resolution* (New York: W.W. Norton and Co., 1974).

Chapter 8 Assessment

1. For further information regarding the series of FACES instruments contact: David Olson, Ph.D., Family Social Science, 290 McNeal Hall, University of Minnesota, Minneapolis, MN 55108.

2. Alan S. Gurman, Ph.D., and David Kniskern, Psy.D., eds., *Handbook of Family Therapy* (New York: Brunner/Mazel, 1981).

3. Bradford Keeney, "What Is an Epistemology of Family Therapy?" *Family Process,* 21:153-168, p.161.

4. Lawrence Sanders, *The Seduction of Peter S.* (New York: Putnam, 1983).

5. For further information write: Institute for Behavioral Medicine, Golden Valley Health Center, 4101 Golden Valley Road, Golden Valley, MN 55422.

6. Charlotte Kasl, "Women and Sexual Addiction," (1984), p. 11.

7. James Orford, "Towards a Theory of Sexual Dependency," *British Journal of Addiction*, 73 (1978): 310.

Chapter 9 Intervention and Treatment

1. Fitjof Capra, *The Turning Point* (New York: Bantam Books, 1983), 83.

2. Bunny Dahl, *From the Inside Out and Other Metaphors* (New York: Brunner/Mazel, 1983), 123.

3. John Updike, *A Month of Sundays* (New York: Knopf, 1975).

4. Fitjof Capra, *The Turning Point* (New York: Bantam Books, 1983), 83.

5. Jay Haley, *Ordeal Therapy* (San Francisco: Jossey-Bass, 1984), 22.

6. Excerpts from *Abstinence and Boundaries in SAA: Tools for Recovery* (Minneapolis: Sex Addicts Anonymous, 1986).

7. O. Hobart Mowrer, "The Mental Health Professions and Mutual Help Programs: Co-optation or Cooperation" in *The Self-Help Revolution*, ed. Alan Gartner and Frank Reissman (New York: Human Sciences Press, 1984), 139-154.

8. Gershen Kaufman, *Shame: The Power of Caring* (Cambridge: Schenkman Publishing Co., Inc., 1980), 144.

9. A good summary of this and other strategies can be found in G. Alan Marlatt, *Relapse Prevention* (New York: The Guilford Press, 1985).

10. Rudolf Moos and John Finney, "The Expanding Scope of Alcoholism Treatment Evaluation," *The American Psychologist,* October, 1983, 1041.

11. M. Scott Peck, *The Road Less Traveled* (New York: Simon and Schuster, 1987), 73.

12. Paul Tillich, *The Shaking of the Foundations* (New York: Charles Scribner's Sons, 1948), 161-162.

About the Author

Patrick J. Carnes, Ph.D., is the Senior Fellow in residence at the Golden Valley Institute for Behavioral Medicine at Golden Valley Health Center, in Minneapolis, Minnesota. Dr. Carnes was the primary architect of the center's inpatient program for sexual dependency and now serves as a program consultant there.

Dr. Carnes has also consulted with business, academic, social service, military, and criminal justice organizations. His books include *Understanding Us* (Interpersonal Communications, Inc., 1981), which was recognized for excellence by the National Institute on Drug Abuse; *Out of the Shadows: Understanding Sexual Addiction* (CompCare Publishers, 1983); *A Gentle Path through the Twelve Steps* (CompCare Publishers, 1989); and this volume, *Contrary to Love: Helping the Sexual Addict*. Dr. Carnes is also the author of scores of published articles on addiction. He is a recognized media spokesperson and nationally known speaker on sexual dependency.

Dr. Carnes received his doctorate from the University of Minnesota. He and his four children enjoy boating, hunting, and fishing in the Upper Midwest.